UNEQUAL EXCHANGE, IMPERIALISM
AND UNDERDEVELOPMENT

An Essay on the Political Economy of World Capitalism

By the same author

INDIAN ECONOMIC GROWTH: CONSTRAINTS AND PROSPECTS
Calcutta: Orient Longman, 1973

UNEQUAL EXCHANGE, IMPERIALISM AND UNDERDEVELOPMENT

An Essay on the Political Economy of World Capitalism

RANJIT SAU

1978

CALCUTTA
OXFORD UNIVERSITY PRESS
DELHI BOMBAY MADRAS

Oxford University Press

OXFORD LONDON GLASGOW
NEW YORK TORONTO MELBOURNE WELLINGTON
IBADAN NAIROBI DAR ES SALAAM CAPE TOWN
KUALA LUMPUR SINGAPORE JAKARTA HONG KONG TOKYO
DELHI BOMBAY CALCUTTA MADRAS KARACHI

Printed in India
by P. K. Ghosh at Eastend Printers, 3 Dr Suresh Sarkar Road,
Calcutta 14 and published by R. Dayal, Oxford University Press,
Faraday House, Calcutta 13

To those . . .
who do . . .
to undo it all.

PREFACE

THE quarter of a century following the Second World War has been a period of momentous changes; it would stand out to be a watershed in the history of mankind. As the vast colonial empires went into liquidation in Asia and Africa, a new era dawned in these continents. And with the colonies gone, imperialism rearranged its tentacles; colonialism faded into neo-colonialism. Side by side, the triumph and consolidation of socialism in one-third of the globe opened a profound vista in the annals of human civilization. On a different plane, the frontiers of knowledge are advancing with unprecedented rapidity; fundamental breakthroughs in science and technology have brought enormous productive power within the grasp of human beings; and as a result, the third industrial revolution is well under way in the rich countries. But most of Asia, Africa and Latin America continues to linger in the shadow of underdevelopment. This is the setting of our study.

This essay is an endeavour to analyse certain aspects of neo-colonialism in its global perspective. Unequal exchange is taken as the central point around which the dynamics of this latest phase of imperialism reveals itself with remarkable clarity, although the concept of unequal exchange as such is apt to elude precise and universal definition.

In a sense this book has been in the making for over five years. A number of my papers have meanwhile appeared in the following periodicals: *Frontier, Ekshan, Samatat, Arthaniti, Economic Bulletin for Asia and the Pacific* and *Economic and Political Weekly*. I have also had the opportunity of organizing my thoughts in the course of participating in seminars and conferences—in Calcutta (Seminar on the Political Economy of Indian Agriculture, March 1973), Montreal (Annual Conference of the Canadian Society for Asian Studies, May 1975), Tananarive (United Nations, Afro-Asian Conference on Industrialization and Agricultural Development, July 1975), and Algiers (First Congress of Third World Economists, February 1976). Gradually these bits and pieces started falling into place; and here is the outcome.

I am grateful to all my friends and critics who have helped me with their co-operation, constructive challenge, and guidance. My special thanks are due to Ratan Ghosh for his excellent research assistance. P. K. Bhattacharjee, T. K. Dan, R. K. Pal, and T. N. Naskar typed, with commendable skill, several drafts of the manuscript; through the years they have typed my research papers which have been the building blocks of this essay. To them I express my deep gratitude.

RANJIT SAU

Calcutta
October 1976

CONTENTS

LIST OF FIGURES

LIST OF TABLES

I

INTRODUCTION

SINCE the dawn of history never before has the world seen such unevenness in economic development as it does today. Teeming millions barely survive at the fringe of existence while a few others climb new heights of wealth and power. Neither geographical idiosyncrasies, nor racial attributes, nor any non-immutable natural characteristics, have dictated the economic imbalance. It is by and large man-made.

Rich countries today are mostly laid out along an arc across the northern hemisphere within the range of 40 and 60 degrees of latitude; North America, West Europe, the Soviet Union, and Japan seem to fall in one neat line. The poor, underdeveloped lands, on the other hand, are all located in the south. This north–south dichotomy is no more natural or pre-ordained than any other product of human contrivance. The arc of prosperity was not always like this; it has shifted over time. Beginning from the days of remote antiquity, civilizations had arisen in manifold and varied conditions; bloomed with all their unprecedented achievements in science, technology and productivity; and faded away with the march of time—in the Nile river valley, in the Andean coast and plateau, in the lower valley of the Yellow River, in the Central American tropical forest, in the Indus and Ganges river valleys, and so on.[1] Civilization is not a preserve of any particular group, place or race. The medieval period that spans from the fifth to the fifteenth centuries had also witnessed social, economic and political developments no less in the three continents of Asia, Africa and Latin America than anywhere else in the world. Even in the early part of the modern era that followed the Middle Ages the socio-economic predominance was initially held in some areas of these three continents. Before the eighteenth century the standard of living of the presently underdeveloped lands was almost certainly higher than that in Europe. It was certainly higher in Asia.[2]

The present-day north–south stratification in development is of recent origin—hardly two or three centuries old. The underlying process, of course, started earlier when the outward venture of European mercantilism began at the end of the fifteenth century; and it culminated in the nineteenth century when capitalism entered its advanced stage in Europe.[3] The poor, underdeveloped countries of Asia, Africa and Latin America have been victims of a relentless machination that has robbed them of precious resources, human and natural. If nothing else, this very fact of imperialist plunder is a common denominator which unites them despite their diversities in many respects.[4]

THE THIRD WORLD

It is an irony of history that imperialist countries could subjugate and rule over colonies far beyond their own size. In the early years of this century, the total area of the colonies stood at five times that of the metropolitan countries whose total population amounted to less than three-fifths that of the colonies. These figures are even more striking if the biggest imperialist countries are taken separately. The British colonies as a whole were eight and a half times more populous and about 252 times bigger in territory than Great Britain. France occupied an area nineteen times bigger than her own. The population of the French colonies exceeded that of France by 16.6 million.[5] The extent of the colonial plunder can be vividly seen from a typically illustrative figure: in the year 1914, through direct and indirect operations, the French imperial banks in Algeria and Tunisia reaped profits amounting to 50 per cent of their capital.[6] A sizable part of the blame for the poverty in large areas of the world today can be laid at the door of imperialist exploitation, so much so that one author goes to the extent of holding an apparently paradoxical proposition, namely, the richer a region was during colonization the poorer it is today; and the poorer a region was at that time the richer it is today. 'The greater was the wealth available for exploitation, the poorer and more undeveloped the region today; and the poorer the region was as a colony, the richer and more developed it is today.'[7]

World capitalism is an ensemble of exploitative relations embracing certain countries and classes. Geographically it has two parts, namely, (*a*) the *metropolis* or *centre*, and (*b*) the *periphery*. Through the ages, the periphery has provided the centre the funds for its primitive accumulation, the raw materials for its industry, and the market for its industrial products. The periphery is also known as the *Third World*, while the centre is recognized as the *First World*. As for the *Second World*, it consists of the socialist countries. The geographic composition of these three parts is as follows.[8]

1. Centre or metropolis of world capitalism: the United States and Canada, Europe (excluding the Soviet Union and the People's Democracies), Japan, Israel, Australia and New Zealand.

2. Socialist countries: Soviet Union, European People's Democracies (including Yugoslavia), China, Mongolia, North Korea, Vietnam, Laos, Cambodia and Cuba.

3. Third World or the periphery of world capitalism: Latin America (excluding Cuba); Africa; Asia (excluding its socialist countries, and Japan and Israel); and Oceania (excluding Australia and New Zealand).

This economic and political division of the world is not beyond controversy. Recently an alternative classification has been put forward which would include only the United States and the Soviet Union in the First World; the remaining advanced capitalist countries such as Britain, France, West Germany, Japan in the Second World; and all the others in the Third World. This new classification in effect denies the unity of a socialist bloc. It identifies the Soviet Union as an imperialist super-power on par with the United States. Moreover, it invests the term Third World with a meaning which is far from that of the periphery of world capitalism; it puts together the presently semi-colonial countries which are linked to the world capitalist system with those which have freed themselves from that system and are currently engaged in the construction of socialism. Such a category for the Third World cannot be meaningfully used in the analysis of imperialism and underdevelopment. And that is why here we shall not adopt this rival typology. In a different, broader context, countries such as China, Vietnam, North Korea are certainly members of the Third World, but not of the Third World that is interpreted as the backyard of imperialism.

One may have reservations about the term Third World itself on the ground that it would imply that this group of countries is organically separate and independent from the advanced capitalist countries, which it is not. Likewise, one may feel that the term 'periphery' completely denies any autonomy whatsoever to the countries grouped under it. Having recognized these limitations of the terminology, we bow to usage and accept both of them. Furthermore, it should be borne in mind that the centre and the periphery are not two distinct sets, each homogeneous within itself. There are rivalries and incompatibilities among the advanced capitalist countries; witness the spectre of the American challenge haunting the European bourgeoisie.[9] Our treatment of this group as one unit disregarding the fissures should not be construed as tantamount to the Kautskyite idea of 'ultra-imperialism'.[10] Similarly, the Third World is not actually an assembly of countries which are of the same rank in terms of economic and political prowess; some of them do tend to establish hegemony of their own over the neighbouring states—a phenomenon which has acquired the name of 'sub-imperialism'.

The relative economic standing of the three parts of the world in our classification can be visualized from Table 1 which gives the data as of the mid-sixties. The Third World is spread over one half of the area of the whole world and inhabited by the same proportion of the total world population; but it accounts for only

TABLE 1

SOME FEATURES OF THE THREE PARTS OF THE WORLD

(Per cent: as of 1964)

	Area	Population	Output
1. Advanced capitalist countries: centre or metropolis of world capitalism	23	20	60
2. Socialist countries	26	30	30
3. Third World: periphery of world capitalism	51	50	10
WORLD TOTAL	100	100	100

Source: Jalée (1968), p. 7, for the first column; for the rest, Sweezy (1972), p. 16.

one-tenth of the world output. The metropolis of world capitalism claims about one-fourth of area, one-fifth of population, but
three-fifths of output. The socialist countries have 30 per cent of
the population and of output, but slightly less of territorial area.
The economic distance between the metropolitan centre and the
outer periphery of world capitalism is highlighted by these
figures. The former has six times output but less than half of
population and area as compared to the latter. The periphery has
been reduced to what it is, not in one day but in stages with the
evolution of imperialism.

IMPERIALISM

Historians usually distinguish the epoch of mercantilism from that
of industrial capitalism, i.e. the period of the late fifteenth to the
late eighteenth century from that of the late eighteenth century
onwards. But nowadays it is being argued that in so far as the
process of underdevelopment of the Third World is concerned
'the unity between capitalism and mercantilism is more important
than their differences. . . . For the underdeveloped part of the
capitalist system, relatively little of importance has changed since
mercantilist times.'[11] Indeed, Lenin considered the 1870s as a
turning-point which marked the beginning of the era of imperialism. However, his analysis had a very specific focus on only 'certain aspects of imperialism: the rivalry among capitalist nations in
the age of monopoly capitalism, on the nature of the First World
War and on the revolutionary opportunities of that period.'[12] But
in so far as the centre–periphery interrelationship is concerned the
basic structure had taken shape right in the early days of the
mercantile period, and the 1870s did not mark any fundamental
beginning or end. In a word, viewed in this perspective, world
capitalism, or imperialism, began in the late fifteenth century, and
it continues up to date. It has changed over time; it has gone
through various phases; but it has a remarkable continuity. One
author has suggested the following delineation of *five* stages of
imperialism (Figure 1):

1. From the end of the fifteenth century to the middle of the
   seventeenth century: the rise of commercial capital and the
   rapid growth of world commerce.
2. From the middle of the seventeenth century to the latter

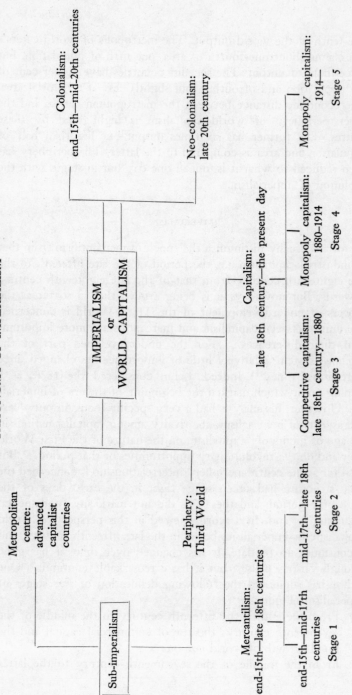

TAXONOMY OF IMPERIALISM

FIGURE 1

part of the eighteenth century: commercial capital ripens into a dominant economic force.

3. From the late eighteenth century to the 1870s: the rise and eventual victory of industrial capital under the spur of the industrial revolution.

4. From, roughly, 1880 to the end of the First World War: the rise and victory of monopoly capital, the territorial division of the globe and the first struggle for redivision.

5. Since the end of the First World War: the beginning of socialism as a rival social system, eventual decolonization and the rise of the multinational corporations.[13]

The tactics of imperialist exploitation have also changed with the stages. In the early stages brute force was the main plank of imperial domination; gradually it gave way to more sophisticated methods as it became evident that unless reproduction took place in the colonies soon there would be very little left to plunder.

The aftermath of the Second World War witnessed decolonization; and now the old methods of colonial rule were no longer applicable. Imperialism changed its colour and continued its exploitation through the medium of collaborating classes of the former colonies. Colonialism shaded off into neo-colonialism. Our interest in this essay is primarily with this latest phase of imperialism.

There are some who are saying that imperialism has lost its economic significance to the advanced capitalist countries; it is now a marginal and diminishing phenomenon. For most of the international flows of commodity and capital are confined within the advanced capitalist countries themselves, whose imports from the Third World do not exceed 3 per cent of their gross domestic product. The quantitative significance of their overseas investment has decreased to an almost negligible level. While before the First World War, Britain used to send abroad between 30 and 90 per cent of its total savings depending upon the year, and France between 15 and 75 per cent, in recent years the average ratio has fallen below 2 per cent. Profits, interests, dividends, and royalties, extracted from the Third World, represent a fraction of one per cent of their gross national product.[14]

This view has been rebutted by the argument that the prices prevailing in the world market discriminate against the exports of the Third World. Should due corrections be made for this *unequal exchange* the above-mentioned figures would be significantly altered, and then the economic importance of trade with, and investment in, the Third World by advanced capitalist countries would become evident.[15] In this essay we shall strengthen this argument by properly formulating the theory of unequal exchange; but at the same time we shall emphasize that the organic link between the Third World and imperialism is much more deep-rooted than what is conveyed by these arithmetic numbers.

METHODOLOGY

The study of imperialism has so far suffered from, to coin an awkward phrase, centre-centricity—first Euro-centricity, and now America-centricity. The dynamics of imperialism is usually sought in that of the metropolitan centre of world capitalism. But the dialectical nature of imperialism cannot be captured in this approach. On the other hand, the recently fashionable theory of conceptualizing the world capitalist system as but a vast machine of single-minded surplus extraction also leaves out certain essential aspects of imperialism, such as the imperative of sustaining continuous expanded reproduction in the periphery where no single class has marshalled unchallenged supremacy, no single class has established full control over the forces of production. The analysis of such a complex situation as the centre–periphery interaction calls for first devising the scientific methodology, and then its scrupulous application.

It is worthwhile to be aware that Marx has not bequeathed universal laws valid for all times and for all modes of production. Marx himself says that he investigated the law of development of one 'economic formation of society' only, i.e. capitalism, and no other. In *Capital* he addresses himself 'to examine the capitalist mode of production and the conditions of production and exchange corresponding to that mode'.[16] He goes on to add that 'up to the present time, their classic ground is England. That is the reason why England is used as the chief illustration in the development of my theoretical ideas.'[17] Many of the fallacious interpretations of Marx, Engels warns us, 'rest upon the false assumption that Marx wishes to define where he only investigates, and that in general one might expect fixed, cut-to-measure, once and for all applicable definitions in Marx's works'.[18] Engels further adds: 'It is self-evident that where things and their interrelations are conceived, not as fixed, but as changing, their mental images, the ideas, are likewise subject to change and transformation; and they are not encapsulated in rigid definitions, but are developed in their historical or logical process of formation.'[19]

The peoples of the world capitalist system are divided into classes *and* countries, each country having a state which enjoys a certain degree of autonomy wherever no single class commands absolute authority over others. Under such circumstances the state boundaries cannot be assumed away, and all the countries belonging to the centre and the periphery of world capitalism collapsed into a single huge hierarchical set-up for surplus extraction. However, if the co-ordinates of Marx's *Capital* are thus obscured in this conjunction of the centre and the periphery of world capitalism, his scientific method remains the only valid guide for analysis. Marx singles out *production relations* from all social relations as being the basic and primary determinant of all other relations including the centre–periphery relations, of which that of unequal exchange is an integral part. This would be kept in view all through our investigation.

What is the fundamental basis of the post-war phase of imperialism when colonies in the strict sense have ceased to exist? In a word, how does neo-colonialism work? If the centre–periphery unequal exchange has been going on for the last four centuries, how is it perpetrated in the neo-colonial era? This is the central question of this essay. We shall try to indicate the order of magnitude of unequal exchange, demonstrate its ramifications, and finally conclude that unequal exchange is in essence a corollary as well as a cause of underdevelopment in the wake of imperialism. As a necessary prerequisite for our final inference we shall also explore the class alignment in the periphery that sustains the entire edifice of world capitalism.

A PREVIEW

We begin with the metropolis. In Chapter 2, we examine the nature of the economic crisis that assails the metropolis, or centre of world capitalism. It is argued that the efforts of bourgeois economists to rationalize and salvage the capitalist system have come to naught. The modern theories of the 'golden age' growth path along which capitalism not only allegedly can perpetuate itself but also do away with the exploitation of man by man are sheer wishful fantasy without any substance. From the days of Adam Smith and Ricardo up to date bourgeois theories have always reflected the contemporary concerns of capitalism. Today when the victory of socialism in one-third of the world has precipitated the crisis of world capitalism from within and without, renewed attempts are being made to theoretically prove its immortality and rationality, and at the same time to carve a way out of the present morass; we have laid bare the futility of these exercises.

The metropolitan centre of world capitalism is burdened with the ever increasing flow of investible surplus, which is another way of saying that the rate of profit shows a tendency to decline. Apart from the safety valve of wasteful expenditures, technological progress is a means of circumventing this crisis. And herein comes the critical role of the periphery which absorbs the obsolescent plant and equipment, and thus helps accelerate the rate of technological progress in the metropolis, and thereby keep up the profit rate in the metropolis.

Chapter 3, at the outset, draws our attention to the fact that unequal exchange has been a many-centuries-old phenomenon. A brief sketch of the colonization of the Indian economy by British imperialism is given in order to highlight also that armed forces had been initially the modality for unequal exchange. In this chapter the theoretical models of centre–periphery unequal exchange as constructed by Emmanuel and others after him are reviewed, and their serious limitations pointed out. We then propose an alternative theoretical model of unequal exchange under competitive market conditions. It is shown that the labour-saving bias of the technological progress in the metropolis further accentuates the unequal exchange. In other words, so long as the Third World countries remain within the world capitalist system they would suffer more and more from adverse terms of trade reckoned at the relative labour contents of the traded commodities, even if competitive conditions were to prevail in the world market. In fact, competitive conditons do not prevail in the world market. The multinational corporations wield considerable monopoly power; besides, a large chunk of the international movement of commodities being only internal transactions of these vertically-integrated enterprises, a sizeable amount of surplus is siphoned off from the Third World through what is called 'transfer pricing'.

The international flow of capital and technology being an important aspect of imperialism, Chapter 4 goes into some details about the nature of technological progress under monopoly capitalism, the technology market, and the propensity of the Third World bourgeoisie to purchase plant and equipment which are meanwhile rendered obsolete in the advanced capitalist countries. An important generalization is made in this chapter about the pattern of the flow of technology in the world.

In the next two chapters attention is focused primarily upon the Third World. Chapter 5, to begin with, critically reviews the bourgeois theories on economic development of the Third World. Then the debate among the Marxists and neo-Marxists with regard to the dominant mode of production is taken up. Is the socioeconomic formation in the Third World fully 'capitalist' in nature? Or, is it 'colonial-postcolonial'? Or, 'semifeudal-semicolonial'? What are the prospects of development of capitalism, if it is not yet fully capitalist? In any case, does the so-called 'non-capitalist path' provide a viable alternative for transition to socialism bypassing the stage of capitalism? Can it be therefore a path that rescues the Third World from the agonies of unequal exchange and underdevelopment?

Chapter 6 briefly shows how an alliance of feudal landlords, local bourgeoisie and imperialism can work in spite of the conflicts of interest among these three classes. It is demonstrated how on the basis of such a coalition of the three ruling classes, imperialism gets the opportunity to deeply entrench itself at various branches of production, and thus to force an unequal exchange on the country concerned. In this sense the roots of unequal exchange are to be found not so much in relatively superficial elements like wage differential or even the monopoly power of the advanced capitalist countries in the arena of international trade as in the basic alignment of the ruling classes in the Third World. By the same token, imperialism cannot but be a system of inflicting unequal exchange and underdevelopment on the Third World.

Chapter 7 finally gives a summary of the discussion and the major conclusions of this study.

2

THE METROPOLIS IN CRISIS

THE basic problem of the metropolitan centre of world capitalism has changed through the ages; and such changes have been reflected in the then prevailing economic theories. Classical economics, for instance, was haunted with the prospect of a stationary state born out of the diminishing returns on the limited land space of Europe. Adam Smith, David Ricardo, John Stuart Mill, writing as they were in the late eighteenth and the early nineteenth centuries, were all concerned about the eventual plateau of prosperity. That was the period when colonies were still only a source of raw materials and a market for the manufactured goods of the metropolitan centre; and not yet an area for investment of capital in order to escape the law of diminishing returns at home.

At the turn of the nineteenth century, a new chapter in economic theory began. By 1871 peace had dawned in Europe after an era of bitter wars among the major powers, following the period of the revolutionary storms of 1848. Meanwhile, the European powers had penetrated deep into other continents. The opening up of Japan by Commodore Perry, the establishment of the treaty system in China, and the ending of the East India Company rule in India had consolidated the network of continuing colonial plunder.[1] Assured with the rolling frontiers in Asia, Africa and Latin America to fend off diminishing returns, the fear of the ultimate stationary state in European economy was left behind. Confident of sustained growth, the once-dismal science of economics now concentrated on such issues as resource allocation and income distribution. Thus began the era of neo-classical economics.[2] The exuberance of the protagonists knew no bounds. The abuses of the capitalist system such as unemployment, cyclical fluctuations in economic activities resulting in periodic lay-off of workers and the ruin of small entrepreneurs, degradation of human labour, were all dismissed as temporary aberrations or were simply glossed over. Capitalism had decisively triumphed and established itself firmly all over the globe.

Came the First World War, the Great Depression, and the Second World War; capitalism passed through crisis after crisis. First in Russia in 1917, and then in parts of Europe, Asia and Latin America, the victory of socialism had meanwhile thrown up an altogether new challenge to world capitalism. Torn with the conflicts both within and without, it needed, more than ever before, a recipe for survival if possible. Indeed, there has been no dearth of writers prescribing ways and means. Below, some of these proposed theoretical solutions would be reviewed, and their limitations pointed out. Then an attempt will be made to identify the nature of the crisis of world capitalism at this stage.

THE PROMISED LAND OF STEADY STATE

Economic theory has a tendency to lag behind facts. The mounting unemployment, poverty and deprivation during the thirties in the metropolitan centre of world capitalism could no longer be brushed aside as a temporary deviation from the promises of full employment equilibrium. Keynes[3] recognized the weakness of capitalism; conceded that it is not a self-correcting system assuring the full utilization of resources; and in so doing he also looked for a remedy thereof. For him, capitalism is like a machine which may not work always with full vigour; but it can be repaired whenever it gets bogged down at a low level of performance. The main thrust of his prescription lies in the creation of purchasing power. Let people even dig holes and fill them up; in the process they will earn some income which will come back to the market as purchasing power and thereby stimulate the production of goods and services. On a more sophisticated plane, Keynes pleads for increased spending on investment, public works, defence and the like, in order to stir up the productive machine of capitalism.

This line of argument is extended by Harrod and Domar[4] into an infinite future. Productive capacity has been built up in the economy through investment year after year. Now, in order to generate demand for the output, further investment is called for. This is an apparently paradoxical solution. The productive capacity is already too high in that there is not enough demand for its products; the profit rate is therefore very low if not nil. Under such circumstances what is required, according to Harrod–Domar, is precisely more investment. That is to say, in terms of the Harrod–Domar formula, should the rate of investment grow up steadily at a certain pace the capitalist system of production need not encounter the so-called realization crisis where demand falls short of supply. This proposition can be demonstrated as follows.

Let Y denote national income, and K the stock of capital, in a certain year. If β is the productivity of capital then it follows that:

$$Y = K\beta. \tag{1}$$

If the productivity of capital is constant, then the level of income changes from year to year as a result of the change in the stock of capital. Denote such an annual change in income by ΔY, and that in capital by ΔK. Again, it follows that:

$$\Delta Y = \Delta K \beta. \tag{2}$$

From the above two equations, one finds the following:

$$\Delta Y/Y = \Delta K/K. \tag{3}$$

That is, the growth rates of income and capital are the same. Also:

$$\Delta Y/Y = \beta \Delta K/Y. \tag{4}$$

To interpret the last equation, note that the stock of capital rises only if a part of the income is saved and invested. In other words, if s is the propensity to save, then:

$$\Delta K = sY. \tag{5}$$

In view of (4) and (5), the growth rate of income, denoted by g, is equal to the product of the propensity to save and the productivity of capital.

$$g = \Delta Y/Y = s\beta. \tag{6}$$

By (3) and (6) it is found that:

$$\Delta K/K = s\beta = g. \tag{7}$$

How does the growth of capital stock at the rate of g per annum prevent the realization crisis? In this system the level of production is being maintained at the point of full capacity utilization; see equation (1). The demand for output has two components, viz. consumption and investment. By equation (5), whatever is left of the total output over and above the consumption demand is being absorbed by the investment demand. Thus total demand perfectly matches with total supply; and the realization crisis is kept off. All this, however, implies that investment must grow every year at a certain rate as given by equation (7). If, for example, $s = 15$ per cent, and $\beta = 1/3$, then $g = 5$ per cent. Continuous growth of investment at the annual rate of 5 per cent would keep off the problem of excess production in this economy, according to Harrod–Domar.[5] Income would then rise at the same rate; and investment as a proportion of income would remain constant.

A more elaborate extension and generalization of the Keynesian theory has come from Joan Robinson. In her own words:

When technical progress is neutral, and proceeding steadily, without any change in the time pattern of production, the competitive mechanism working freely, population growing (if at all) at a steady rate and accumulation going on fast enough to supply productive capacity for all available labour, the rate of profit tends to be constant and the level of real wages to rise with output per man. *There are no internal contradictions in the system.* Provided that political events cause no disturbances, and provided that the entrepreneurs have faith in the future and desire to accumulate at the same proportional rate as they have been doing over the past, there is no impediment to prevent them from continuing to do so. As long as they do, the system develops smoothly without perturbations.[6]

Such an allegedly contradictionless growth path is known as the *Golden Age*.[7] This theorem of Joan Robinson, as it is, claims that the capitalist system of production can continue indefinitely without any breakdown under the weight of its internal contradictions, provided the volumes of production and investment grow at the proper rate. This concept of the golden age is intended to be an answer to Marx's theory of falling rate of profits. Of course, Mrs Robinson underlines the stringency of the conditions under which the golden age is possible, and thereby brings out its remoteness. Nevertheless, she does concede at the theoretical plane the possibility of limitless capitalism.

Since then, the concept of the golden age has blossomed further into a full-fledged panacea of capitalism in bourgeois economics, as we shall gradually see. According to its latest specifications, the golden age witnesses the grand four-fold equality among the rate of profit, and the growth rates of income, of capital, and of employment, which can be demonstrated as follows.[8] Total income is distributed between wages and profits. If W stands for the wage bill, and r for the rate of profit per unit of capital, then:

$$Y = W + rK . \qquad (8)$$

Now assume that the saving and investment in any year is equal to the profits.

$$\Delta K = rK . \qquad (9)$$

It does not necessarily mean that all profits are saved and invested, and all wages are consumed. It is possible that workers also save from wages, and the profit-earning capitalists also consume from profits; on balance, however, total investment in a year is equivalent in amount to the volume of profits.[9] Equation (9) can be rewritten as:

$$\Delta K / K = r . \qquad (10)$$

Equations (6), (7) and (10) then imply the following equality:

$$\Delta K / K = \Delta Y / Y = g = s\beta = r . \qquad (11)$$

Finally, since the golden age is a steady state with full employment the growth rate of population also must be equal to that of income or capital.

The so-called golden rule of accumulation, viz. the coincidence of the rates of profit, growth, and accumulation, has been established also in an n-sector dynamic Leontief model. The authors Weizsäcker and Samuelson pointedly remark that the capitalist economy, if it moves along this trajectory, 'need in principle encounter no eventual breakdown or realization crisis'.[10] The fruits of the labour of Keynes, Harrod–Domar, Joan Robinson, Weizsäcker–Samuelson, and others, have thus culminated in the discovery of an escape route for capitalism from its own internal contradictions, although it must be added in all fairness that all these authors have not contributed in equal measure to this frantic search.[11] Indeed, bourgeois economics now claims to have found a corridor of internal growth: *the Golden Age of steady state where $r = g$*. This is perhaps the most ambitious achievement of bourgeois economics so far. We shall show the emptiness of this claim in a few moments.

THE SAGA OF THE GOLDEN AGE

Not just the immortality of capitalism, but much more is promised in the golden age. There is no exploitation of man by man in the capitalist golden age, it is further asserted. The fundamentals of this proposition can be displayed in a simple way. Consider an economy which produces only one commodity with the help of a primary factor of production, namely, labour. To produce one unit of the commodity, suppose it takes b units of labour, and a of itself as current input. Let the wage rate, in terms of the said commodity, be denoted by w, and the rate of interest or profit by r. Suppose that gestation lag is one period; and that wages are paid at the end of the period, but the other input, a, has to be paid for in the beginning. The commodity itself is the *numeraire*; so its price is one. Accordingly, the price equation is given by:

$$1 = a(1+r)+bw. \qquad (12)$$

This shows that, for a given set of a and b, the wage rate and profit rate are inversely related; if one goes up the other falls down along a downward sloping straight line.

There is an identical relationship between the growth rate of output g and the per capita consumption denoted by c. Let x be the output of the commodity this year, and $x(1+g)$ the output next year. Now, x is partly consumed, and partly saved and invested. Production next year would require an investment this year to the extent of $ax(1+g)$. Assuming that average consumption per unit of labour is c, the total consumption this year is given by bxc. Thus,

$$x = ax(1+g)+bxc \qquad (13)$$
$$\text{or,} \quad 1 = a(1+g)+bc. \qquad (14)$$

The similarity between equations (12) and (14) is remarkable, and reflects the underlying duality, viz. that the wage/profit relationship and the growth rate/per capita consumption relationship are the images of each other.[12]

In Figure 2, AB represents equations (12) and (14) in turn. Suppose that the economy is in a steady state so that the parameters w, r, c and g are invariant through time. Let R denote the specific position of this economy with regard to both equations

WAGE/PROFIT AND PER-CAPITA-CONSUMPTION/ GROWTH-RATE FRONTIERS

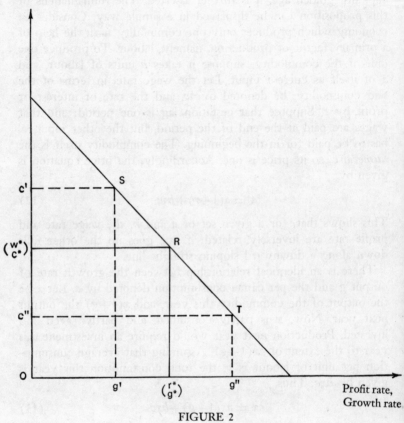

FIGURE 2

(12) and (14). The growth rate is g^*, and the profit is r^*; evidently, $r^* = g^*$. Similarly, $c^* = w^*$. This is the golden age.

Alternatively, let R remain the point for (12), but now suppose S is the point for (14). Then the growth rate is g' which is *less than* the profit rate r^*; likewise the wage rate w^* is *lower than* the per capita consumption c'. This means that although the workers are producing enough to sustain permanently a certain steady stream of per capita consumption, they are consuming less than that. Somebody else then must be depriving them of a part of the fruits of their labour. To put it differently, when the growth rate is *below* the profit rate, the workers are obviously being exploited.

By the same token, should the growth rate *exceed* the profit rate the workers in turn must be exploiting some other group of persons in the society. Consider points R and T, the former still representing the wage/profit point and the latter the growth rate/per capita consumption point. The growth rate g'' is higher than the interest rate r^*, and the per capita consumption c'' is lower than the wage rate w^*. That is to say, the workers are receiving an income which is larger than what the system can afford for the given amount of work with the pre-determined technology. Under such circumstances, it is the workers who seem to be exploiting others; so goes the argument.

These two alternative situations are intended to highlight the observation that when R represents *both* the wage/profit and the growth rate/per capita consumption profiles, i.e. when the profit rate does not diverge from the growth rate, then the wage rate is at par with the maximum sustainable per capita consumption. Each worker then gets all that the system is capable of giving, with the specified technology. Where is the exploitation then? This is the golden age of capitalism which thus brings the exploitation of man by man to an end. This saga of the golden age is enunciated with somewhat more rigour as follows.

Consider an economy that produces one commodity with two current inputs as mentioned above. Output is growing steadily at an annual rate g. Labour force is keeping pace with it; and full employment is maintained throughout. Although the gestation lag is one period, wage is paid at the beginning of the year, unlike in the previous case. Once having entered the system, a worker stays on for ever. In the first year of his entry he is employed and fed with the output that has been produced by somebody else. Thereafter for ever he produces an annual gross output that is adequate not only to sustain his own wage (consumption) w, but also to bear his share of the burden of *employing* and *feeding* the new entrants to the work force, viz. g, whose labour would fructify at the end of the year. *This is an essential condition for remaining on the full employment steady growth path.* At the beginning of period t, production starts with L number of workers and a certain amount of the other input. The volume of output at the end is x. Meanwhile the number of workers has gone up to $L(1+g)$. Now x is to be divided into two parts: one part would be paid out as wages to $L(1+g)$ workers, and the other part would be ploughed back as input for the expanded production in the next period. So, it follows that:

$$x = ax(1+g) + wL(1+g) \tag{15}$$

$$\text{or,} \quad x = w(1+g)L/[1-a(1+g)]. \tag{16}$$

Setting $L = 1$ in (16), it is found that the gross output per worker is given by $w(1+g)/[1-a(1+g)]$.

The output of each worker thus has two components; one component is consumed by him and his share of the new entrant, viz. g, and the other component is used as an input with which he and the new entrant work. Keeping this in view, what is the direct and indirect labour content of the consumption bill $w(1+g)$ which is made available in period t? The direct labour requirement for it is $bw(1+g)$, in $t-1$. And the other input requirement is *not* just $aw(1+g)$, but $a(1+g)w(1+g)$, in period $t-1$. Because it is not enough to produce just for consumption (wage), provision has also to be made for the growth of output at rate g, i.e. the input with which the newcomer in the labour force in period t would work is to be made in period $t-1$. Once this is understood, the rest is quite simple. Repeat the process backward infinitely. What are the input requirements, under the conditions of steady growth, for producing $a(1+g)w(1+g)$ of output in period $t-1$? Again, the direct labour amounts to $abw(1+g)^2$; and similarly the other input to $a^2w(1+g)^3$, both in period $t-2$. Furthermore, for producing the commodity by the amount of $a^2w(1+g)^3$ in period $t-2$, it takes $ba^2w(1+g)^3$ of labour, and $a^3w(1+g)^4$ of the commodity itself in period $t-3$. And so on. All this can be presented schematically as Figure 3.

Thus resolving the input requirements of the commodity into labour alone, and summing up the infinite stream of labour as given in the middle row of Figure 3, the *total labour* that is necessary to support a constant permanent consumption flow of w per worker is found to be:

$$bw(1+g)/[1-a(1+g)]. \tag{17}$$

The worker receives the fruits of this amount of labour. And how much labour does he supply in return per year? He supplies one unit, for which he is paid the wage. Now whether the worker is exploited, or he himself is an exploiter, depends upon how the direct and indirect labour content of his steady annual consumption as measured by expression (17) compares with the amount of labour he supplies.

RESOLVING THE COMMODITY INPUT INTO LABOUR

Output for consumption in period $t = w(1+g)$

...	$a^4w(1+g)^5$	$a^3w(1+g)^4$	$a^2w(1+g)^3$	$a(1+g)w(1+g)$	Commodity input
...	$ba^3w(1+g)^4$	$ba^2w(1+g)^3$	$abw(1+g)^2$	$bw(1+g)$	Labour input
...	$t-4$	$t-3$	$t-2$	$t-1$	Time

FIGURE 3

The expression of (17) can be interpreted in another way. The process of production in the economy is duly synchronized in that the worker, in any period t, produces not only what he consumes in the current period but also what is required for inputs in all the future periods to come. The entire top row of Figure 3 is telescoped into each single period, as it were; to which the production of $w(1+g)$ for immediate consumption is to be added. Thus one gets the gross output of a worker as measured by equation (16), with $L = 1$. The labour coefficient being given by b, the expression of (17) can be derived by multiplying (16) with this coefficient.

Now the degree of exploitation, E, is defined by a comparison between the labour content of the worker's consumption on the one hand and the supply of his labour on the other. Precisely, the ratio of (*i*) the actual amount of his labour supply, and (*ii*) the direct and indirect labour content on his annual consumption, under the conditions of full employment steady state, is defined as the degree of exploitation E, *plus* one. Thus in view of (17):

$$1+E = 1 \left/ \frac{wb(1+g)}{1-a(1+g)} \right.$$

$$\text{or,} \quad 1+E = [1-a(1+g)]/wb(1+g) . \tag{18}$$

If E is positive, labour is being exploited; if it is negative, labour is said to be exploiting others; if $E = 0$, there is no exploitation. This theory has been formulated by Weizsäcker.[13]

This is the new concept of exploitation as it has appeared in the literature of the so-called neo-neoclassical economics. In a moment we shall see that this definition has nothing to do with the Marxian version. At any rate, armed with this novel idea, the neo-neoclassical economist then pronounces that there is no such thing as exploitation in the golden age of steady growth of capitalism. The proof is rather simple. If the price of the commodity is one, and the wage rate is measured in terms of this commodity, then the price equation becomes:

$$1 = (1+r)(a+bw) \qquad (19)$$

where r is the profit or interest rate. The slight discrepancy which creeps in between this equation and the other price equation (12) arises because of the difference in the timing of wage payment. Now wage is being paid at the beginning of the year, whereas in (12) it is paid at the end. This is a minor issue which need not detain us. In any case, the interesting thing to note is that if the value of r as given by equation (19) is substituted in the place of g in equation (18), the value of E would be driven to zero. That is to say, in the capitalist golden age of steady state, where $r = g$, the degree of exploitation of labour E is precisely nil. Encouraged by this finding, Weizsäcker goes on to declare: 'Capitalist exploitation seems to be comparatively easy to overcome. Sufficient accumulation of capital by the government can drive the rate of profit down to the rate of growth of the system where capitalist exploitation no longer exists.'[14]

In effect, the prospect of an exploitationless golden age boils down to this: by assumption, all wages are consumed and all surplus is invested; whatever is produced in the system is therefore consumed in the ultimate analysis by none but the workers themselves. So the degree of labour exploitation is exactly zero. This neo-neoclassical proposition of Weizsäcker–Samuelson is old wine put in a new bottle; it echoes an observation that was made by Adam Smith, Ricardo and Mill long ago. Now only the context has changed; Smith, Ricardo, Mill referred to the more general framework of any state of the economy,[15] whereas Weizsäcker–Samuelson consider only the steady state. The classical economists argue that whatever is produced in the economy is ultimately consumed by the workers themselves so long as the capitalists plough back all the surplus that is generated in production. They start out with the erroneous observation that the price of a commodity has only three components, viz. wages, profit and rent. Since profit and rent are but two forms of the same surplus it may be said that according to the logic of the classical economists the price resolves itself into two basic parts, viz. (*i*) wages or variable capital, and (*ii*) surplus. This being true for every commodity, it is true also for all the commodities together. That is to say, the gross product of the economy consists of these two basic parts. Since the surplus is reinvested this part also goes back eventually to the workers themselves. This is how Smith concludes that 'even though each individual capital is divided into a constant and a variable part, the capital of society resolves itself only into variable capital, i.e. is laid out exclusively in payment of wages. ... The whole of that part of the surplus-product, which is converted into capital, is consumed by the working class.'[16] Ricardo reproduces this theory of Adam Smith almost verbatim: 'It must be understood that all the productions of a country are consumed'[17] by the labourers. Mill also maintains the same view. 'The capital itself,' he observes, 'in the long run becomes entirely wages, and when replaced by the sale of produce becomes wages again.'[18]

The main source of the error lies in the classical doctrine that the price of a commodity 'either immediately or ultimately' resolves itself entirely (that is to say, without leaving any commodity residue) into wages and surplus (profit and rent).[19] It ignores the element of constant capital that is included in the price. This error is at the root of the absurd conclusion that all products are ultimately consumed by the workers, and that in a sense there is no exploitation as such in a capitalist society, on or off the steady state path.

END OF THE PARABLE

As mentioned earlier the neo-neoclassical concept of exploitation has nothing in common with the Marxian definition. It may now be shown more rigorously. Furthermore, it will be demonstrated that exploitation in the Marxian sense exists in the golden age steady state of Joan Robinson, Weizsäcker, Samuelson, and others.

Recall the economy that produces one commodity with two inputs.[20] In the terminology of Marx, total output has three parts, viz. constant capital, variable capital, and surplus.

$$x = ax + wbx + u \qquad (20)$$

where u stands for surplus. The rate of exploitation of labour, denoted by e, is defined by Marx as the ratio of surplus labour and necessary labour, or the ratio of unpaid labour and paid labour.[21] So:

$$e = u/wbx \qquad (21)$$

$$\text{or,} \quad 1 + e = (1-a)/wb . \qquad (22)$$

It may be noted here that so long as the wage rate reflecting the value of labour power remains the same, *the degree of exploitation of labour as defined by Marx is numerically independent of the level and the growth rate of output*, as indicated by equation (22). This does not mean that the growth of output and accumulation has no organic relation with the degree of exploitation. Indeed, the exploitation of labour would determine the volume of surplus and accumulation, and thereby would have its bearing upon the scale of expanded reproduction. To repeat, the degree of exploitation of labour is the ratio between surplus labour and necessary labour; and as such it is unrelated to the way in which the surplus is finally *used* by the capitalist between consumption and accumulation.[22] Even if the surplus is entirely invested, the exploitation of labour in the Marxian sense continues to exist. The sharp distinction on this issue between Marx on the one hand and Smith, Ricardo and Mill on the other is now clear; and so also is the distinction between Marx and Weizsäcker.

It appears that if $g = 0$, Weizsäcker's index of the degree of exploitation E as given by equation (18) coincides with the Marxian e as of equation (22). This may give rise to the false supposition that the former is a generalization of the latter, or that the latter is relevant only in a static economy. So long as the surplus is positive, the coefficient e of (22) is indeed positive, no matter whether the economy is one of simple or expanded reproduction. It is possible to interpret this parameter from the comparative view-point of the worker's labour supply in relation to the total labour content of his consumption of w, the wage rate.

To produce w in period t, now without regard to the conditions of steady growth, the input requirements are simply: bw amount of labour and aw of the commodity, in period $t-1$. Again, the production of the commodity input aw in period $t-1$ calls for abw of labour and a^2w of the commodity in period $t-2$. And so on. Summing up the stream of labour inputs we get the total labour content of w as follows:

$$bw+abw+ba^2w+ \ldots = bw/(1-a) . \qquad (23)$$

The worker supplies one unit of labour in exchange of the wage rate. Now, if $(1+e)$ is defined as the ratio between (*i*) the amount of labour he supplies, and (*ii*) the total labour content of his consumption, then in view of (23), we get again exactly the same measure of e as given in equation (22).

The exploitation of labour in the Marxian sense continues to exist even in the golden age steady state, because surplus labour is still realized in the sphere of production. The numerical equality between the growth rate g and the profit rate r is of no help in eliminating exploitation. The algebra of this content is rather simple. First, we know that the profit rate is given by:

$$r = u/(ax+bxw) \qquad (24)$$

or, in view of (20),

$$r = [1/(a+bw)] - 1 . \qquad (25)$$

Should the entire surplus be re-invested as a result of which output grows at rate g, then the total output x in period t is disbursed as follows: $ax(1+g)$ provides the commodity input for production next year, and $wbx(1+g)$ constitutes the corresponding wage bill. Thus:

$$x = ax(1+g)+wbx(1+g) . \qquad (26)$$

Therefore, $\qquad g = [1/(a+bw)]-1 . \qquad (27)$

Here, indeed, r and g are equal. But then the coefficient e of (22) must be positive, in the event r and g are positive.[23] The golden age of capitalism therefore provides no escape from labour exploitation; and to the extent exploitation leads to the appearance of contradiction, the golden age cannot be a regime with 'no internal contradictions in the system', notwithstanding the assertion of Joan Robinson to the contrary.[24]

Be that as it may, a serious question arises with regard to the very theoretical feasibility of the golden age steady state. Should the capitalists consume a part of their profit income, their propensity to save, denoted by s_c, becomes less than one. Now, there is a fundamental relationship, due to Pasinetti, that holds in any steady state:[25]

$$g = rs_c. \tag{28}$$

With s_c less than one, r must exceed g. Hence, it is impossible to reach the golden age.[26] Furthermore, the growth rate having fallen behind the profit rate, workers become the victims of exploitation even of the Weizsäcker variety.

In any case, the absurdity of the model of a golden age steady state as the theoretical proof of the infinite durability and exploitationless benevolence of capitalism is laid bare ever more sharply when it is recognized that in this stylized model of capitalism there is no place for capitalists as such. Where are these sinews of capitalism in the Leontief input–output matrix of the Weizsäcker–Samuelson models?[27] Does the number of capitalists in the economy grow uniformly at the rate of g per year keeping in line with output and employment? Or, does the volume of their respective capital smoothly swell all along the golden age trajectory? It may be recalled that according to Marx the monopoly of capital becomes a fetter upon the mode of production. Centralization of the means of production and the growth of the working class at last reach a point where they become incompatible with their capitalist integument. The Weizsäcker–Samuelson models are oblivious to such questions. How can a model analyse the dynamics of capitalism over an infinite time horizon without having the class of capitalists anywhere in the picture? The moment this error is rectified and class relations are taken account of, the golden age steady state in addition to being a never-never land, thanks to the Pasinetti condition, turns out to be an empty exercise, to say the least.

THE PRECIPICE OF REALITY

Over a century ago during the heyday of capitalism, Marx through his scientific analysis laid bare the law of motion of capitalism and pronounced its ultimate replacement by a superior mode of production in the course of history. As an oblique antidote to his theory arose the so-called neo-classical economics of William Jevons, Carl Menger, Leon Walras, Alfred Marshall, Knut Wicksell. According to Marx, primitive accumulation, the starting point of the capitalist mode of production, has been historically marked by unequal exchange, plunder, and outright expropriation by force. However, as triumphant capitalism attains its pure form, perfect competition prevails in the market. With the law of value in operation it becomes a system of 'equal exchange'; that is to say, under pure capitalism, only 'equivalents' in terms of the embodied socially necessary labour time change hands at the market place. Now, labour itself becomes a commodity; and it is exchanged at its value. In other words, no matter how much he produces, the wage a worker receives is just enough for his survival. And herein lies the clue to the generation of surplus value which originates in the sphere of capitalist production, not in that of exchange.

The *value* of a commodity produced under capitalist conditions is measured by the labour time that is socially necessary for its production. It can be broken down into three constituent parts, namely, constant capital (q), variable capital (v), and surplus value (u). The first part merely represents the value of the materials and machinery used up; thus it consists of the fixed and circulating capitals of common parlance. The second part is essentially the wage bill which reflects the value of labour power that is engaged in production of the commodity. And the third component is the surplus value to be appropriated by the capitalist. If π is the notation for the value of a commodity, we get:

$$\pi = q+v+u . \qquad (29)$$

Under the law of value, commodities are exchanged in proportion to their values. If commodity A contains a value of 100 units, and commodity B 50 units, then the exchange rate would be $A = 2B$; only like is to be exchanged with like. Now a complication creeps in. The mobility of capital in search of profit leads to the equalization of profit rate in every branch of activity. Here the capital employed by the capitalist is given by the sum of constant and variable capitals, $(q+v)$. Should the profit rate be r, then the price p of a commodity, which is conceptually distinct from its value, is to be as follows:

$$p = q+v+r(q+v) . \qquad (30)$$

From this point of view, the *price* of a commodity also has three constituent parts, viz. constant capital, variable capital, and profit. It may be recalled here that the classical economists failed to recognize that the first of these three elements cannot be resolved in the final analysis into the other two so long as there is no commodity which can be produced by labour alone, unassisted by means of production or unprovided with the means of subsistence.

The profit rate is the same throughout the system. Furthermore, free movement of labour ensures that the rate of exploitation of labour also would be uniform in all areas of employment. The *rate of exploitation* is given by the ratio (u/v) (*vide* equation (21) above). However, the method of production varies from commodity to commodity in the sense that the *organic composition of capital*, i.e. the ratio $q/(q+v)$, may not remain constant across the board. There follows the well-known conclusion that the price of a commodity may not tally with its value. Indeed, the prices determined under the conditions of uniform profit rate, constant rate of exploitation of labour, but different organic compositions of capital, are *not* proportional to the respective values of the commodities. A commodity with a higher organic composition of capital will have a higher price in relation to its value. In the market it is the price which sets the rate of exchange; and as such, rarely does the exchange rate correspond to the value of a commodity. Looked at from another angle, it follows that the surplus value of a commodity as of equation (29) may not be equal to the volume of profit realized therefrom in terms of equation (30). In other words, should p diverge from π there is no reason why u will be at par with $r(q+v)$. However, what is true for a single commodity may not be so for all together.

The search for an 'invariable standard of value'—a unit of accounting which is invariant with regard to the rate of profit —began with Ricardo. Marx called it the 'average commodity', a commodity whose own organic composition of capital is exactly equal to the average organic composition of capital in the economy as a whole. The price of this commodity then will be equal to its value, irrespective of the uniform profit rate prevailing in the economy. Should such an 'average commodity' be used as the *numeraire* for computation of prices, the aggregate price of all the commodities taken together will be equal to the aggregate value.[28] Moreover, the aggregate surplus value will be identical in quantity with the aggregate profit. In symbols:

$$\Sigma\pi = \Sigma p \tag{31}$$

$$\Sigma u = r\Sigma(q+v) . \tag{32}$$

Although equation (32) is not a rigorous proof thereof, yet it correctly indicates the true source of profit, which is neither the marginal productivity of capital, nor the reward for waiting or abstinence, but the unpaid labour.

The conversion of values into prices of commodities has remained an area of controversy in the shape of the 'transformation problem'. Piero Sraffa's latest contribution[29] is presumably going to resolve this issue. Sraffa constructs a 'standard system' where 'the various commodities are produced in the same proportions as they enter the aggregate means of production', and therefore 'the rate by which the quantity produced exceeds the quantity used up in production is the same for each of them'.[30] The mixture of outputs of the standard system is called the *standard commodity*. And the net product of this commodity employing the whole annual labour of the actual system is defined as the unit for measuring prices. Evidently, the price of this commodity itself is identical with its value,[31] and hence when used as a *numeraire* it preserves the equations of (31) and (32).

There are basically two types of crisis in capitalist production. One is called the *falling tendency of the rate of profit* and the other the *realization crisis*. Despite the apparent resemblance, the two problems are fundamentally different.[32] In the Marxian theory of capitalism the tendency of the profit rate to fall is deduced on the assumption that the law of value is fully in operation; that is, the capitalists are realizing the surplus value in production which is consummated in market exchange. Now, with value coinciding with price, equations (29) and (30) imply that:

$$r = \frac{u}{q+v} = \left(\frac{u}{v}\right)\left(1 - \frac{q}{q+v}\right). \tag{33}$$

In other words, the rate of profit is mathematically a product of the rate of exploitation on the one hand, and one minus the organic composition of capital on the other. Hence, the profit rate would vary directly with the rate of exploitation, and inversely with the organic composition of capital. Under the capitalist mode of production, the latter tends to rise, and accordingly the rate of profit acquires a tendency to decline.[33]

When the capitalists find themselves unable to sell the commodities at a reasonable rate of profit, they fail to realize the surplus value to the full extent. This is known as the realization crisis. Obviously, the law of value under such circumstances is no longer in force; and yet the net effect of the crisis once again does express itself as a decline in the rate of profit. This time the impact is felt initially as a reduction in the element u, as it were, in equation (33). So far as the individual capitalist is concerned, to him indeed both the crises appear as similar phenomena of declining profitability of capital. Nevertheless, they do differ in respect of their causality. In any case, the analytical validity of the falling tendency of the profit rate in response to a relative rise on the part of constant capital has been proved elsewhere.[34] It is also an observed fact that the organic composition of capital has increased over the centuries. But this bit of empirical information *per se* need not imply that the profit rate must have declined in consequence, the reality of the capitalist world being far from the model of the law of value. This brings us to the realization crisis which raises its head where the law of value ceases to operate. As we shall see below, this segment of Marx's theoretical deductions has been amply borne out by the testimony of history, especially over the last one hundred years.

Propelled by its internal logic, the capitalist regime entangles all peoples in the net of a world market, and with this it assumes 'the international character'. Furthermore, one capitalist always swallows up many; and eventually competitive capitalism gives way to monopoly capitalism. And in fact so it happened. The decade of the 1870s is a landmark in the history of world capitalism. This was the era of the emergence of monopoly capital, facilitated as it was by the epoch-making developments in transport, communication and industrial chemistry. The new technology provided the framework, and all too often the opportunity, for the quite normal tendencies of capitalist industry towards concentration of power.[35] In the wake of this 'second industrial revolution' as it is sometimes called, a shift took place from a capitalism characterized by dispersed small competitive units to one in which large concentrations of economic power dominated the industrial and financial scene. Not that the world saw the birth of monopoly for the first time; it had seen an apparently similar phenomenon before—at the threshold of modern industrial capitalism. The very early period of industrial capitalism in Britain and Germany witnessed monopolies in many of the 'new' trades and a capitalist domination over the guilds through some sort of putting-out system. Modern industry was then marked by the prevalence of monopolistic formations, many of which were grafted on to earlier systems of production and were protected by high transport costs. Then followed a long period of competition, the first theorists of which were the classical economists; and this competitive phase in turn was superseded by the more recent phase of industrial-cum-financial concentration with its large and oligopolistic business formations, maturing in the 1870s.[36] With the vastly improved communication and transport system of railway and steamship, the extension of imperialist control over almost the entire world completed the process of creating the world market which produced and reproduced the international division of labour most favourable to the centres of industry and finance. For the first time in history, the investment decisions throughout the world were co-ordinated in one place, London, and subjected to a single strategic conception. It thus became technically possible to spread capital evenly throughout the world. In other words, capital accumulation after 1870 could have proceeded via capital-widening rather than capital-deepening; that is to say, the capital–labour ratio as it is commonly called nowadays could have remained constant and a far larger number of people could have been activated as industrial workers.[37] But, instead, true to its immanent law, the organic composition of capital in the centre of world capitalism kept on rising. For reasons to be explained below, meanwhile capitalist development in colonies and semicolonies either did not get off the ground or did not proceed very far.[38] The centre of monopoly capitalism having decided to steadily increase the so-called capital–labour ratio at home, the producer goods sector had to innovate continuously *labour-saving* machinery.[39] This has had far-reaching implications as will be shown below.

This crisis of world capitalism in its monopoly stage since the 1870s had already cost the world two global wars, *inter alia*. Now, in the years following the Second World War, capitalism seems to have entered a new stage with certain distinguishing features, of which three stand out very clearly. For the first time in its chronicle, the capitalist mode of production is actually confronted with a superior mode of production, thanks to the victory of socialism over nearly one-third of the world. It has now met from outside a challenger that is by no means inferior to it. Secondly, there has been an unprecedented convergence or integration, if you like, among the triple elements in the body polity of the centre of world capitalism, viz. the army, the industry, and the state bureaucracy. This has followed from the inherent tendency of capitalism to fall into the realization crisis, and in turn it has further reinforced the same. The last, but certainly not the least important, characteristic of the current epoch of world capitalism dated since the Second World War is the appearance of the giant *transnational corporations* on the scene.[40] These giants, known variously as multinational corporations, international enterprises or firms, and the like, have been looming large in the horizon for a while; and lately they have been rising fast. Defined as companies with production facilities in more than one country, transnational corporations account for a rather small proportion of employment in their respective home countries—barely 8.7 per cent in the USA, 7 per cent in Great Britain, and between 3 to 4 per cent in France and Germany.[41] But their economic ramifications travel far beyond what these tiny ratios might suggest. For instance, as Table 2 shows, the top three transnationals, viz. General Motors, Standard Oil, and Ford, together account for annual sales equal to the GNP of India. Taken severally, individual company-sales are equivalent to, or exceed, the GNP of even advanced small West European countries. Most of the countries of underdeveloped Asia have GNP values less than the annual sales of the top transnationals. As for the value added, as distinct from sales, each of the top ten transnationals has crossed the level of 3 billion dollars per year which is more than the GNP of some 80 countries of the world. The value added by all transnational corporations in 1971 was estimated to be of the order of 500 billion dollars, which was one-fifth of the GNP of the world, outside the socialist countries. Further projections are still more staggering. The net output of the transnational corporations has been increasing at a rate roughly twice the growth rate of the GNP of the non-socialist world. Within a quarter of a century, i.e. by the year 2000 A.D., the production of transnationals would come to about 60 per cent of the non-socialist world GNP.[42]

TABLE 2

SALES OF SOME TRANSNATIONAL CORPORATIONS AND THE GROSS NATIONAL
PRODUCTS OF SOME COUNTRIES
(Year: 1970)

(thousand million dollars)

Country	GNP	Transnational	Country of origin	Sales
India	48.97	General Motors	USA	18.75
Holland	31.28	Standard Oil, N.J.	USA	16.55
Sweden	30.77	Ford	USA	14.98
Belgium	25.88	Royal Dutch/Shell	Holland—UK	10.97
Switzerland	20.31	IBM	USA	7.50
Denmark	15.75	Unilever	UK—Holland	6.88
Austria	14.37	Philips	Holland	4.16
Norway	11.39	ICI	UK	3.50
Finland	10.22	Boeing	USA	3.04
Greece	9.39	Hoechst	Germany	1.42
Ireland	3.89	Alcan Aluminium	Canada	1.36

Source: For GNP figures, OECD, *Main Economic Indicators*, and Government of India, *Economic Survey* (for India's GNP only); and for
the corporate figures, *Fortune*. Cited in Tugendhat (1971), p. 20,
and Chattopadhyay (1975), p. 21.

Transnational corporations constitute a qualitatively potent
departure from the traditional order of international transactions.
Trade in commodities, flows of portfolio investments, and exchange of technology, across the boundaries of nation states, have
been known for ages. And now, apart from their impact on trade,
capital flow, and technology transfer, these corporations have
added another dimension to the world economy, viz. international
production through subsidiaries. Later there will be many more
occasions to make reference to various aspects of the transnationals. Suffice it to emphasize here that while the Weizsäcker–
Samuelsons are spinning the fantasy web of the perfectly competitive golden age trajectory, the iron grip of monopoly capitalism over the world economy has been tightening through the
last hundred years, and at an accelerating rate in the post-war
period. Its tentacles spread over far-flung areas, its business operations in various countries of the world have now been subjected

3

to a single strategic command of a transnational corporation. What it lost in Cuba, for instance, was sought to be recouped with a vengeance in the then South Vietnam; what it suffered in Vietnam is again redeemed with compound interest in Chile; and so the game of exploitation goes on. Armed with an enormous surplus at home and abroad, the transnational corporation can afford not to pay any heed to the monetary-fiscal measures of the local government such as high interest rate, credit squeeze, and all that. Keynes laid out his theory on the premise of perfect competition; and Harrod–Domar worked out their formula for steady growth in very much the same vein, having assumed that full capacity utilization is a precondition to be fulfilled.[43] With the increasing intensity in the tempo of monopoly capitalism, the set of all such postulates has fallen by the wayside. The transnational corporations have drastically curtailed the operation of perfect competition; and as such they are not under any compulsion to expand output up to the point of full capacity. No wonder, the outer limits of Keynesianism have been rapidly approached in the advanced capitalist countries.

Capitalism, true to its character, has amassed in the metropolitan centre a vast array of productive forces. Today, the capacity to produce far outstrips the system's ability to absorb the output. The profit rate remains depressed, and tends to slide down. The *normal* state of monopoly capitalist economy is therefore stagnation.[44] On pain of possible extinction, monopoly capital then devises ways and means of circumventing the ever-present threat of a crisis; and in so doing it only sharpens the contradictions all the more. One can conceptualize the situation as follows. As huge surpluses are extracted, there arises the problem of finding profitable investment opportunities. With single-minded devotion to the principle of profit maximization, monopoly capital scans the horizon; the zero-sum game of an expensive sales campaign at home, an elaborate space programme, or an escalating military budget with an eye on the little wars here and there in the world, are all a great help to alleviate the *malaise* for the time being. But the second round of finding profitable outlets for an even bigger surplus soon begins. And thus the cycle goes on.

Briefly, the spectre of the realization crisis is haunting the metropolitan centre of world capitalism. Large sums of surplus are piling up in search of investment outlet. The situation has its own contradictions. Price rigidity being the characteristic feature of an oligopolistic market, the giant enterprises indulge in innovations to reduce cost and to launch new products for a place in the consumer's budget. Wages are allowed to move up for a twofold purpose: first, to create a market for a variety of new items of consumption, and secondly, to wipe out small competitive firms, which would crumble under the pressure of a swelling wage bill.[45] Consequently, the inherent upward trend of the organic composition of capital gets a fillip as the rising wages induce ever more labour-saving technological progress.[46] This in turn reinforces the crisis by further impinging upon the rate of profit. The short-run palliative intensifies the contradictions in the long run.

World capitalism with its metropolitan centre and the outer periphery is a dialectical unity. The crisis of one part cannot be understood in isolation from the contradictions of the other. This chapter has concentrated upon certain specifics of the centre; the next chapter will dwell on one aspect of the centre–periphery interrelationship, namely, the unequal exchange of commodities.

3

UNEQUAL EXCHANGE

CAPITALISM cannot but be a worldwide system. Its primitive accumulation draws sustenance from colonies and semicolonies; then its expanding reproduction seeks markets throughout the globe. Finally, in the era of monopoly capitalism, as we shall see below, it also needs a dumping ground for obsolete technology.

It was in the exclusive context of the European countries that Marx observed: 'The country that is more developed industrially only shows, to the less developed, the image of its own future.'[1] Elsewhere he could correctly foresee the future of the three other continents, as witness the following statement: 'A new and international division of labour, a division suited to the requirements of the chief centres of modern industry, springs up and converts one part of the globe into a chiefly agricultural field of production for supplying the other part which remains a chiefly industrial field.'[2] It was indeed during the period of the Industrial Revolution of the eighteenth and nineteenth centuries that the international specialization between industrial and agricultural countries was decided; the world became split into two groups,[3]—one, the industrial 'town'; and the other the agricultural 'country'.[4] And thus was sealed the fate of the countries of Asia, Africa and Latin America, for a long time to come, on the basis of such an international division of labour. 'The foundation of every division of labour that is well developed, and brought about by the exchange of commodities, is the separation between town and country. It may be said that the whole economic history of society is summed up in the movement of this antithesis.'[5] So also is the case with the history of world capitalism.

PILLAGE THROUGH THE AGES

The movement of the antithesis between town and country on the world scale is dramatically exemplified by the process of colonization of the Indian economy by British imperialism. Here was the first capitalist power creating, and transforming, the largest colony in the world.[6] There are two crucial coordinates around which the process evolved. The first is the mode of production in India, especially the system of extraction of surplus, or, in a word, the exploitation; and the other is the nature of British imperialism which was itself subject to evolution as the British economy was transformed under the impact of the Industrial Revolution. Reckoned in these terms, the colonial–metropolitan antithesis went through four distinct phases over two centuries, beginning from 1757 and extending up to 1947, each phase covering about half a century.

To begin with, the mode of extraction of surplus took the form of levy of land revenue by the conqueror, the East India Company, who 'found in their conquests the ultimate bliss that every merchant dreams of: to be able to buy without having to pay, and yet to be able to sell at the full price'.[7] The entire land revenue was gross profits, as it were, from which the necessary expenses for maintaining government and army, and law and order —the costs of maintenance of the existing system of exploitation —had to be deducted in order to yield the net profits. These profits were now invested to purchase Indian commodities, exercising the full monopsony power of a conqueror, which in turn were sold in markets throughout the world with an enlarged profit margin. The Indian 'tribute'—a word freely used at the time for the land revenue—thus increased manifold before it reached England. This drain of wealth disrupted the Indian trade pattern and crippled the economy. Computed at the prime cost in India, the drained-out tribute from 1783–84 to 1792–93 amounted to as much as 9 per cent of the GNP per annum.[8] Let it be noted here for comparison that at about this time in Britain the total rate of capital formation was probably no more than 7 per cent of its national income. Taking the amount of Indian tribute to be about £4.7 million at sale prices, it amounted to over 2 per cent of the British national income in 1801. At this critical stage of the Industrial Revolution, India was furnishing an amount to Britain that was almost 30 per cent of the latter's total national saving transformed into capital. Continuing primary accumulation from India thus played a vital role in the capitalist development of Britain.

In so far as the transfer of wealth took the form of export of eastern Indian commodities, it resulted in a radical disturbance of

the entire trading pattern of India. Earlier the principal export of
Bengal used to be transported overland westward: much of the
muslin, and a third of the silk. The great silk manufacturers of
Gujarat prospered on the silk import from Bengal. Now the bulk
of the raw silk, cotton and silk manufactures of Bengal was exported to Europe in consequence of the tribute, thus dislocating
the inland trade of India, and rendering the indigenous merchant
capital idle and forcing it to seek refuge in the acquisition of
landed property.

The British colonial policy underwent a shift in the first half
of the nineteenth century. The objective changed from seizing
Indian commodities to seizing the Indian market. By 1800, England
was on the threshold of completing the conquest of the cotton
textile industry by the machine. During the next thirty years the
extension of the machine to most other sectors was to be similarly
accomplished, culminating in the construction of railways in the
1830s and 1860s. The required capital could not yet entirely be
generated through internal sources; hence the need for continuing
primary accumulation was felt all the more. As such, the pressure
for tribute could not be relaxed. But simultaneously, a market for
the burgeoning British industry also had to be found. The Lancashire cotton textile industry overpowered the worldwide market
for Indian textiles; not yet satisfied, it invaded India's own home
market. A similar urge governed other new industries as they
came up with expanding production.

The extraction of tribute and the capture of the Indian market,
both at home and overseas, were the duality of the economic as-
sault upon India that marks the second stage of British colonialism
in India, set by the progress of industrialization in England and
of *de-industrialization* in India. This two-pronged attack suffered
from its own contradictions. The heavy burden of tribute on land
pauperized the agricultural proletariat, impoverished the peasants
and denuded the *zamindars*. The effective demand for British
industrial goods shrank in proportion. Meanwhile, the industries
of India had succumbed to the keen competition from British
manufactured products; and the consequent de-industrialization
then seriously affected the entire mechanism of the transfer of
wealth from India to Britain, jeopardizing thereby the mode of
exploitation through tributes. Hitherto, the realization of tribute
from India had taken the form of export of Indian manufactures;

but now a severe check was put to these exports by the disappearance of India's industries. By 1830 the problem was acute; and then a solution was found in opium. A triangular arrangement of trade was set in motion. Opium was exported from India into China, and, in return, from China tea and silk were despatched to England. In 1855 the Indian opium trade came to £6.23 million, which paid for three-fourths of the £8.50 million import of tea and silk from China into England.[9] The dominance over China had thus become indispensable for the economic exploitation of India.

About the middle of the nineteenth century a new page in the history of British colonialism in India was turned, recording the full-blown phase of British imperialism. Having completed the victory of the machine in every branch of the economy at home, British capital overflew into India. The 'net foreign investment' of Britain that was already equal in size to 42 per cent of the net domestic capital formation at home during the 1860s went up to 48.5 per cent during the 1870s and to 80 per cent in the 1880s; then after a trough in the next decade and a half it reached the peak of 114 per cent during 1905-14. British capitalism was thus gradually transformed into Monopoly Capitalism. There was apparently a partial reversal of the flow of wealth that had gone so long in one direction only. But the reversal of the flow was, of course, superficial: the principal and returns on account of this capital flowing back into Britain were, in time, to rival the size of the Indian tribute.

By 1871 the railway mileage in India was roughly 5,000 miles; within ten years it doubled; and it doubled again into 20,000 miles in a decade and a half thereafter. India, perhaps the poorest country in the world, was then in competition with the richest, in railway mileage. With the railway lines piercing through the Indian sub-continent, the heavier products of British industry such as metal manufactures (hardware, cutlery, etc.) and machinery and tools now began to be imported in large quantities. The railways did not simply facilitate imports by carrying them cheaply; as bulk no longer remained a barrier to transport, they also assisted exports of such items as foodgrains, raw cotton, oilseeds, tea, jute, hides and skins. By the 1880s the process of the de-industrialization of India had been more or less completed; and then began that of a *colonial* commercialization of agriculture—colonial, because it was meant for meeting the needs of the factories in Britain. There was a double shift in Indian agriculture to the production of raw materials for England, firstly a shift in relative acreage from food-grains to non-food crops, and then again another shift within the acreage under foodgrains to crops for export.

Meanwhile, the dominant British industrial interests brought about in 1858 the abolition of the East India Company's rule over India, and in its place the establishment of direct government by the Crown. Under the new regime the emphasis moved away from the levy of tribute through land revenue to the exploitation of India as a market and as a source of raw materials. It was during the second half of the nineteenth century that the modern Indian landlord was created and an alliance was formed between him and imperialism.

But imperialism also contributed to the formation of two other classes, the nascent bourgeoisie and the industrial proletariat. The irreconcilable contradictions that emerged between imperialism and its junior ally, the landlords, on the one hand, and the bulk of the Indian people including the bourgeoisie, the working class and the peasantry, on the other, laid the seeds of the struggle for national liberation. This was the fourth and final phase of British imperialism in India, covering the period 1900–1947.[10]

The course of imperialist exploitation in other parts of Asia, Africa and Latin America was not exactly the same in all details as that in India. Africa was forced to supply human beings as slaves to the metropolis of imperialism; Latin America was robbed of precious metals, mineral resources and agricultural raw materials. Despite variations over time and across the continents, one thing is clear: *To the extent there was any exchange of goods between the outer periphery and the metropolitan centre of world capitalism throughout the four centuries, it had always been an unequal exchange to the detriment of the former.*[11] The outline of Indian history *vis-à-vis* British imperialism, as given above, makes this point quite clear. The unequal exchange indeed has a history. One wonders—how could this go on for such a long time, over such a vast area, on such a large scale!

The Third World countries are richly endowed with natural resources as well as human resources. Yet they are poor, evidently not because of a curse of nature since they are not lacking in natural wealth—least of all in raw materials for heavy industry.

They are poor partly because this natural wealth has been, and still is being, plundered by imperialism for the needs of its own industrialization at the expense of those countries from which it slips away in its raw state.[12] As for human resources, half of the world lives in the Third World. Important as these initial endowments may be, they recede more and more into the background when compared with differences that are the outcome of the uneven development of productive forces in various countries. The unequal development of productive forces creates different economic types and different production spheres, thus increasing the prevailing international division of labour.[13] Since the Industrial Revolution of the eighteenth-nineteenth centuries when the world was split up into a 'town' and a 'country', it has been one single process with all its change and continuity.

The imperialist ways of plundering the mineral resources of the Third World have all too often been direct, crude and transparent. It is perhaps easier for the newly independent former colonies and semicolonies to identify and put an end to this part of the pillage, if they so wish. But the imperialist mechanism of exploiting the human resources of the Third World, however, had been comparatively camouflaged, and, at present, is quite subtle. Unequal exchange is a major component of this mechanism which works, not in a vacuum, but in the medium of a certain collaboration of classes as we shall elaborate in due course. In proportion to the subtlety and pervasiveness of this process, it is equally difficult to lay one's hand on the phenomenon, to measure its extent, and to single it out for elimination.

TENTACLES OF IMPERIALISM

The three continents of Latin America, Asia and Africa were drawn into the world capitalist system in that order. Different countries with their respective endowment of resources fell into the network at different points of time. Accordingly, there is some degree of heterogeneity in their experiences as part of world capitalism. However, the sum total of their history as colony or semicolony would bear out a few broad generalizations regarding the net effect of imperialism on them. India in particular would be a case in point.

First, a large chunk of income is siphoned off every year from the colony in the name of tribute, profit, royalty, etc. At the turn of the eighteenth century, such an outflow amounted to 9 per cent of the GNP of India, whereas, in comparison, about that time the rate of capital formation was 7 per cent of the national income in Britain, for instance. Second, the above-mentioned outflow in effect takes the form of export of commodities. Within the physical limits of feasibility, with or without the support of the armed might of imperialism, the commodities to be exported by a colony are determined by the requirements of the headquarters of imperialism. In consequence, the agriculture and industry of the colony are rendered subservient to the factories and consumers in the metropolis. Third, the mineral resources and other raw materials of the colony are plundered by imperialism, without letting the former have the full benefits thereof. This takes away the material foundation upon which manufacturing, chemical or engineering industries could have grown up in the colony. Fourth, as the manufactured goods of the metropolitan centre assail the colonial market, all too often with the backing of the military strength of imperialism as it happened in the case of textiles in India, the industrial structure of the colony falls apart, and is then reorganized only to complement that of the metropolitan centre of world capitalism. Fifth, the colony being a captive market for the metropolitan manufactured products, the technological base of the industries there cannot but be dictated by the compulsions of the metropolitan industries, no matter what the local conditions are.

Of course, one must add to this list the bearing of imperialism upon the class relations in the Third World. Since it will be a major theme in our subsequent analysis, we may ignore it for the time being. Looking at the five-point impact of imperialism as enumerated above in the course of making a generalization from the historical experience, one is struck by the fact that these observations are valid even today. This is not to say that history repeats itself mechanically or that it does not move ahead. All it means is that, despite changes in the form and modality of imperialist exploitation, the Third World in effect continues to remain a semicolony of the metropolitan centre of world capitalism. Lately, imperialism has resorted to new forms of exploitation. The net result on the Third World, however, is much the same. The colonial–metropolitan, or, if you like, the centre–periphery, relationship now revolves around four axes as follows.

First, the capital flow. The export of capital to colonies was considered by Lenin to be one of the major characteristics of modern imperialism. Up to the year 1914, Britain was the biggest foreign investor. Since 1946, the USA with its share of 60 per cent of all foreign direct investment in the world, has come to the top. The nature of investments has however changed in the meantime. Formerly, the capital flow was primarily in the form of portfolio investment, i.e. purchase of shares in foreign companies. In the wake of transnational corporations, establishing subsidiaries overseas has also become quite significant. However, the outflow of royalty, profit, dividend, etc. from the Third World certainly dwarfs the amount of capital inflow into it. So the net flow is in fact negative from the viewpoint of the Third World. Foreign capital in the Third World is a device of transferring the surplus to the metropolitan centre.[14]

Second, the transnational production. Transaction of business at the international plane dates back to the Middle Ages when banking was conducted on international lines. Worldwide trading was known a long time ago; the East India Company of Britain is a leading example. In the nineteenth century, companies from several countries, notably Britain and the USA, exploited the raw materials and natural resources of Asia, Africa and Latin America on a vast scale. From about 1860 onwards manufacturing companies began to establish production facilities outside their own countries, and by 1914 many of today's giant transnational corporations were already operating in several countries. However, during the last twenty-five years or so, there has been a fundamental change in the situation: the most striking characteristic of the modern transnational company is its central direction. The subsidiaries are no longer run as separate enterprises each of which has to stand on its own feet. All the operations of a transnational company, including those of its subsidiaries, have been subjected to a central command, with remarkable indifference to the interests of the host countries.[15]

Third, the flow of technology. The pace of technological progress in the advanced capitalist countries has sharply accelerated during the last quarter century. The Third World countries, on the other hand, are looking for modern technology. So a coincidence of 'needs' has taken place, and as a result the international flow of technology has assumed a significant proportion. In another chapter we shall investigate this matter further.

Finally, trade. Indeed, it is the trade of commodities which mediates all the above three, viz. capital movement, international production and technology transfer. Apart from being a medium for these three, trade has also an independent identity as an exchange of goods and services without necessarily consummating in the process any of the above three. This only confirms the overwhelming importance of trade as a crucial axis for the dynamics of centre–periphery relationship.

The imperialist objectives in each of the four modalities of colonial exploitation—foreign capital, transnational production, technology transfer, and trade—when considered separately, are mutually conflicting to a certain extent, although their underlying equation is one of complementarity. This dialectical interface among them may be here briefly touched upon. To the extent a sizeable part of the surplus of a semicolony is transferred to the metropolitan centre through these mechanisms, and consequently its development is retarded, its potentialities as a market for the goods of the centre are reduced; the same thing happens to the prospects for sending to it the obsolete plant and equipment from the metropolis. It is incorrect to say that, in view of imperialism, industrialization is impossible in the Third World; or that its economy must stagnate or even regress. For it is to the interest of imperialism that an economic expansion of a particular nature occurs in the semicolony, so as to absorb its discarded commodities including plant and equipment. Trade thus plays a central role in the entire ensemble of centre–periphery links; and, as noted earlier, the other three means of imperialist exploitation not only ultimately work through the vehicle of international trade, but also order its basic nature. In this chapter, we are concerned with only trade as such; the factors having bearing upon it would be taken up for consideration subsequently. History shows that the trade between centre and periphery had always been one of unequal exchange in the past; and one may argue that it is going to be so also in future. Let us see why. Before that, we need to know the volume and content of the centre–periphery exchange.

TRADE AND PRODUCTION

First of all, it may be noted that the two-way trade between the metropolitan centre and the outer periphery amounted to 52 billion dollars in 1964.[16] In the year 1962, on the other hand, the total long-term capital, including official donations, private investments, and the credits extended by such bodies as the International Bank for Reconstruction and Development, that came into the Third World, amounted to 5.9 billion dollars.[17] Now, just to have an impression of the quantitative importance of unequal exchange, suppose that the extent of overpricing of imports and of underpricing of exports from the Third World was of the order of 10 per cent. If so, the surplus acquired by the advanced capitalist countries through this method alone was as much as 5.2 billion dollars in 1964, which is over 80 per cent of the long-term capital inflow into the Third World during 1962. *In case the margin due to unequal exchange is 20 per cent, the surplus thus extracted by the metropolitan centre from the outer periphery far exceeds its long-term capital investment in the latter.* Are there any empirical indicators of the possible measure of the margin?[18] In the Colombian pharmaceutical industry, for example, the weighted average overpricing of products imported by foreign-owned subsidiaries amounted to 155 per cent while that of national firms was 19 per cent, during the late sixties. Chile as well as Peru had suffered such overpricing in their pharmaceutical industry to the extent of more than 300 per cent in some cases. The electronics industry in Colombia and Ecuador had the same experience. Moreover, the rubber and chemical industries of Colombia recorded a weighted average of overpricing in the imports of foreign-owned subsidiaries to the tune of 40 per cent and 20–25 per cent respectively.[19] Such is the magnitude of the surplus thus transferred that there are instances where the absolute amount of overpricing by the foreign firms operating in a Third World country amounted to a figure of six times the royalties and twenty-four times the declared profits.[20] The overpricing of imports into the Third World and the underpricing of its exports therefore appear to be instrumental in effecting the transfer of a huge quantity of surplus from the Third World. Here the prevailing world price is being taken as the benchmark for computing the degree of over- or under-pricing. But the capitalist world market itself has evolved through the ages a bias against the weaker Third World countries. And if that built-in bias also is kept in view, the quantum of surplus transfer through unequal exchange is likely to go up still higher.

The trade relation of the outer periphery of world capitalism with the metropolitan centre is given in Table 3. In 1964 the

TABLE 3

VOLUME AND DIRECTION OF WORLD EXPORTS, 1964

(Per cent)

	Total exports (million dollars), with % within brackets	Exports to		
		Advanced capitalist countries	Socialist countries	Third World
1. Centre: advanced capitalist countries	116,015 (68)	74	4	22
2. Socialist countries	20,222 (12)	20	65	15
3. Periphery: Third World	34,725 (20)	74	6	20
Total	170,962 (100)	67	12	21

Source: Jalée (1968), p. 29.

Third World's export was about 35 billion dollars, of which three-fourths went to the advanced capitalist countries, and only one-fifth was among its own countries. The advanced capitalist countries as a group did just the opposite: three-fourths of their exports were within the group, and one-fifth was delivered to the Third World. This gives a measure of the unequal strength of the two groups of countries in the field of international trade. As for the composition of the Third World's exports, foodstuffs contribute 30 per cent, raw materials of agricultural and mineral origin 30 per cent, fuels 25 per cent, base metals 5 per cent, and manufactures, machinery, and miscellaneous 10 per cent. However, about 60 per cent of its imports from the advanced capitalist countries consist of manufactured and machinery items.[21] And of course it is the Third World which supplies the raw materials for these industrial goods. Of the respective total imports of the advanced capitalist countries, the Third World as a source of supply accounts for 92.7 per cent of crude oil, 86.8 per cent of bauxite, 85.5 per cent of tin, 74.1 per cent of manganese, 64.5 per cent of phosphates, 57.8 per cent of copper, and so on.[22] Raw materials and foodstuffs of agricultural origin are also an area where the Third World continues to be a primary source of supply to the metropolitan centre of world capitalism. Some 98 per cent of coffee, jute and copra, between 90 and 95 per cent of tea and peanuts, over 75 per cent of sugar and rubber, imported into these advanced countries, come from the Third World.[23]

Apart from the volume, composition and direction of the Third World's export, what is very striking is the influence it seems to exert upon the pattern of production in the Third World. It appears as if the entire economy is oriented towards meeting the export demands which, in any case, are determined by the needs of the metropolitan centre of world capitalism. During the decades of the fifties and sixties the export sector of the Third World had expanded well ahead of the other sectors of the economy. The extractive industries which produce the major raw materials from the subsoil are growing rapidly in the Third World while the secondary industries which produce consumer goods and equipment are growing only at a modest rate. Expansion seems to be in the same order in the field of agriculture as well. There is rapid growth in basic products which are exported to meet the needs of imperialist countries; side by side there is stagnation or regression in the production of food for local consumption. One is reminded of the colonial commercialization that took place in India in the late nineteenth century; the same pattern continues today throughout the Third World. Even in a period of rapid political decolonization, the international division of labour that was delineated during the eighteenth-nineteenth centuries, far from being modified, has grown even sharper.[24]

UNSUCCESSFUL ATTEMPTS TO THEORIZE

One may have a vague impression of the meaning of the term 'unequal exchange'; but an attempt to find a precise definition for it meets with serious difficulty. To define unequal exchange, one must first of all clarify what is meant by equal exchange; and that is not an easy task. Under pure capitalism, with the law of value in full force, equivalents are exchanged— equivalents in terms of the socially necessary labour time embodied in the commodities. But here again a problem crops up in case the organic composition of capital is not uniform throughout the economy. Prices then cease to be equiproportional to values; and the rate of exchange between two commodities being determined by their relative prices, values no longer retain any relevance at the market place. This may be explained through simple numerical examples.

Table 4 gives the calculation of value and price under two situations, one with the same organic composition of capital for both commodities, and the other with different compositions. Numerical figures, to begin with, have been so chosen as to satisfy the following: the rate of exploitation must be uniform; and so should be the rate of profit as well. Constant and variable capitals are measured in value terms, but are retained as such for price calculation as well.[25] Partly in deference to equations (31) and (32) of the preceding chapter, but mainly for convenience, total value is taken as equal to total price of the two commodities; likewise total surplus value and total profit are taken as equal. Now, in the first case, 4.1 in Table 4, price coincides with value. The two commodities then would be traded in the ratio of 2:1; and it would be an instance of exchanging the equivalents in terms of the labour content. The next case, 4.2 in Table 4, however, is different. Commodity 1 has a higher organic composition of capital than the overall average, i.e. 3/5. Consequently, it would relatively gain in price. The values of the two commodities are in the proportion of 50:20; but their prices are such that they would be exchanged in the market at the rate of 49:21. Clearly, the seller of commodity 1 is giving less labour content in his merchandise than what he is receiving from the other commodity in return. One form of unequal exchange thus emanates from the difference in organic composition of capital.

Typically, the method of production of agricultural goods requires a relatively smaller constant capital in comparison with industrial goods. Should the rate of profit be equalized between two trading countries having the same rate of exploitation of labour, the country specializing in the export of agricultural goods therefore would suffer a loss of surplus in the process of exchange.

4

TABLE 4

VALUE AND PRICE CALCULATION

(Case 4.1) Equal Exchange: Same Organic Composition of Capital; Value = Price

Commodity	Constant capital q	Variable capital v	Surplus value u	Value $\pi = q+v+u$	Rate of exploitation u/v	Organic composition of capital $q/(q+v)$	Rate of profit $r = \Sigma u/\Sigma(q+v)$	Price $p = (1+r)(q+u)$
1	100	50	50	200	1	2/3	150/450 = 33.33%	200
2	200	100	100	400	1	2/3	do	400

(Case 4.2) Primary Form of Unequal Exchange: Different Organic Composition of Capital; Value ≠ Price

Commodity	Constant capital q	Variable capital v	Surplus value u	Value $\pi = q+v+u$	Rate of exploitation u/v	Organic composition of capital $q/(q+v)$	Rate of profit $r = \Sigma u/\Sigma(q+v)$	Price $p = (1+r)(q+u)$
1	100	50	50	200	1	2/3	200/500 = 40%	210
2	200	150	150	500	1	4/7	do	490

Surplus would be transferred from there into the country which exports industrial goods, although the profit rate remains the same in both the countries. This position was taken by Otto Bauer as early as 1907 and by Henryk Grossmann in 1929.[26] In criticism, Sweezy concedes that 'the conclusion indeed follows from the premise'; then he hastens to add, 'but the premise is incorrect'.[27] Sweezy continues: 'It is no more true that trade equalizes profit rates between two countries than it is that trade equalizes profit rates between two *monopolized industries* within a single country.'[28] He thus assails the so-called primary form of non-equivalent exchange which springs from the fact of diversity in organic composition of capital on the ground that competition does not prevail in international trade.

Emmanuel however grants the assumption of perfect competition, but dismisses the above-mentioned theory of non-equivalent exchange in its primary form as too broad since it holds not only in trade between countries but also within the same country among different sectors of the economy. As such, according to him, it cannot capture the specific problem of imperialist exploitation of one country by another.[29] Emmanuel then proceeds to build up his theory of unequal exchange which is characterized by differences in organic compositions as well as in wages.[30] Referring to equation (30) of the previous chapter, it is found that the price of a commodity is a multiple of the sum of constant and variable capitals, the multiplier being given by simply one *plus* the rate of profit. If, for one reason or another, the wage rate is reduced, *ceteris paribus*, the price of the commodity will be lower as the variable capital declines. So it will command, in exchange, less labour than it was doing before. This logic can be extended to the case of two countries producing, for instance, one commodity each. Thus one gets the unequal exchange in the strict sense, according to Emmanuel. There are institutional barriers to the mobility of labour across countries; as a result, wage differentials between nations still persist even though the profit rate is equalized in the wake of international trade.[31] In his own words:

Regardless of any alteration in prices resulting from imperfect competition on the commodity market, unequal exchange is the proportion between equalization of profits between regions in which the rate of surplus value is 'institutionally' different—the term 'institutionally' meaning that these rates are, for whatever reason, safeguarded from competitive equalization on the factors market and are independent of relative prices.[32]

Briefly, Emmanuel takes wages as the independent variable of the system. Wage-difference between countries is accepted as a given fact, and is assumed to surpass the difference in labour productivity, if any. Now, the low-wage country would export its commodity at a rate, governed by the Marxian theory of price determination, which would effect an exchange of commodities with unequal labour contents.

Numerical examples of Table 5 can illustrate the point. Case 5.1 gives an instance of unequal exchange of the primary form, i.e. one which is due to the difference in organic composition of capital. As in the two earlier cases, the figures for q, v and u are arbitrarily taken subject to the condition that the rate of exploitation is the same for both commodities. Assuming the equality of total price and total value, the overall profit rate is calculated, with which one can find the prices. Under case 5.1, the two commodities according to their prices would be exchanged at the rate of 286:214, whereas their respective values would warrant the ratio of 300:200. Clearly there would be a hidden transfer of value from the country that produces commodity 2 to the one which produces commodity 1. Again, the origin for this unequal exchange can be traced to the discrepancy in the organic composition of capital.

Now, suppose that wages in the country producing commodity 2 are cut in half; case 5.2 in Table 5 presents the results. The rate of exploitation goes up for commodity 2 while the organic composition of capital is equalized across the board. Their prices would make the two commodities exchange at 1:1, whereas their values would call for the rate of 3:2. Here again the lower-wage country of commodity 2 would lose in terms of value. This time the organic composition of capital cannot be blamed. The villain of the piece is now the lower wage rate. Should it go with also lower organic composition of capital, then it would be a formidable combination to the detriment of this poor country. Such is the theory of unequal exchange as formulated by Emmanuel.

One of the difficulties with Emmanuel's model is that its construction is totally illogical, so much so that there would be no exchange at all in his model, let alone unequal exchange. Consider the two countries in isolation. In the country of commodity 1,

TABLE 5

Unequal Exchange: Primary Form and à la Emmanuel

(Case 5.1) Unequal Exchange: Primary Form

Commodity	Constant capital q	Variable capital v	Surplus value u	Value $\pi = q+v+u$	Rate of exploitation u/v	Organic composition of capital $q/(q+v)$	Rate of profit $r = \Sigma u/\Sigma(q+v)$	Price $p = (1+r)(q+v)$
1	100	50	50	200	1	2/3	150/350 = 43%	214
2	100	100	100	300	1	1/2	do	286

(Case 5.2) Unequal Exchange: à la Emmanuel

Commodity	Constant capital q	Variable capital v	Surplus value u	Value $\pi = q+v+u$	Rate of exploitation u/v	Organic composition of capital $q/(q+v)$	Rate of profit $r = \Sigma u/\Sigma(q+v)$	Price $p = (1+r)(q+v)$
1	100	50	50	200	1	2/3	200/300 = 66.66%	250
2	100	50	150	300	3	2/3	do	250

without trade, the profit rate is: $50/(100+50) = 33.33$ per cent; similarly, in the other country it is: $150/(100+50) = 100$ per cent. As trade takes place, the uniform profit rate settles in the middle, 66.66 per cent. But, why should the bourgeoisie of the latter country voluntarily engage in trade when it knows full well that the profit rate will decline?[33] Therefore, there would be no exchange under competitive conditions in the Emmanuel model. This problem is not peculiar to the numerical example we have chosen. Looking at equation (33) of the previous chapter one can see that the bourgeoisie would not trade with another country where the rate of exploitation is lower and/or the organic composition of capital is higher; for that would reduce the profit rate. So long as trade between the metropolitan centre and the outer periphery of world capitalism is conceived of as just a mechanical way of bringing together two countries to exchange without affecting the basic conditions of production this problem is bound to remain. Let it be emphasized that it is a necessary condition for voluntary trade to occur that the profit for the bourgeoisie of *both* the countries must improve; otherwise there would be no trade.

Another type of approach has been made to the theory of unequal exchange using the Sraffa-type model of price formation. Its author is Braun.[34] Here wages are no longer the independent variable; nor is perfect competition the rule. Now price would be the independent variable, manipulated as it is by the metropolitan centre exercising its monopoly power. Consider two countries called A and B, the former being the advanced capitalist country and the latter the backyard of imperialism. In the formal model of Braun, the economies of A and B were initially operating in mutual isolation with their respective technologies and price systems governed by Sraffa equations.[35] Somehow the two economies are brought together through trade, and a single profit rate prevails everywhere. The insights of the Sraffa model can be drawn upon for the problem at hand. Partly by theoretical reasoning and partly by simulation, Braun deduces the following four propositions:

(*i*) In the joint economy of A and B, profit rate varies inversely with wage rate.

(*ii*) By assumption, profit rate is uniform in both the countries; but wage rates may be different. With a given profit rate ruling in A and B, wage rates in the two countries must be inversely related. The reason is that once a certain profit rate is fixed the weighted average of the wage rates in A and B are immediately determined in view of the above proposition (*i*). Should the wage rate in country A rise, that in country B must fall so as to maintain the predetermined weighted average in consonance with the pre-assigned value of the profit rate. Obviously, the set of equations has two degrees of freedom.

(*iii*) The wage rate of one country being given, that of the other country and the overall profit rate are also inversely related. This is a simple corollary of the preceding theorems.

(*iv*) If the wage rate of a country varies, *ceteris paribus*, the price of a commodity produced there would also move in the same direction; and *vice versa*.

With these conclusions at hand, Braun tries to build up his theory of unequal exchange as follows.

The metropolitan centre has tremendous monopoly power in the world market which is used to keep down the prices of goods exported by the poor country B. Hence arises the unequal exchange. What are the consequences? In view of proposition (*iv*) above, it leads to a lower wage rate in country B. Moreover, taking account of proposition (*ii*) it is found that as wage rate in country A improves, the income of workers in country B keeps on falling. Unlike Emmanuel, Braun however does not clarify why the exchange is deemed unequal, and in what sense. Rather, what he provides is a formal explanation of the deteriorating terms of trade of poor countries, accompanied by rising wages in imperialist countries and falling wages in the Third World.

But the same question crops up again. Will there be any trade at all in the model of Braun? The answer is No. The uniform profit rate that prevails in the joint economies of A and B in the wake of international trade must belong within the range defined by the two individual profit rates obtained in A and B respectively in the absence of trade. Why then would the bourgeoisie of the country with the higher profit rate engage in trade with the other country? Not only that; as the simulation exercise of Braun shows,[36] trade in his model, in addition to reducing the wage rate in the poor country B, goes on impinging also upon the volume of *profit* in B, in response to the rising wages in country

A. The bourgeoisie of *B*, unless they are prone to self-immolation, should better withdraw from such trade, if they have got somehow involved in it in the first place.[37]

Despite their logical flaws the models of Emmanuel and Braun emphasize two important facets of the disadvantageous position of the poor countries of the Third World. The countries of the metropolitan centre of world capitalism wield tremendous monopoly power, and with this power or otherwise they transfer value from the Third World; this is the essence of the phenomenon known as unequal exchange. One may ask: Does the export sector of the Third World observe the rules either of the Marxian theory of price determination as claimed by Emmanuel, or of the Sraffa system of price formation as claimed by Braun? To put it differently, is not the export sector, much like the rest of the economy, far from being capitalist in nature? To this Amin answers as follows:

The exports of the Third World are not in the main agricultural products from backward sectors with low productivity. Out of an overall total of exports from the underdeveloped countries of $35 billion (in 1966), the *ultramodern capitalist sector* (oil, mining and primary processing of minerals, modern plantations—like those of United Fruit in Central America or Unilever in Africa or Malaya etc.)—provides at least three-quarters, or $26 billion.[38]

That is to say, mineral and agricultural raw materials and foodstuffs indeed are the major export items of the Third World; but these are produced under the capitalist mode of production, often with foreign capital. Hence the formulas of Emmanuel and Braun are not out of place, though misconceived they might be. This may or may not be correct in fact; in any case it remains an open question as to how the concept of unequal exchange is to be formulated when a capitalist sector trades with a, say, primarily feudal one. For, outside the capitalist mode of production, the labour content or value has no role in the equation of prices.

A FRESH APPROACH

Emmanuel's attempt to demonstrate the occurrence of unequal exchange *even* under the conditions of perfect competition has not met with success. However, the possibility of unequal exchange at the theoretical plane can be proved in the following way. The importance of the foreign trade sector in the national economy varies from country to country. So a full-blown general equilibrium model embracing two economies in their entirety is not necessarily called for, although it can be done. Soon after a Third World country is integrated into the system of world capitalism, its economy is transformed by and large to suit the requirements of the metropolitan centre. The commodities to be exported are decided upon, and the method of production thereof is also worked out accordingly. The export commodities may be altogether new items of production, or may be products of the old traditional type. In the era of neo-colonialism, however, a Third World country is politically independent, and enjoys a degree of economic flexibility. Although remaining within the orbit of world capitalism, it gains some measure of economic choice. Suppose that it identifies a commodity, new or old, as a profitable item of export, whose output is denoted by x. To simplify the matter, let it require only two inputs for production, viz. an amount a of itself, and b of labour, per unit of output. Money wage rate (previously it was real wage) is represented by w, and profit rate by r. Production takes one period. Wage is paid at the end of the period, but input a has to be paid for at the beginning. If p stands for the price of the commodity, then:

$$p = bw + ap(1+r)$$
$$\text{or,} \quad p = bw/[1-a(1+r)] . \qquad (34)$$

It resembles equation (12) of the previous chapter.

An advanced capitalist country imports x, and exports another commodity by the amount y to the Third World country. To keep the focus on unequal exchange only, we assume a balance in trade. Let the unit of measurement of the commodity exported from the advanced capitalist country be so chosen that its price also is equal to p, so that in the event of balance in trade, we get:

$$xp = yp . \qquad (35)$$

For production, every unit of y requires amount $(a+\Delta a)$ of itself, and $(b-\Delta b)$ of labour as input. In this country, however, the money wage rate is higher; suppose it is kw, where $k > 1$. To begin with, it is furthermore assumed that the profit rate is equalized in the wake of international trade; this assumption will be relaxed later. Like equation (34), we get the following for the price of y:

$$p = (b-\Delta b)kw/[1-(a+\Delta a)(1+r)]. \qquad (36)$$

From equations (34) and (36) it follows that:

$$b/[1-a(1+r)] = (b-\Delta b) \cdot k/[1-(a+\Delta a)(1+r]. \qquad (37)$$

Since it is known that $k > 1$, equation (37) yields the following inequality:

$$b/[1-a(1+r)] > (b-\Delta b)/[1-(a+\Delta a)(1+r)]. \qquad (38)$$

Let it be noted that in view of the choice of units, commodities x and y are traded at the rate of 1:1; see also equations (34) and (36). But (34) and (36) also imply the inequality of (38). As we shall show below, the two sides of (38) are the total labour contents per unit of x and y respectively; and therefore here is an instance of *unequal exchange* even under perfectly competitive conditions in the market.

The method of resolving the commodity input into an infinite stream of labour inputs has already been outlined above. Now properly weighing the labour inputs with the profit rate,[39] the ultimate series of labour inputs per unit of x adds up as follows:

$$b+ab(1+r)+a^2b(1+r)^2+ \ldots = b/[1-a(1+r)] \qquad (39)$$

This is the term at the left hand side of (38). Similarly, the other term of (38) is the labour content per unit of y. Hence, the Third World country is giving away more labour than it is getting back in trade. This is then an unequal exchange.

In order to gain more insight into this theory, the above model may be looked at in another way. Consider for the moment x and y as the same commodity produced in two countries with two different techniques, viz. (a, b), and $(a+\Delta a, b-\Delta b)$, the latter being less labour-intensive in view of the higher wage rate in the country concerned. It has the same price everywhere; and hence may be used as the *numeraire*. It is now interesting to note that from (38) we get:

$$\Delta b/\Delta a > b(1+r)/[1-a(1+r)]. \qquad (40)$$

This inequality only highlights the condition that for the phenomenon of unequal exchange to hold the substitutibility between labour and the other commodity input has to be of a sufficiently high order. This observation will help us later to understand the place of technological progress in the theory of unequal exchange.

The model can be extended to any number of commodities. If a_{ij} stands for the amount of commodity i required to produce one unit of commodity j ($i, j = 1, 2, \ldots n$), b_j for the corresponding labour input, r the rate of interest and w the money wage rate, then the price of j is given by:

$$p_j = b_j w + (1+r) \sum_{i=1}^{n} a_{ij} p_i \qquad (41)$$

$$(j = 1, 2, \ldots n) .$$

This equation is the many-goods analogue of equation (34). In matrix notation:

$$p = bw[I - \{I - (1+r)\ A\}]^{-1} \qquad (42)$$

where p and b are vectors, A the $n \times n$ technology matrix $[a_{ij}]$, and I the identity matrix, w and r being the wage rate and interest rate respectively.[40] These goods are produced in one country, and are to be traded with those of another. The other country similarly produces another set of goods under the conditions of a higher wage rate but equal interest or profit rate. All these goods are exchanged between the two countries according to their price ratios. However, let it be noted that price is a multiple of the wage rate prevailing in the country concerned as shown in (42). When two commodities are exchanged between two countries maintaining trade balance, their total prices must be equal. But there is a difference in wage rates; so the respective multipliers of wages in the price equations also must be different. For the commodity produced in the country with a lower wage will have a higher multiple. And this multiple is nothing but the sum of the direct and indirect labour contents duly weighed with the profit rate according to their timings of occurrence in the production pocess. Hence the country with the lower wage rate gives out more labour than what it gets back under balanced trade *even* with perfect competition in full force.

Having thus demonstrated the validity of the model of unequal exchange in the many-goods case, our subsequent discussion may revert to the two-goods case, for simplicity. It is true that fixed capital like machinery has not been fully taken into account in price equation (34). Of course, coefficient a may be interpreted broadly so as to include depreciation of machines also as a cost component. Still another problem remains; the capitalist reckons the profit rate on the total capital tied-up; not just on the amount of capital used-up as measured by the coefficient a. Such considerations may be duly brought into the model, but evidently the fundamental conclusion in respect of unequal exchange will remain unaffected. However, the algebra will clutter up quite a bit.[41]

A more important question is whether the assumption of profit equalization between the countries is tenable. All evidence points to the contrary. Baran and Sweezy, for instance, report that the profit rate in the USA is only a quarter of that abroad.[42] Similarly, Kidron finds that the profit rates of foreign companies are higher in India than in their respective home countries.[43] The Third World is thus characterized by a lower wage rate as well as a higher profit rate. How does this affect the conclusions drawn from (37)? The way profit rate enters into the denominator a higher value of r, *ceteris paribus*, would raise the value of the entire expression. The computation of the labour content of the exports from the Third World would thus tend to be somewhat exaggerated on this count. However, the wage differential between the Third World and the metropolitan centre is so wide, i.e. the parameter k of (37) is numerically so large, that the inequality of (38) will in fact be well pronounced, much beyond swamping the effect of any discrepancy between the profit rates. On balance, the Third World therefore pays more and gets less in terms of the labour content of traded commodities. Let it be emphasized, however, that although mathematically unequal exchange owes its origin to the postulate of wage differential between two countries, raising the wage rate of the poor country to the level of the rich country's is certainly no answer to the problem. It is no exaggeration to say that unequal exchange between the metropolitan centre and the outer periphery of world capitalism is a phenomenon many centuries old; in modern times such exchange is effected partly by the relative cheapness of labour in poor countries and partly by the outright monopoly power of rich countries. It is predicated upon a certain matrix of class collaboration at home and abroad; it is a manifestation of a deep-rooted *malaise* of the world capitalist system. And that is the major burden of this essay.

THE RISING INEQUALITY

Such is the inherent logic of world capitalism that the degree of unequal exchange, instead of narrowing down, tends to grow over time. All the elements of the system are laid out in a way that only deepens the inequality between the rich and poor countries. The point will be clear if one keeps equations (34–42) in view. As mentioned earlier, there are compelling reasons for the wage rate in the metropolitan centre to keep on rising; that is, parameter k in equation (37) moves up. As a result, *ceteris paribus*, the inequality of (38) becomes all the more acute. Now the twin problems of rising surplus and a swelling wage bill are sought to be mitigated through labour-saving technological progress, which means that $\Delta b/\Delta a$ of expression (40) tends to be higher and higher, thereby intensifying the inequality of exchange all the more. The labour-saving nature and the fast pace of technological progress have other consequences as well, which will be taken up in due course. Meanwhile, let us note that as huge stocks of machinery get obsolete every year the metropolitan centre looks out for a profitable dumping ground; and thus the centre and the periphery continue to remain connected through a one-way transfer of technology. The periphery thereby witnesses a particular form of industrialization that primarily suits the timepath of obsolescence in the metropolitan centre.

In addition to inducing labour-saving technological progress the very upward shift in the wage rate also compels the profit-seeking firms in the metropolitan centre to move along the isoquant within the limits of the existing technology for a higher capital–labour ratio, thereby increasing $\Delta b/\Delta a$ of expression (40) above. This is the third factor which operates to widen the gulf between the centre and the periphery.

Obviously, these three processes which lead to growing inequality in exchange reinforce one another. The flow of hidden transfers from the periphery to the metropolitan centre of world capitalism as a result assumes the form of an ever-rising tide.

TIP OF THE ICEBERG

The world trade market is far from a textbook model of perfect competition; depending upon the commodity concerned, it has all the traits of monopoly, oligopoly, monopsony, oligopsony and several other departures from competition. For a Third World country, however, trade is a tussle with giants. A striking feature of recent origin is that an increasing part of world trade has become an internal transaction within the same vertically integrated transnational corporation. It is estimated, for instance, that as much as two-fifths of manufacturing exports from Latin America come from subsidiaries of the United States transnationals.[44] On the other hand, the transnational corporations hold a dominant position in US exports, and they are also the main exporters of technology.[45]

The so-called multinational or transnational corporations manipulate their accounts so as to locate profits wherever it is most advantageous to them; and on occasion, usually of course to avoid taxation, they declare low profits in underdeveloped countries regardless of the scale of activities.[46] They overcharge the imports into the Third World country and undercharge the exports therefrom. The resultant unequal exchange of course cannot be theoretically captured in a model of competitive trade. Nevertheless the quantitative significance of the hidden flow due to the malpractice of 'transfer pricing' by transnationals can hardly be exaggerated. Trade in technology is also tied up with this process; almost invariably a contract of technology sales stipulates the purchase of intermediate products from the seller of technology, who then charges excessive prices for these products. For instance, 'from research in Colombia and extrapolating from a sample that included 25 per cent of the imports of 40–50 per cent of the pharmaceutical industry, it was estimated that the country paid for intermediate products in 1968 close to US $20,000,000 solely due to *price differentials* above those available in the "international" market for the same products. Price differentials were observed in each of the sectors studied, which included chemicals, electronics and rubber products.'[47] The overwhelming importance of transfer pricing as a means of draining away surplus from the Third World can be gauged from the fact that in the Colombian pharmaceutical industry what was taken away through overpricing of intermediate products was about 25 times the amount that was declared as profits of the subsidiary of the parent multinational corporation, or nearly 6 times the royalties received. To quote: 'Defining as effective returns to the parent corporation the sum of reported profits of the subsidiary, royalty payments and intermediate product overpricing, the following data can be inferred from our sample of the Colombian pharmaceutical industry. *Reported profits constituted 3.4 per cent of effective returns, royalties 14.0 per cent and "overpricing" 82.6 per cent.*'[48]

What is visibly extracted by transnational corporations in the form of profit or royalty is overwhelmingly dwarfed by what they expropriate from the Third World by way of surreptitious transfer pricing. The former is but the tip of the iceberg. The dice is thus very much loaded in the world capitalist system against the Third World: competitive trade—the Third World gives away more labour content than what it gets in return; trade with the giant multinationals—surplus is squeezed out of the Third World through various means such as technology tie-up and transfer pricing. Either way, *uneven development* therefore is an inevitability within world capitalism.[49] The underdevelopment of the periphery is a precondition for the development of the centre. How can the periphery develop if so much of surplus is drained away from it?

NECESSITY AND FREEDOM

Can the metropolitan centre of world capitalism not develop without causing underdevelopment of the periphery? Has not the volume of trade of the centre with the periphery declined relatively almost to the point of being nonconsequential? Is the inflow of dividend, royalty and profit from the periphery into the centre not almost negligible in relation to the latter's gross domestic product? As for the outflow of investment from the centre into the periphery, that also has been considerably reduced in comparison with what it was as a proportion of gross domestic savings. For a definitive answer to these queries one has to wait till the end of our analysis. Meanwhile we may briefly mention the place of unequal exchange assigned by Rosa Luxemburg and Evgeny Preobrazhensky in their theoretical models of capitalist expansion and of the primitive socialist accumulation, respectively.

In Marx's schema of capitalist development unequal exchange marks the beginning of the historical process, primitive accumulation, accomplished through loot, plunder and fraud, being its starting point. But then, in the subsequent phase of pure capitalism 'equivalent exchange' is the rule which might be distorted in practice due to the difference in the organic composition of capital. Rosa Luxemburg, however, contends that unequal exchange is a perennial feature of capitalism, not just of primitive accumulation alone. Her argument runs as follows. In expanded reproduction the surplus value cannot be realized unless there is a demand for the product from outside. The value of all commodities, and hence of the total social output, consists of constant capital, variable capital and surplus value. The constant capital is realized through replacement purchases by the capitalists themselves; the variable capital is realized through the expenditure by workers of their wages; so much is clear. But how is it with surplus value? A part of it is purchased by the capitalists for their own consumption; another part they wish to accumulate; and here is the difficulty: 'where is the demand for the accumulated surplus value?'[50] The capitalists certainly cannot realize the surplus value which they wish to accumulate by selling it to workers, for the latter exhaust their wages in realizing the variable capital. They cannot sell it to themselves for consumption, because in that case the system would revert to simple reproduction. 'Who, then, can be the taker or consumer for the social portion of commodities the sale of which is a necessary prerequisite of capital accumulation?' Luxemburg proceeds to argue that the part of surplus value which is to be accumulated can be realized only by sale to non-capitalist consumers, that is to say, to consumers who are completely outside the capitalist system. 'The realization of the surplus value for the purposes of accumulation is an impossible task for a society which consists solely of workers and capitalists.'[51] Capitalism therefore requires two markets: one, internal, and the other, external. She goes on to add that the exchanges within the internal capitalist market are of equivalents, but those between the capitalist and non-capitalist systems which constitute the external market for capitalist accumulation are a matter of 'force, fraud, oppression, looting', i.e. unequal exchange of every conceivable form. In her own words:

Thus capitalist accumulation as a whole, as an actual historical process, has two different aspects. One concerns the commodity market where surplus value is produced—the factory, the mine, the agricultural estate. Regarded in this light, accumulation is a purely economic process, with its most important phase a transaction between the capitalist and wage labourer. In both its phases, however, it is confined to the *exchange of equivalents* and remains within the limits of commodity exchange....

The other aspect of the accumulation of capital concerns the relations between capitalism and the non-capitalist modes of production which start making their appearance on the international stage. Its predominant methods are colonial policy, an international loan system—a policy of spheres of interest—and war. Force, fraud, oppression, looting are openly displayed without any attempt at concealment.[52]

She laments that bourgeois liberal theory takes into account only the former aspect: the realm of 'peaceful competition', the marvels of technology and pure commodity exchange; it separates it strictly from the other aspect: the realm of capital's blustering violence which is regarded as more or less incidental to foreign policy and quite independent of the economic sphere of capital.[53]

On the theoretical plane Luxemburg's contention is erroneous. Sweezy argues that it is not possible to sell to non-capitalist consumers without also buying from them. Who is to buy the commodities 'imported' from the non-capitalist milieu? If there were no demand for the exported commodities in the first place, how can there be demand for the imported commodities? At best, the surplus value can change its form or composition, but the problem of its realization still remains.[54] It is, however, theoretically possible for capitalism to overcome this dilemma on its own internal strength. Accumulation by itself involves adding to variable capital which, when spent by workers, helps in turn realization of the surplus value.[55] Despite this refutation by Sweezy, Luxemburg has a point which has been validated by the records of history. The Lancashire cotton textiles industry in the nineteenth century, for instance, would have been stifled if it were left to the mercy of the British home market alone; and the history of capitalist development in Britain would have been quite different if the Indian market was not available for absorbing the products of British industry. The colonies not only supplied British capitalism with funds for primitive accumulation but also helped resolve its realization problem throughout the centuries.[56]

If there is a grain of truth in Rosa Luxemburg's thesis, then unequal exchange with the Third World countries has been going on since the dawn of world capitalism up till now, and it would continue as long as world capitalism is there. Unequal exchange is then indispensable for the capitalist system. Does it cease with the victory of the socialist revolution? If the country under reference belongs to the Third World, it continues to be a victim of unequal exchange so long as it participates in the world trade market dominated by capitalist countries, and as long as it remains bounded by the international division of labour delineated centuries ago. If it is a country of the metropolitan centre of world capitalism, however, it would find itself in a different position on the morrow of the socialist revolution. It can no longer exploit the Third World through unequal exchange; but in the changed context it has to resort to unequal exchange only internally, against the non-socialist sector of the economy. As Preobrazhensky formulates the relevant law, a phase of *primitive socialist accumulation* has to be passed through before socialist transformation can be accomplished all over the economy. '*Primitive socialist accumulation*', according to Preobrazhensky, 'means accumulation in the hands of the state of material resources mainly or partly from sources lying outside the complex of state economy.'[57] The law of primitive socialist accumulation is in conflict with the law of value in that the former calls for *non-equivalent exchange* of values between the socialist and the non-socialist sectors of the economy. It requires that the terms of trade be tilted more and more against the non-socialist environment in order to channelize surplus towards the socialist sector. Primitive socialist accumulation is no less imperative for a Third World country either; in fact it is much more so. 'The more backward economically, pettybourgeois, peasant, a particular country is which has gone over to the socialist organization of production, and the smaller the inheritance received by the socialist accumulation fund of the proletariat of this country when the socialist revolution takes place', points out Preobrazhensky, 'by so much the more, in proportion, will socialist accumulation be obliged to rely on alienating part of the surplus product of pre-socialist forms of economy.'[58] That is to say, an underdeveloped country of the Third World will have a bigger task of primitive socialist accumulation, and for that it will have to rely even more on the internal unequal exchange against the non-socialist sector within the economy.

Unequal exchange between countries, in one form or another,

5

therefore prevails from the beginning of the era of mercantilism till the end of the period of capitalism. During socialist construction a special type of non-equivalent exchange within the economy of the country comes into operation under the Preobrazhensky law of primitive socialist accumulation. Unequal exchange of every form will cease to exist only when socialism would hold full sway throughout the world. The class base of capitalist unequal exchange between countries having then disappeared, and the task of primitive socialist accumulation having been accomplished, the productive forces of all the parts of the world would develop to the fullest extent under socialism; no longer would there be either any necessity or any grounds for unequal exchange, externally or internally.

Be that as it may, to return to the main theme of this essay, unequal exchange between the metropolitan centre and the outer periphery, mediated as it is partly through the prevailing wage differential and partly through the monopoly power of the former within the current set-up of world capitalism, has far-reaching effects on the periphery. Unequal exchange is a powerful modality for transferring surplus from the poor countries of the Third World to the rich advanced capitalist countries. In consequence, the rate of accumulation in the Third World suffers; and with it suffers the ability of the Third World to effectively utilize and develop its natural and human resources. The contradictions of the metropolitan centre of world capitalism further accentuate and increasingly intensify the unequal exchange between the centre and the periphery. As a result, the latter becomes ever more dependent upon the former. In the process the peripheral countries of world capitalism experience a sort of expansion in agriculture and industry that is neither consistent with their resources nor responsive to the genuine aspirations of their peoples. But then the question which immediately comes to one's mind is: How then has it been going on for so long?

4

FLOW OF CAPITAL AND TECHNOLOGY

COMMODITY trade and capital flow were the two links with which colonies had been kept in economic bondage with the metropolis since the beginning of the modern phase of imperialism. The export of technology came into the picture much later, notably after the Second World War, in its most significant dimension. Not that the trade in commodities and the export of capital did not have any technological connotation; certainly they assailed the indigenous colonial method of production. What is, however, new in the present set-up as compared to the earlier experience is that technology itself has now assumed an identity of its own in international transactions. Though not organically separate from commodity or capital, it has acquired a world market with its own distinction. One simple example will perhaps illuminate the point. When you go to purchase a Boeing jet or to borrow one million dollars you know the totality of what you are looking for; but when you go to buy the technology for producing a particular type of jet engine, for instance, you cannot be sure how much of the technology is given to you and how much is withheld. It is like a blind purchase; all too often one does not know what to ask for. The import of technology of course ultimately manifests itself in the import of commodities, and, on occasion, in the borrowing of capital as well. But the three are not the same.

The metropolis of world capitalism today is in the midst of the third industrial revolution, the hallmarks of which are embedded in computers, electronics, cybernetics and similar vehicles of automation.[1] If the waves of the first two industrial revolutions had largely bypassed the outer periphery there is no reason why those of the latest one could not do the same. Not completely though; in the changed perspective of the post-colonial era of formally independent nation states the sweep of the industrial revolution of the metropolis this time is likely to leave a stronger imprint on the Third World, stronger but not necessarily of the appropriate type.

SCIENCE AND TECHNOLOGY

Technology is the method of production in industry, mining, agriculture; science is the store of knowledge. The organized application of science to advance technology is a relatively new thing. Until the middle of the nineteenth century the connection between science and technology was tenuous. The periods when science flourished did not coincide with those when technology was taking rapid strides. When they did move ahead together it was not necessarily at the same place. On balance, science was far more indebted to technology than vice versa. Magnetism, for example, was known as an empirical fact, and had been used to construct compasses for centuries before the physicists began to study the subject in the eighteenth and nineteenth centuries. It was during the second half of the last century that science and technology began to draw somewhat close together, and science began to take the lead in some fields. Nonetheless, the relation between science and technology during this period was on the whole quite remote. The distance narrowed towards the end of the nineteenth century; and commercial research laboratories began to appear. These laboratories, set up by industry as they were, constituted a significant departure from previous days when invention was mainly the work of independent inventors who were not then completely replaced but whose relative importance gradually diminished. In the 1890s it was still the era of *private* science, that of the small laboratory of the professor or the back-room of the inventor. The next stage, first evident in the twenties and thirties of the new century, was the age of *industrial* science, that of the research laboratory, university department and research institute subsidized by industry. The third stage is that of *government* science which took shape during the Second World War; the expenses for research and development had run into hundreds of millions of dollars which only the government together with the assistance of monopoly firms could furnish.[2]

Today, the government is by far the largest source of funds for scientific research and technological development; and it is the requirements of the state which sets the line for the advancement of science and technology. In 1963 the US federal government, for instance, accounted for over 65 per cent of all the resources spent on research and development in that country; and almost 90 per cent of those government funds came from the Department of Defence, the National Aeronautics and Space Administration (NASA) and the Atomic Energy Commission (AEC).[3] The compulsions of the hot and cold wars have provided the impetus for such deployment of resources by the government. Military ambitions have called the tune; and science and technology have followed suit. One of the greatest marvels of modern science, the computer, for instance, was first conceived as a military project. Work on the first electronic computer, ENIAC, began at the University of Pennsylvania in 1942 and was completed in 1946. It received financial support from the US Army and was mainly designed to calculate trajectories of shells and bombs. Thereafter, rapid progress was made in logic design, memory storage, and programming. Eventually, the computer became technically as well as commercially feasible for a wide range of scientific and business applications.[4]

State patronage to scientific research and development is no less generous in other advanced capitalist countries either. It is estimated that the State's share in the total expenditure of the country on this count is 69 per cent in France, 64 per cent in Great Britain, 40 per cent in West Germany and 37 per cent in Belgium, against 65 per cent in the United States as mentioned above.[5] Undoubtedly, the growing economic and military strength of the socialist countries has impressed the advanced capitalist countries, and prompted them to invest more and more in science and technology. The trail-blazing Sputnik that was put in space by the Soviet Union must have delivered the *coup de grâce* to the complacency of the capitalist states.

One of the outstanding characteristics of science in this century is far more immediate and rapid application of scientific discoveries. Research expenditure not only speeds up the pace of scientific advancement, but also *shortens* the gap between the laboratory and the production line. The time lag between the scientific invention and the manufacture of the item tends to be reduced; this tendency can be discerned from the following examples: [6]

> 112 years for photography (1727–1839)
> 56 years for the telephone (1820–1876)
> 35 years for the radio (1867–1902)
> 15 years for radar (1925–1940)
> 12 years for television (1922–1934)
> 6 years for the atomic bomb (1939–1945)
> 5 years for the transistor (1948–1953)
> 3 years for the integrated circuit (1958–1961).

These are only examples to highlight the underlying trend; the actual situation, however, is not always as smoothly exponential as it may appear from above. For profitability remains the basic criterion for innovation; and an inordinate delay in application or even complete suppression of scientific potentialities is not uncommon. The lag is known to be shorter for consumer products than that for producer goods; and it is shorter for those developed with government funds than those developed with private funds. The fact of the matter is that the science on which the bulk of twentieth century technology is based is still nineteenth century science—in power production, in electricity, and in chemistry; production techniques depending primarily upon more recent scientific discoveries have made their appearance in minor, albeit striking, roles. There is much more yet to come from what has already been achieved in twentieth century science. The potentialities are immense, only if the economic system can make proper use of them. [7]

Rapid and profound advances in science and technology of production, transport and communication have reduced geographical and temporal distances; have brought far-flung worldwide business operations within the technical feasibility of control and command from the headquarters located in New York, London, Paris, Bonn, Rome or Tokyo; and have thereby placed in the hands of the giant transnational corporations unprecedented capabilities for exploiting the Third World. If monopoly capitalism was born in the 1870s, [8] it has thus come of age within a century, in the 1970s.

MONOPOLY CAPITALISM AND INNOVATION

The first Industrial Revolution of the eighteenth century paved the way for competitive capitalism; the second Industrial Revolution, of the nineteenth century, facilitated the birth of monopoly capitalism. The third Industrial Revolution, of this century, has arrived in the midst of the decline, but not yet the demise, of monopoly capitalism as a world order. What is the nature of science and technology in this new era? Where is it leading to, and with what result for the metropolitan centre and the outer periphery of world capitalism?

Innovation is the pioneering application of scientific discoveries. The quantum and direction of innovations under capitalism are set forth by considerations of private profitability. Vast possibilities of production may remain untapped if they are not commercially profit-making; on the other hand, there would be a mad rush to exploit scientific inventions for piling up profits without regard to social costs. Capitalism thus acts as a brake on progress, and at the same time unleashes uncontrolled forces of technological development. Between these two faces of capitalism there seems to fall a shadow of paradox. It is reconciled if we remember that there are stages of capitalism. The mad haste of exploitation, threatening the very basis of the human resource of labour on which it was built, was characteristic of the first and second Industrial Revolutions. The brake was on in the mature economy of the inter-war period.

What of the present time? The two indictments are, in a sense, both valid, and the paradox is resolved as follows: 'Capitalism works with mad haste to exploit commercially certain profitable applications of the technological and scientific development. It does very little itself, however, to stimulate and keep up this development, which would have receded to a low ebb but for one factor: war—or the armaments race.'[9]

An analysis of the research and development activities of US industries throws considerable light on these issues.[10] First of all, a large and increasing proportion of research and development (R&D) performed within the US industries sector itself is financed by the federal government. In 1953, about 40 per cent was supported in this way; in 1963, about 60 per cent.[11] Secondly, the maximization of expected profit is evidently the most important determinant of a firm's selection of R&D projects. Thirdly, the firm keeps a relatively short time horizon. According to a McGraw-Hill Survey in 1958, 39 per cent of the large firms expected their R&D efforts to pay off in less than three years, and another 52 per cent of the large firms in more than three but less than five years.[12] The bulk of the research projects in the laboratory are therefore expected to be completed well within less than four years.[13] Fourthly, in addition to being quick-yielding the R&D projects are by and large risk-free, the estimated probability of technical success being as high as 0.80 on an average. Fifthly, these fast and safe projects are indeed extremely high-yielding, if successful. Sixthly, the speed of diffusion of new techniques between firms as well as between various branches within the same firm is likewise governed by the supreme criterion of commercial profitability.[14] Finally, the major emphasis of innovation is on developing new products or on improving the existing products, and very little on developing new processes. It is a misnomer to call these activities research and development; they are primarily efforts for product development. The McGraw-Hill Survey of business plans for new plant and equipment in 1962 reported that in all manufacturing industries combined, about 47 per cent of firms were engaged in R&D for the purpose of launching new products, 40 per cent for improving the existing products, and barely 15 per cent for devising new processes.[15] Innovation for the advancement of production technology thus is at the low end of the scale; luring the consumer's dollars appears to be the primary target of innovation; and all else is incidental. After all, the consumer goods market covers between eighty to ninety per cent of the gross national product.

Conceptually, difference is not the same thing as change. The difference between competition and oligopoly or monopoly with regard to their impacts on innovation has been a matter of controversy for long. An important, but hitherto neglected, dimension has been added to the debate recently by Sylos–Labini; it relates to the mechanism of diffusion of the fruits of technical progress under alternative market structures.[16] The classical economists, Adam Smith and Ricardo, have analysed the distribution of gains of advancement in technology under competitive market conditions. In their scheme, agriculture is subject to the law of diminishing returns, as a result of which the prices of agricultural products tend to rise. By contrast, industry offers considerably more scope for division of labour and other forms of technical progress; consequently, industrial prices decline over time, not only in absolute terms but also in relation to the agricultural commodities. The benefits of advanced technology are thus distributed in the form of falling prices, with constant nominal incomes. This mechanism of benefit propagation is not only all-pervasive in the sense of carrying the fruits of technical progress to every corner of the economy, to all consumers and producers, but it is also self-equilibrating in that the workers who might be displaced in the wake of technical progress are immediately re-absorbed as the firms, encouraged by lower costs, expand their investment.[17]

Things are very different when oligopolistic elements are present in the market. Price is no longer flexible downwards; it is rigid. Introduction of new techniques then leads to higher nominal incomes, with a more or less constant price level. Instead of being evenly spread out throughout the economy, the additional incomes accrue to a few pockets. To the extent the wage bill rises it poses no problem, inasmuch as it is spent by workers on consumption, so that aggregate demand also goes up *pari passu*. But if the additional income takes the form of profits, the economy may stumble on the rock of insufficient aggregate demand. A part of the incremental profits would be consumed. But what about that part which is saved? In case there is no external factor to stimulate the *ex ante* investment to rise to the level of the extra savings the economy *à la* Keynes will fail to reach an equilibrium that would reabsorb the workers who have been dislodged in the advent of the new technique. Only if the economy is growing, under the influence of some exogenous forces such as public spending or expanding export market, will the technological progress be neutral or labour-using in effect. In an oligopolistic market the normal feature of technological progress is therefore *labour-saving*, not only in comparison with the classical mechanism of competition, but also in an absolute sense.[18]

The Sylos–Labini mechanism of *labour-displacing* technological progress as outlined above grinds on with increasing ferocity as monopoly capitalism with the oligopolistic elements ascends higher stages. There is yet another factor which compels the technology to pursue a labour-saving route. The investment decision of a monopolist (oligopolist) is guided not by the profit rate of the project under consideration but by what may be called the *marginal* rate of profit. That is to say, just as in the case of an expansion of output the monopolist must take into account the effect on his old business, so in the case of technological innovation he cannot neglect the depreciation in value which his already invested capital may suffer through being outmoded. Accordingly, '*labour-saving* becomes more than ever before the goal of capitalist technology and the rate of introduction of new methods will be so arranged as to minimize the disturbance of existing capital values. In other words, new methods will have an even stronger *labour-saving* bias, and for the most part new equipment will be put in the place of old only when the latter wears out and needs to be replaced anyway.[19] In short, technological progress in the regime of monopoly capitalism is designed in such a way that the existing plant and equipment are used to the maximum possible extent, and the least possible is expended on new capital goods or on labour.

Finaly, the third factor which imparts a labour-saving bias to the monopolist's technology is the pressure of rising investible surplus at his disposal. If the volume of his profits is going up at the rate of, say, 10 per cent per year it is just arithmetically impossible to find as many people to employ with constant capital–labour ratio.

The nature of technological progress under monopoly capitalism was briefly alluded to in the previous chapter. Now the full theoretical reasoning behind it has been given. Another observation which emerges from this discussion is as follows: the State has assumed the primary responsibility for promoting scientific and technological advancement in the metropolitan centre of world capitalism; the basic objective of this endeavour lies in the sphere of military preparation. Basking in the fall-out of this vast programme of the State, *the monopoly capitalists indulge in quick-yielding relatively risk-less, highly profitable ventures; and thereby combat the falling tendency of the profit rate in the face of swelling investible surplus.* All this adds up to a rather fast rate of technical progress which impinges more upon the consumer goods than upon the producer goods. However, in absolute terms the net effect of technological progress upon the producer goods sector is quite significant so as to accelerate the pace of obsolescence. And yet there still remains a vast reservoir of scientific knowledge acquired in recent decades which has not yet been fully harnessed to the service of mankind. Only its surface has been scratched so far; most of the twentieth century technique of production even today draws upon nineteenth century science.[20]

OBSOLESCENCE

Despite the usual hesitation of a monopolist to innovate, his penchant for quick and high profits leads to a rapid development of consumer products, and, in its train, to a fast turnover of producer goods. Obsolescence creeps into the plant and equipment, and their economic life gets exhausted well before the expiry of the technical longevity. This much is simple enough. There is however another element at work which may induce the monopolist to retire the plant and equipment even earlier; it is the possibility of selling the near-obsolete machinery to the capitalists in the Third World. Such an opportunity not only helps stabilize the profit rate in the metropolis; it also paves the way for continuous technological advancement there, which again keeps the rate of profit from tumbling down. Before elaborating these propositions, let us first of all see the extent of obsolescence in the capital goods structure of the metropolis.

A study conducted by the McGraw-Hill Department of Economics in the year 1958 revealed that only less than one-third of the plant and equipment of US industry was modern in the realistic sense of being not more than eight years old; two-thirds were definitely obsolete. It would cost at least $95 billion to replace all outmoded facilities with the best new plant and equipment available at that time. The rapidity of technological progress and the inexorable toll of obsolescence can also be gauged from the following facts which turned up in the McGraw-Hill study. A 1958 metal-working tool was on an average about 54 per cent more productive than one that could be purchased in 1948. A combination of new freight cars and modern freight yard equipment could reduce operating costs up to 50 per cent. New instruments that automatically direct the flow of chemical or other raw materials could often reduce costs enough to pay back the cost of the controls in one year. These savings were rarely possible in older plants.[21] That was the position in US industry in 1958. Since then the rate of technological progress has certainly accelerated; the current situation regarding obsolescence can be easily visualized.

If the replacement of obsolete machinery is inadequate and slow in the US, how is it in other countries of advanced capitalism? Britain, in particular, is way behind the United States in this respect; and this lag is singled out as a major cause for productivity difference. 'There is some evidence to suggest,' comments one observer, 'that one of the chief reasons for Anglo-American productivity differences lies in standards of obsolescence. It is a common theme in Productivity Mission Reports that the productivity of the best plants in the United Kingdom is comparable with that of the best plants in the United States, and that the difference lies in a much higher proportion of plants employing outmoded methods in the United Kingdom—a much greater 'tail' of low productivity plants. Such a situation is consistent with a higher standard of obsolescence in the United States which ... follows from a higher level of real wages.'[22]

Having recognized the extent of obsolete plant and equipment in the metropolitan centre of world capitalism, let us note that the access to an overseas market where outmoded machinery can be sold produces the following three-fold result: (*a*) it raises both wages and profit rate[23] (that is to say, the wage–profit frontier shifts up, a formal proof of which is given in footnote 23); (*b*) it further expedites the obsolescence at home; and (*c*) it facilitates the launching of a new production process or a new consumer product, which in turn props up the rate of profit. The last two points can be explained in the following way.

Consider a machine which is operated by labour alone, so that there are no other operating costs than the wage bill. The physical life of the machine is given; and the productivity remains constant all through. In Figure 4, the horizontal axis represents calendar time; the machine is produced and installed in year *O*. It is known that a new model of the machine would supersede the present one, either because a more profitable production technique will come into being in due course or because the current brand of the product would go out of fashion; in any case the current machine will sooner or later disappear from the scene. In Figure 4, *DD* denotes the constant annual output, and *WW* the correspond-

OBSOLESCENCE IN THE METROPOLIS AND RESALE OF
OBSOLETE MACHINERY TO THE PERIPHERY

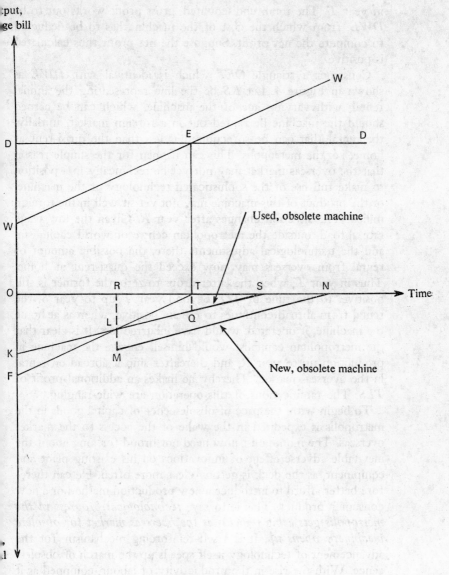

FIGURE 4

ing wage bill that steadily goes up as more labour is needed to maintain and operate the machine with the passage of time, or the wage rate climbs up. It follows that the machine will be scrapped in year T. The total, undiscounted, gross profit works out to be DWE, from which the cost of the machine has to be deducted to compute the net profit. Suppose the net profit thus calculated is positive.

Construct a triangle OFT which is identical with DWE as shown in Figure 4. Let KS be the line representing the annual rental, with varying age of the machine, which can be earned should the machine be rented out in a foreign market. Initially, the rental that can be so acquired is less than the quasi-rent at home, i.e. the metropolis. This can happen for the simple reason that the overseas market may not yet be technically in a position to make full use of the sophisticated technology of the machine, or the product of this machine may not yet sit well in the foreign milieu. The situation changes after year R. Given the low wage rate abroad, outside the metropolitan centre of world capitalism, and the technological adjustments there, the possible amount of rental from overseas may now exceed the quasi-rent at home. Thus in year T, when the latter drops to zero, the former is still positive, to the tune of TQ. Beyond year T up to year S, the rental from abroad continues to remain positive, whereas at home the machine, if operated, would have incurred loss. It is clear that the metropolitan capitalist would himself engage the machine in production up to year R, and thereafter ship it abroad on rental in the overseas market. Thereby he makes an additional profit of TLS. The ramifications of this operation are wide-ranging.

To begin with, the pace of obsolescence of capital goods in the metropolis is expedited in the wake of the access to the market overseas. The monopolist now need not brood for long about the inevitable adverse effect of innovations on his existing plant and equipment, as the deck is getting clear more often. He can therefore better afford to introduce a new production method or a new consumer product. This is to say, *technological progress in the metropolis gets a big impetus as the overseas market for obsolete machinery opens up.* It is a self-reinforcing mechanism, for the advancement of technology itself speeds up the march of obsolescence. With the rise in the productivity of labour, equipped as it is with more modern machines, the wage rate tends to be higher and higher; and so the wage-bill line *WW* in Figure 4 becomes steeper, even though the machine under reference continues to have the same annual output.[24] Triangle *DWE* shrinks as a result, so does the identical twin, namely, *OFT*. Accordingly both the points, *T* and *R*, move leftward in view of the technological progress.

At this stage we must keep in mind the clear distinction between 'obsolete' and 'old' or 'used'. Note that an obsolete machine need not always be an old machine or an used machine; it can very well be unused and new at the same time. So far we have seen how it is to the advantage of the metropolitan capitalist to sell or rent out used *and* obsolete machines to a country where the wage rate is lower and hence the rental is higher. Now we shall examine the possibility of such trade in *new* but obsolete machines. Previously, the machine under reference was produced in year *O*, and was used in the metropolis up to year *R*; thereafter it was sold or rented out in the foreign market, i.e. the Third World. The production of this type of machine in the metropolis was discontinued immediately after year *O* since it was known that technical progress would bring forth a more productive machine to supersede this one. It is, however, quite conceivable that after year *R* not only the used machine but also a new machine of the same brand would be quite profitable in the Third World where the wage rate is lower. Let *MN* in Figure 4 be the line representing the annual rental of the new but obsolete machine of the metropolis when it is deployed in the Third World with effect from year *R*. Thus old as well as new machines which are meanwhile rendered obsolete in the metropolis would flow into the Third World. Under such circumstances the production of these obsolete machines would continue in the metropolis; and the plant and equipment which were engaged in producing them in year *O* would not be dismantled at least till year *R*. Thus there would be an all-round improvement in profitability in the metropolitan centre of world capitalism, as the Third World absorbs old or new but obsolete machinery discarded in the former.

But why will the Third World be at all interested in old, used machines? In fact, 'many underdeveloped countries buy a considerable quantity of second-hand machinery from advanced economies'.[25] In recent years not just used machines but 'complete manufacturing units' which have become outdated in advanced capitalist countries are being bodily lifted from there and transplanted in poor countries, small such as Taiwan, Hong Kong, South Korea, and Mexico, as well as big such as Indonesia, India and Brazil.[26] This is a development of great significance which would bear an in-depth analysis. One easy explanation of such shipment lies in the rising cost of maintenance with the age of the machine. Since the wage rate is generally lower in underdeveloped countries, and even that of skilled labour is comparatively low in many of them, particularly in Latin America and some parts of Asia, the cost of maintenance may be much less in these economies. It would explain why many underdeveloped countries may be ready to buy what the advanced capitalist economy finds too expensive to maintain. Similarly, a fall in the absolute productivity of a machine with age can be more easily absorbed in the underdeveloped economy, thanks to its lower wages. A fall that will wipe out all profits in the advanced economy may still allow a profit margin in the low-wage underdeveloped country. All this is fairly obvious.[27] We shall now take a more interesting case and find that the trade in old machines would take place, even if there were no obsolescence due to technical progress or rising wages; even if the machine works with unchanged efficiency over its whole life in either country; and even if the wage rates in the two countries are equal; but provided the profit rate in the underdeveloped country is higher for one reason or another.

Let the machine yield the same net output in both types of economy at a constant annual rate throughout its life. To begin with, suppose the wage rate is lower in the underdeveloped economy, and the profit rate is higher, in comparison with the advanced metropolitan country. The net output of the machine being the same but wages being different, the annual gross profit of the machine is higher in the lower wage economy. If P and r are respectively the gross profit of the machine and the ruling profit rate in the advanced economy; and if P' and r' are the corresponding notations for those in the underdeveloped economy, then by our assumption, $P' > P$, and $r' > r$. In the underdeveloped economy, the present value of the gross profit of the machine one year before the end of its life is:

$$P'/(1+r').$$

The same for the machine two years before the end of its life is:

$$P'/(1+r')+P'/(1+r')^2 .$$

In the advanced economy, on the other hand, the market price of an asset is determined by the present value of the income stream to be generated by it. Accordingly, there the market price of the one-year-to-go machine is:

$$P/(1+r) .$$

Similarly, the price of the other type of machine is:

$$P/(1+r)+P/(1+r)^2 .$$

Now compute the ratio of the present value of the gross profit in the underdeveloped economy to the market price of the same machine in the advanced economy. The ratio for the one-year-to-go machine is:

$$\frac{P'}{(1+r')} \bigg/ \frac{P}{(1+r)} = \frac{P'(1+r)}{P(1+r')} \tag{43}$$

For the two-year-to-go machine it is:

$$\frac{P'/(1+r')+P'/(1+r')^2}{P/(1+r)+P/(1+r)^2} = \frac{P'(2+r')(1+r)^2}{P(2+r)(1+r')^2} \tag{44}$$

If $r' > r$, the ratio as given in (43) is higher than that of (44); i.e. between the two the older machine with one year to go is more profitable for the capitalist in the underdeveloped economy, so long as the profit rate there is higher than that prevailing in the advanced economy. This conclusion remains valid even if $P = P'$, vide equations (43) and (44); in other words, the relative advantage of the older machine in the underdeveloped economy arises in this model not from the wage differential as such, but from the difference in discount rates, r and r'. This result can be extended to machines of less or greater age, showing that profitability increases with age.[28] Furthermore, should obsolescence due to technical progress or rising wages be introduced in this model the conclusion will be again reinforced.[29]

In the third world, the wage rate is much lower and the profit rate considerably higher[30] in comparison with the advanced capitalist countries; besides, technical progress and rising wages in the latter are continuously taking their toll of obsolescence. Under such circumstances, *the class interests of the bourgeoisie of the advanced capitalist countries neatly converge with those of the bourgeoisie of the Third World. The metropolitan bourgeoisie is eager to dispose of its old, obsolete plant and equipment, and its counterpart in the outer periphery of world capitalism is equally interested in welcoming the outmoded, second-hand stuff.* Some cross-section data about the extent of used machinery in the fixed assets of Japanese industries during the fifties are given in Table 6. If these data can be taken as broadly representative of the state of affairs in the countries of the Third World also, then a few extremely significant conclusions follow. Evidently, the smaller the firm size the bigger is the incidence of used machinery on its capital structure. Small capitalists therefore look up to the bigger capitalists of the same country and/or to the capitalists of the foreign countries for the supply of used machinery. If so, not only the big but also the medium and small bourgeoisie of the Third World will be dependent on the bourgeoisie of the advanced countries in so far as the flow of used machinery is concerned. Thus *the economic interests of all the sections of the Third World bourgeoisie—big, medium and small—are tied up with those of the metropolitan bourgeoisie.* This inference will be later corroborated with more substantive evidence.

The data of Table 6 indicate another momentous feature of the

TABLE 6

Proportion of Used Machinery in Total Investment in Fixed Assets in Japanese Industry

(Per cent)

Scale by number of employees	1954	1955	1956	1957	1958
4–9	48.8	40.2	34.3	n.a.	n.a.
10–19	44.1	40.8	29.9	n.a.	n.a.
20–29	39.5	34.3	28.7	n.a.	n.a.
30–49	35.0	28.9	26.1	26.8	26.5
50–99	31.5	22.0	22.3	21.9	20.9
100–199	23.0	16.3	16.8	14.5	13.8
200–299	15.2	9.1	9.9	9.3	10.0
300–499	13.9	10.1	9.1	7.4	7.6
500–999	11.2	5.2	4.2	4.6	6.3
Over 1000	4.6	4.1	4.9	3.3	3.1

Source: M. Shinohara, *Sangyokozo (Industrial Structure)*, 1959, p. 120; cited in Sen (1962), p. 346.

flow of technology. To the extent the cross-section pattern of Table 6 can be construed as reflecting the intertemporal, inter-country movement of used and obsolescent machinery, it appears that *technology tends to filter down across the layers of economies, beginning at the top, then into less and less developed economies in a descending order.*[31] This hypothesis will again be substantiated with more evidence later.[32]

TECHNOLOGY MARKET

The world market of technology is extremely skewed. In the early sixties, three countries, namely, the USA, the UK and West Germany, accounted for over 90 per cent of all royalties internationally received.[33] Among the three, the USA is by far the largest recipient of royalties, which were in the range of 600 to 750 million dollars during 1961–1962, whereas the UK could boast of about 150 million dollars and West Germany some 70 million dollars or so.[34] According to an estimate of the OECD, the United States received roughly ten times as much in technological payments from abroad in 1961 as went out in payments to other countries.[35] During 1958–62 the annual growth rate of the US receipts of royalties was about 15 per cent.[36] Of the eight countries with the highest output per head in the world, only the United States has a surplus on its technological balance of payments account.[37] Moreover, this country tends to dominate world trade most in those industries that are the most research-intensive. The contribution of US subsidiaries in Europe, as a proportion of output produced, is most pronounced in the science-based industries. For instance, 75 per cent of computers sold in Europe and an even larger proportion of integrated electronic circuits come from US companies; so do one-half of the pharmaceuticals bought by the UK national health service.[38] Such are the clear indices of the overwhelming predominance of the United States in the world of technology and in the technology of the world.

Who are the main exporters of technology in the USA? Of course, the transnational corporations. They are the most important spenders of research and development funds; naturally they are almost the sole exporters of technology in the US; and indeed they receive 90 per cent of the net inbound flows of royalties and fees, which reached nearly 2.3 billion dollars in 1971 as compared to some 0.6 billion dollars a decade earlier.[39]

A large part of the internationally traded technology, certainly most of the sort sold to the Third World countries, implies on the part of the sellers 'cutting and taping together' bits of knowledge which, when appropriately combined and promoted, could lead to the successful launching of modified or new products and processes. This form of innovative activity requires technical and other skills which are quite distinct from the activities of the so-called 'centres of excellence' of research oriented towards the frontiers of scientific know-how. 'A systematic study undertaken in the petrochemical industry indicated that, during the period when technology was most likely to be sold to developing countries, the original producers of a particular product or process accounted for only one per cent of the total licensing of know-how. The remaining 99 per cent was divided between "followers" of commercial producers (52 per cent) and engineering firms (47 per cent). Similarly know-how in electronics sold to developing countries by technology-intensive companies like Philips International or General Electric generally includes know-how on products that have been in commercial usage for some time (such as transistorized components for TV or radio). Such technology is available to other firms which are not necessarily technology-intensive, in Belgium, Spain, Japan etc.'[40] In so far as the technology imported into the Third World is concerned, its market therefore is at least potentially competitive from the sellers' point of view; but in fact it is highly concentrated, approaching a monopolistic situation. And in such a market structure, bargaining power appears to be the determining factor for prices and 'quantities' of the technology exchanged. Weak and occasionally subservient, the Third World countries import the technology all too often with many a string attached, such as restriction on export, compulsion of purchasing intermediate products from the sellers of technology at inflated prices, and the like.[41] When the technology comes through the subsidiary of a transnational corporation the position is still worse.

Which section of the Third World bourgeoisie—big, medium, or small—is the leader in technology import? Is it true that it is mainly the big bourgeoisie that has links with foreign technology, and that the medium and small bourgeoisie of the Third World are relatively independent on this count? Though important, these questions are difficult to answer, because identification of the various strata of the bourgeoisie is not so easy. For instance, most of the technology imports into India are made by firms that are small or medium even by Indian standards.[42] But there need not be any one-to-one correspondence between the size of a firm and the stratum of the bourgeoisie who owns it. The big bourgeoisie may and does set up small firms for a variety of reasons such as getting official allocation of scarce inputs, special credit facilities, etc. Despite such difficulty of identification certain observations can be made as a first approximation on the basis of the data presented below.

The Reserve Bank of India periodically reports the financial statistics of some two thousand joint-stock companies operating in India. There are two types of such companies depending upon whether or not a company's shares are available for transaction in the stock-exchange; if available, the company belongs to the category of 'public limited'; if not, it is 'private limited'. They are further classified according to their paid-up capital: (*i*) small, if the paid-up capital is Rs 0.5 million or less, (*ii*) large, if it is Rs 10 million or more, and (*iii*) medium for the intermediate range. The data of two subgroups, usually falling within the broad group of 'large' companies, are also separately available; they are called (*a*) foreign-controlled rupee companies, and (*b*) branches of foreign companies in India. The RBI publishes financial statistics of seven kinds of joint-stock companies as shown in Tables 7 and 8. Some characteristic features of five of them as of 1969–70 are listed in Table 9. With our awareness of the limitations of the approach, we shall, as a modest beginning in the absence of a better method, identify the *top* bourgeoisie with the large and medium companies, and the *middle* bourgeoisie with the small companies. Note that the medium companies as defined by the RBI cover a wide range. It is conceivable that the lower tail of the medium-size companies belongs to the middle bourgeoisie and the upper tail to the top bourgeoisie. As such a detailed breakdown of data is not available, occasionally we may relate the medium companies with the middle bourgeoisie also; it may be then slightly confusing but it is in the nature of the subject. In any case, the main findings of this section would remain valid.[43]

To begin with, do the data reveal any qualitative difference in the behaviour and performance of the small companies on the one

TABLE 7

Mean and Standard Deviation of Profit Rates

Types of companies (Ltd.)	Period	Profit after tax/net worth	Gross profit/net sales	Gross profit/total capital employed
Small private	1963-4/1968-9	4.4(1.8)	4.6(0.8)	7.7(1.2)
Small public	1956-7/1969-70	4.6(2.4)	5.1(0.9)	7.0(1.1)
Medium and large private	1958-9/1970-1	9.9(2.5)	6.9(1.1)	10.9(0.9)
Medium and large public	1956-7/1969-70	9.2(1.3)	9.3(0.8)	9.4(0.9)
Large public	1965-6/1970-1	9.9(1.0)	10.3(0.7)	10.0(0.6)
Foreign-controlled rupee companies	1957-8/1968-9	11.4(1.2)	11.3(0.9)	12.7(0.8)
Branches of foreign companies	1957-8/1968-9	n.a.	5.6(1.3)	7.7(0.8)

Note: (1) Figures in brackets are standard deviations from the mean.
(2) The rates of profit after tax/net worth of small private limited companies and foreign-controlled rupee companies are respectively for 1963-4/1967-8 and 1960-1/1968-9. Gross profit/total capital employed for large public limited companies relates to the period 1965-6/1968-9.

Source: Reserve Bank of India, *Bulletin.*

TABLE 8

SHARE OF WAGES IN OUTPUT OF COMPANIES IN INDIA

Year	Small private limited	Small public limited	Medium and large private limited	Medium and large public limited	Large public limited	Foreign-controlled rupee companies	Branches of foreign companies
1950–51				66.61			
1951–52				63.55			
1952–53				71.65			
1953–54				69.96			
1954–55				67.33			
1955–56			66.32	63.42			
1956–57		68.51	64.74	64.07			
1957–58		78.21	64.63	68.39			
1958–59		72.49	63.22	66.73		54.12	67.74
1959–60		71.19	61.72	62.91		54.35	66.26
1960–61		71.30	59.85	61.02		52.36	68.60
1961–62		73.52	59.16	60.96		52.97	68.92
1962–63		72.69	58.31	60.72		52.38	69.27
1963–64	69.87	71.92	57.83	59.69		52.04	64.65
1964–65	69.02	71.45	59.35	61.33		51.04	68.57
1965–66	64.86	71.75	58.11	60.81	54.72	49.40	69.42
1966–67	73.02	72.12	59.92	60.44	54.64	49.57	69.83
1967–68	75.67	72.41	62.08	64.26	57.92	50.19	66.21
1968–69	68.57	74.82	63.47	65.17	59.21	52.38	66.35
1969–70		74.82	62.77	62.35	56.91	51.79	75.72
1970–71					55.93		

Source: Reserve Bank of India, *Bulletin*.

TABLE 9

Some Features of Joint Stock Companies in India, 1969-70

(Rs million)

Per company	Small : public	Small : private	Medium and large : private	Medium and large : public	Large : public
1. Paid-up capital	0.5 or less	0.5 or less	Over 0.5	Over 0.5	10 or more
2. Annual gross profit	0.06	0.07	1.0	3.7	15.0
3. Annual gross sales	1.5	1.9	16.0	43.0	151.0
4. Assets	1.0	1.3	9.0	39.0	147.0
5. Total assets of all companies	3,491.0	8,349.0	23,457.0	59,475.0	41,038.0

Note: Paid-up capital is the RBI criterion for classification of companies; row 1 gives the criterion. Rows 2–4 are the actual data of gross profit, gross sales and assets, per company, as of 1969–70. Row 5 gives the total assets of all the companies by each group.

Source: Reserve Bank of India, *Bulletin.*

hand and the medium and large companies on the other? Table 7 presents mean and standard deviation of three indices of profitability as computed from balance-sheets and income–expenditure statements. It is found that the profit rate of small companies is not only much smaller, but also highly volatile in comparison with medium and large companies; as the table shows, the mean profit rate of the former is lower but its standard deviation is comparatively high. If anything, it indicates the weak and precarious position of the middle bourgeoisie, provided, of course, one accepts the identification of the economic status of the small, public or private limited companies with that of the middle stratum of the bourgeoisie. So much about the performance; now consider the behaviour. Income distribution is an important aspect of behaviour; and here also the difference is fundamental. The share of wages in net output is appreciably higher in small companies than in medium and large ones; *vide* Table 8.[44]

Now a word about the differentiation of the bourgeoisie. It is estimated that the average annual gross profit per small company is in the neighbourhood of Rs 0.1 million, while per medium and large private limited company it is Rs 1 million; per medium and large public limited company Rs 3.7 million; and per large public limited company Rs 15 million (Table 9). We see from the income tax statistics of Table 10 that the companies with assessed income of over Rs 0.5 million had substantially advanced their position in the ten years between 1957–58 and 1966–67. At the beginning of the period they earned slightly over three-fourths of the total income of all companies put together; by the end of the period their share reached nine-tenths. In number also they have multiplied quite fast, in fact fastest of the whole lot. All the other companies, each earning Rs 0.5 million or less, had invariably lost ground; the smaller the company the worse it had fared. This is an eloquent testimony as to how sharp the competition is between the big companies on the one hand and the smaller ones on the other. It suggests that the process of differentiation of the bourgeoisie is going apace.

There is evidence that, battered in the struggle for survival, *the middle bourgeoisie of the Third World are turning to foreign technology and capital for succour.* About a quarter of the firms that imported foreign technology into India up to 1967 had sales under Rs 10 million in that year; and another two-fifths had sales between Rs 10 and 50 million. Only about a tenth of the firms importing technology recorded sales over Rs 100 million.[45] In Table 9 we find that only large public limited companies, in terms of the RBI classification, had sales over Rs 100 million; the average for the medium as well as large public limited companies was only Rs 43 million; and that for medium and large private limited companies was far below, Rs 16 million, during 1969–70. It can therefore be concluded that the middle bourgeoisie who presumably own the small companies (and perhaps a few of the medium companies also) accounted for an overwhelming proportion, approximately nine-tenths, of all imports of technology from abroad.

There is another source of information about foreign collaboration in India which also sheds some light on this question. The Reserve Bank of India in 1965 conducted a survey which was in the nature of a census of all public and private limited companies with foreign company-capital participation and of all companies having foreign technical collaboration.[46] Three forms of collaboration were kept in view, namely, subsidiaries, minority foreign capital participation, and pure technical collaboration. In the *subsidiary*, the unit is incorporated in India but the majority control is by a single foreign company. The extent of foreign control in subsidiaries ranges anywhere between the 51 per cent minimum and the 100 per cent wholly foreign owned. As for *technical collaboration* it refers to such facilities provided by the foreign partner as technical services, licensing, franchise, trademarks and patents. Now, Table 11 shows that the joint-stock companies having any form of foreign collaboration—subsidiary, minority foreign capital participation or pure technical collaboration—and with capital of Rs 50 million or over constituted between 10 and 15 per cent of all such companies. That is, more than 85 per cent of all Indian companies having foreign connection of any sort are relatively small in size, with below Rs 50 million of capital. For comparison with the RBI classification it may be seen in column 4 of Table 9 that during 1969–70 the assets per large public limited company was Rs 147 million while the average for medium and large together was only Rs 39 million. In 1963–64 these figures must have been correspondingly smaller. So the cut-off point of Rs 50 million of capital as used above is not too high. In any case, if only purely technical collaboration

TABLE 10

Shares of Companies' Total Income Assessed for Taxation

(Per cent)

Income grade (Rs thousand)	1957–58	1959–60	1964–65	1966–67	Growth rate Number of companies	Growth rate Total income
Up to 12.5	0.80 (42.97)	0.86 (44.37)	0.52 (44.87)	0.38 (37.53)	22.9	147.7
12.5–25	1.13 (12.41)	1.11 (21.83)	0.63 (11.89)	0.59 (10.96)	7.3	9.5
25–50	2.22 (12.26)	2.07 (12.34)	1.15 (10.83)	1.06 (11.87)	8.6	8.8
50–100	4.00 (11.06)	3.39 (10.01)	1.85 (8.88)	1.99 (11.38)	19.0	18.7
100–500	15.78 (14.14)	14.10 (13.15)	10.19 (14.77)	9.90 (17.15)	26.4	23.1
above 500	76.00 (7.16)	78.45 (7.27)	85.64 (8.73)	86.16 (11.07)	49.2	55.4
Total	100.00 (100.00)	100.00 (100.00)	100.00 (100.00)	100.00 (100.00)	90.9	180.8

Note: (1) Figures in brackets are percentages of the total population of companies assessed.
(2) The growth rates of companies and of total income as given in the last two columns are for the year 1966–67 relative to 1957–58.

Source: Government of India, Statistical Abstract of India.

TABLE 11

Number of Companies in India with Foreign Collaboration and Their Capital and Net Worth by Size of Company, 1963–64

Size of company (total capital employed) (Rs million)	Subsidiaries			Minority foreign Capital participation			Pure technical collaboration		
	Number of companies	Total capital (Rs million)	Total net worth (Rs million)	Number of companies	Total capital (Rs million)	Total net worth (Rs million)	Number of companies	Total capital (Rs million)	Total net worth (Rs million)
Up to 2.5	64	66	23	118	117	59	75	70	29
2.5–10	61	357	136	122	665	347	72	406	160
10–50	65	148	601	89	1993	936	61	1428	573
50–100	16	1092	543	21	1549	713	16	1060	460
Over 100	18	3132	1533	17	4385	1534	12	2640	1163
Total	224	6127	2836	367	8709	3589	236	5604	2385

Source: Reserve Bank of India (1968), pp. 13, 42, 70.

is considered, according to Table 11 over 60 per cent of the companies having such collaboration had capital of Rs 10 million or less. To sum up, *the middle layer of the bourgeoisie is an important channel for the penetration of foreign capital and technology in the Third World*. It also appears that if *giant corporations are the oligopolistic sellers in the world technology market, the private buyers from the Third World are but minuscule companies*. Both these conclusions are of immense significance.

CAPITAL FLOW

Technology is often carried with the flow of capital. For instance, it is estimated that more than a quarter of US research and development was made available to the UK economy through the media of American subsidiaries.[47] Again, in Indonesia the technology used by foreign investors in that country could have been obtained without necessarily being attached to foreign investment, had the Indonesians searched the world market adequately. In the absence of such initiative by local firms, technology reached Indonesia through foreign direct investments.[48] On occasion, it is also the dearth of necessary foreign exchange which compels a poor country to combine the import of technology with the borrowing of foreign capital.

A few glimpses into the order of magnitudes involved may be of help. The *net flow* of long-term private capital from capital-exporting countries worked out to $2.6 billion per annum on the average during 1951-1964; that of official donations and capital, $4.1 billion; the total thus came to $6.7 billion per year.[49] For most of the post-war period, the USA and UK have supplied between them 80 to 90 per cent of the world's international capital.[50] It is, however, well known that the bulk of the *gross* outflow of private capital is invested among the advanced capitalist countries themselves; proportionately little, 24 per cent during 1958–60 to be precise, flows into the Third World.[51] Thus not only world trade but also international capital flows are increasingly becoming an internal matter of the metropolis of world capitalism.[52] The dependence of the Third World on the metropolis for foreign capital, however, continues unabated. 'Of the total capital imports absorbed in 1965 by the less developed countries, 49 per cent originated from the USA, 25 per cent from

Western Europe, 6 per cent from international institutions and 3 per cent from the Sino-Soviet bloc.'[53] *Prima facie* it may appear that resources are flowing from the advanced capitalist countries into the Third World by way of foreign capital; but in fact the situation is just the reverse if the outflow of profit, dividend, royalty, etc. are taken note of.

Foreign capital in the Third World has always been an imperialist instrument of extracting surplus. It seems that there is a historical formula for it: *for any given steady inflow of foreign capital per year, 70 per cent more than that would flow out from the Third World continuously*. In other words, if the annual inflow of capital is one dollar, the annual outflow in the form of profit and dividend would be one dollar *and* seventy cents. Call it the *seven-tenths rule* if you like; you would be borne out by history. In the period 1870–1913, Britain, for instance, invested abroad a net amount of £2.4 billion; during the same period the income from foreign investment flowing into Britain came to £4.1 billion—precisely 70 per cent more than the principal. Or take the tremendous outburst of foreign investment from the USA during the post-war period, 1950–1963: the net flow of capital from the USA, $17.4 billion; the flow of income into the USA, $29.4 billion —almost exactly 70 per cent more than principal.[54]

The secrets behind the seven-tenths rule are being explored. The US direct investment abroad, for example, operates in the following manner. It gathers around itself a certain amount of capital from local sources, but it always retains the control over the assets so as to capture the 'perpetual' flow of profits. The American capital and the local capital are combined roughly in the ratio of 60:40; but here also there is a catch. In calculating the total value of capital investment by the American corporation the intangibles such as trade-marks, patents and know-how are taken as equivalent to twice the actual invested capital. In some other cases know-how, blueprints and so on are considered as one-third of capital investment, and then another one-third in equity is supplied by the corporation by providing machinery and equipment. The third secret, even more striking, is the way US direct investments abroad are financed. During 1957–1965 some $84 billion were used to finance the expansion and operations of US direct foreign investments. 'Of this total, only a little more than 15 per cent came from the United States. The remaining 85 per cent was raised outside the United States: 20 per cent from locally raised funds and 65 per cent from the cash generated by the foreign enterprise operations themselves.'[55]

As mentioned above, the flow of official donations and capital ($4.1 billion per year) is more than 50 per cent above that of private capital ($2.6 billion per year). For the Third World countries as a group of borrowers, the quantitative significance of official donations and capital is somewhat greater than private capital as such. 'In 1959–64, those countries [of the Third World] with a *per capita* national income of $350 or more in 1962 received equal proportions of their foreign capital from private and official sources; those with a *per capita* national income of $150 or less received 91 per cent of their receipts from official loans and donations.'[56] It would appear that the Third World is thus escaping from the excruciations of private foreign capital; or at least, the official donations and capital are mitigating some of the blunt edges of private capital. Here again the actual state of affairs is far from it. Official capital imported into the Third World quite often stipulates that purchases are to be made from the lending country, as a result of which the borrower has to pay a much higher price for the imports than what prevails in the world market. The extent of such over-charges is estimated to be 30 per cent in some cases. This reduces the quantum of net effective capital from the viewpoint of the borrower; but it subserves the interests of the capitalists of the lending country. Official capital, or 'aid', as it is euphemistically called, is more fundamentally 'a concession by the imperialist powers to enable them to continue their exploitation of the semi-colonial countries; it is similar in its effects to reforms within capitalist countries, in the sense that the exploiting classes relinquish the minimum necessary in order to retain their essential interests.'[57] The so-called 'aid is merely a form of subsidy for international companies paid for by taxpayers of the imperialist countries. An obvious case is aid which is tied to exports from the country providing it, . . . goods which are financed by tied aid are usually very much more expensive than those which can be bought elsewhere. Aid also partially finances the profits and interest which are remitted in increasing amounts from the Third World.'[58] Aid promotes the interests of imperialism in quite a few ways. 'It may enlarge the overseas market for the products of the private companies of the imperialist powers; and it can be used to secure the creation of facilities such as roads, harbours and training institutions, to commit the Third World's own resources to such projects, and thus to make the operations of these companies more profitable.'[59] 'In its general role as preserver of the capitalist system, aid can act in more indirect and complex ways than as a mere bribe or concession to sweeten the pill of exploitation.... The availability of "official aid" increases the likelihood that the governments of Third World countries will tolerate the continuation of massive outflows of private profits and interest on past debts. It may also help to create and sustain, within Third World countries, a class which is dependent on the continued existence of aid and foreign private investment and which therefore becomes an ally of imperialism.'[60] These are no mere conjectures of hypothetical possibility; these are the conclusions drawn from actual observation of the Latin American scene.

SUMMING UP

The discussion so far can be summed up as follows. To preserve and promote the world capitalist order, the State in the metropolitan centre engages itself in military preparation. Large amounts of resources are committed to military-oriented research and development. The private capitalists take full advantage of the scientific and technological knowledge thus produced. Guided by the objective of profitability they indulge in process and product innovations which are relatively risk-free, quick-yielding and highly remunerative. It is a characteristic feature of monopoly capitalism that the innovations under this regime must be labour-saving in nature, for both microeconomic and macroeconomic reasons. At any rate, the tendency of the rate of profit to fall is stemmed by rapid introduction of product and process innovations.

A monopolist, of course, hesitates to adopt any technological change, in view of the adverse effect on the capital value of his already existing plant and equipment. But fortunately for him, his opposite number in the Third World is quite eager to purchase old and obsolete production facilities. And it helps both ways—profitability improves in the metropolitan centre; and profitability improves in the outer periphery of world capitalism, despite the fact that the Third World capitalist, when he goes to buy technology and borrow capital, is confronted with giant monopoly corporations which overcharge prices and otherwise manipulate the transactions to the detriment of the former. The imported technology that comes to the Third World, all too often, has a number of strings attached to it—export-restrictive clauses, tie-in clauses on intermediate products, etc. However, a large part of the technology imported into the Third World involves on the part of the sellers 'cutting and taping together' bits of knowledge which leads to the launching of modified or new products and processes. This form of innovative activity does not require the same kind of expertise as the activities of the so-called 'centres of excellence' of research oriented towards the frontiers of scientific know-how. As a result, most of the traded technology is supplied, not by the original producers, but by their 'followers' and other engineering firms.

The United States is by far the most important exporter of technology and capital. Besides, it is observed that the overwhelming bulk of the world flows of trade, capital and technology take place within the group of advanced capitalist countries—between the USA on the one hand and Western Europe, Japan and Canada on the other. No wonder, commodities, capital and technology that enter the world market, all tend to move together in the same direction, for one complements the other two. In sum, *two major currents in the international flow of technology towards the Third World are clearly discernible : one directly from the USA, the other filtering through Western Europe and Japan.* Either way the net result is that the Third World gets by and large obsolete technology as well as second-hand machinery.

To recall the two earlier chapters in the light of the present one, the labour-saving technological progress in the metropolitan centre helps intensify the degree of unequal exchange in the centre–periphery international trade. Both wage and profit rates improve in the wake of product and process innovations in the metropolis. As the wage differential between the centre and the periphery widens, so does the gulf between the labour contents of their exports even under the conditions of balanced trade in a competitive market. Furthermore, technological changes in the metropolis in effect strengthen the transnational corporations and increase their monopoly power. The unequal exchange in the centre–

periphery international trade as a result is intensified by yet another notch. In addition to the visible outflows from the Third World in the form of profit, interest and royalty, an increasingly enormous but invisible stream of surplus is being drained out of the Third World by way of unequal exchange. This continuous haemorrhage cannot but retard the economic development of the Third World, and thereby reduce it ever more to an object of imperialist exploitation through various means.

The phenomenon of unequal exchange apparently arises even under competitive conditions from the fact of wage differential; it does not, however, mean that raising the wage rate in the Third World is the answer to it. Unequal exchange in one form or another is a historical fact many centuries old; it is predicated upon a certain layout of class reciprocity; and herein lies the fundamental root of unequal exchange. To understand this part of the story let us look at the dynamics of the Third World.

5

THIRD WORLD IN TRANSITION

THE Third World countries of Asia, Africa and Latin America as
a group are potentially more powerful than the advanced capitalist
countries. They are definitely larger in population and territory,
and no less endowed with natural resources. The population of
the metropolitan centre of world capitalism is only one-third or
so of that of the outer periphery today. In the past there was a
time, not long ago, when the sun did not set in the empire of a
tiny country consisting of one island with a few million people;
when it was dusk in one part of the empire it was dawn in the
other. How is it then possible that so many were, and are, sub-
jugated by so few for so long? This aspect of the world capitalist
system remains by and large an unexplored area. The theories of
imperialism so far have been essentially centre-centric—first Euro-
centric and now US-centric. The internal dynamics of colonies
or semicolonies that makes imperialism feasible has yet to be
analysed in depth.[1]

The Third World countries of Asia, Africa and Latin America
are a group with enormous diversity in size, population and other
socio-economic features. And yet there is a common thread which
holds them together: they have been subjected to imperialist exploitation of one form or another; they have suffered the plunder
of their invaluable resources, human as well as natural; and they
are appalled today at the yawning gap between their potentialities
and the actual performance. The preceding quarter of a century
has been an eventful era of rapid changes in the three continents.
Colonial outposts have fallen one by one; newly independent
states have taken their place in the comity of nations. But in what
direction are the Third World countries heading? Where are they
now anyway in the co-ordinates of historical progression? One
half of the world lives in the Third World; and certainly the

future course of the peoples of this part would determine the make-up of human civilization in the years to come. This is therefore no idle curiosity.

Till about half a century ago it used to be held that capitalism in its thirst for an ever expanding market and with its overflowing surpluses would cross the frontiers of its original home in Europe and assail the whole world; and that, as a result, one day the entire globe would bloom with the glories of capitalist development. The country that is more developed with capitalism only shows, to the less developed, the image of its own future. Cheap commodities produced under the conditions of efficient capitalism would batter down the Chinese Walls of pre-capitalist formations in distant lands; and the penetration of foreign capital would further erode their very foundations. One day therefore the line between a pre-capitalist colony and the capitalist metropolis would wither away; and the world would see only one ceaseless system of capitalism. But then, this will only be the prelude to the eventual collapse of the entire system under its own weight.[2]

History has not exactly taken this route. Capitalism has emerged in many parts of the world beyond its original home; indeed it has been stirred by cheap commodities and profit-seeking capital that came from the centre of world capitalism. Yet, over the last four centuries the roots of pre-capitalist formations have not been entirely transformed everywhere in Asia, Africa and Latin America; on the contrary, they have been strengthened at some places, though modified to a certain extent so as to suit the needs of world capitalism. On this issue however there is hardly any unanimity. In fact, this is a topic of fierce controversy among Marxists as well as non-Marxists. The point at issue is: how does one characterize the present situation in the Third World which has gone through four centuries of colonial exploitation? Is capitalism the dominant mode of production there? If not, then what is it? What are its characteristics? What is the nature of the current phase of transition of the Third World?

BOURGEOIS APOLOGIES

The bourgeois school, in its characterization of the Third World, operates on *three* strands: one, of which Theodore Schultz[3] is the principal mentor, considers the Third World as already fully capitalist, as the closest approximation to the neoclassical competitive model; the second, headed by Arthur Lewis,[4] concedes half, and calls it a dual economy; while the third one finds very little of capitalism anywhere now, but holds that the future of the Third World lies through capitalism.[5] In fact, the common element among these three viewpoints is their conviction that the Third World has to proceed along the capitalist line if it wants to achieve economic development. We shall take these up one by one.

Private industrialists are birds of the same feather all over the world, be it in Lima, Tananarive, Calcutta, Rome or New York. They maximize profit; they seek out areas of expansion; and the big among them tend to swallow up the smaller fry. However, the farmers apparently do not fall in line with one another across the continents. It may seem that the American ranchers have practically nothing in common with the impoverished tenants of Bengal. But here comes the surprise. Econometric models have been fitted, and mathematical calculations made, to show that the behaviour pattern of farmers is the same the world over.[6] From the poorest peasant in the tiny paddy field of Indonesia to the affluent farmer in Europe or America, they are all alike in that they regulate the crop pattern, resource allocation, investment decision, in a word, all their economic activities, according to the same laws of the market. Only the digits vary, but the model is the same. For instance, if the price elasticity of land allocation by cotton farmers in the USA is numerically 0.67, that of their counterparts in the Punjab is also positive; only the magnitude is different, namely, 1.62.[7] Indeed, the agricultural sector in the Third World is a fair prototype of the neoclassical competitive system. Resources are being utilized by farmers satisfying the first-order conditions of efficient production. The marginal productivity of labour is not zero, as withdrawal of labour from the agricultural sector would reduce the volume of output, just as it is predicted in a theoretical model of competitive equilibrium. Farmers respond to the stimulus of market prices in releasing their supply of outputs. And above all, as investors they are as shrewd as the stock-brokers in the Wall Street of New York; if the volume of their transactions is low that is of course a separate matter. Schultz is so moved that he says: 'Like a trading floor on which commodity futures are bought and sold, one observes throughout the world different groups of suppliers and demanders of agricultural factors of production haggling over the price.'[8] Third World agriculture, although a part of this Walrasian iteration, however, is somewhat dull in trading. 'Toward the rear of the stage, close to the entrance,' continues Schultz, 'there is a stand marked "traditional agriculture". The group at this stand is the quietest of the lot; there are few transactions.'[9] It is a neoclassical competitive model, no doubt;[10] but somehow it has got stuck in a low level equilibrium. 'No appreciable increase in agricultural production is to be had by reallocating the factors at the disposal of farmers who are bound by traditional agriculture.'[11] This is a summary of the view held by Schultz and his associates— for short, the Chicago group. In terms of this view, the distance that separates a subsistence peasant of the Third World from a millionaire farmer of the metropolitan centre of world capitalism is only one of material inputs—tractor, fertilizer, high-yielding varieties of seeds, insecticides, etc.; and that is all. Institutions do not matter; production relations are either uniform throughout the world, or are irrelevant.

According to the Chicago view, then, competitive capitalism prevails throughout the Third World economy—in agriculture as well as industry. So much so that, for example, the actual situation of the Chilean economy during the year 1958 was only 15 per cent short of the optimal equilibrium; 'reallocating existing resources . . . [of Chile] . . . would raise national welfare by *no more than* 15 per cent.'[12] The peasants are 'poor but efficient'— efficient according to the rules of the capitalist game; and the industrial capitalists are everywhere the epitome of capitalism. This Chicago view as propagated by Schultz and his associates may be flattering to the gullible in the Third World who are titillated by what look like compliments paid to the poor peasants. But in fact it conceals a trap. For it implies that only material inputs matter; nothing else is of any consequence for achieving economic advancement. From here it is but one small step to the conclusion that the advanced capitalist countries with their enormous productive capacity should therefore be invited to provide material 'assistance' to the underdeveloped countries of the Third World. Not only that; it further implies that feudalism, semi-feudalism and all such categories are totally beside the point when one considers the question of economic development, which only needs tractors, fertilizers, seeds, pesticide, steel, cement, automobiles, etc.[13] In the same vein, programmes of institutional change such as land reforms are considered as only distractions from the main agenda of the day.

The Chicago view is no more than idle window-dressing; its empirical evidence is dubious and its theoretical construction is open to serious question.[14] To recall, it denies, as it must for its internal consistency, the existence of surplus labour, i.e. labour with zero marginal productivity; and it posits the full utilization of available resources as it is in a smooth competitive equilibrium model. Such a postulate or inference flies in the face of actual facts in a Third World country like India. The question of surplus labour in Indian agriculture need not detain us here at all.[15] Let us instead pass on to the question of full utilization of a very scarce factor—land. It is our contention that thanks to the production relations there is an enormous *excess capacity* in land in a country like India. It may sound strange, but the evidence is there for all to see. Out of some 350 million acres of net cropped area, barely 50 million acres, or 14 per cent, is cultivated more than once per year. If one crop takes on an average four months, 86 per cent of India's agricultural land then remains idle for 66 per cent of the time per year.[16] To put it differently, nearly 60 per cent of the cropped area is, as it were, not at all used,[17] assuming that all land could have been cultivated throughout the year for three crops consecutively. Indeed, the arithmetic is slightly exaggerated, but the basic argument is valid. Big farmers have the least intensity of cropping in their land; *the bigger the farm size the lower is the intensity of cropping*. Table 12 in the first few columns presents the data for six states as revealed by the Farm Management Studies in India during the late sixties; while in the last two columns it gives the figures for the state of Rajasthan in 1971–72, then under the influence of the so-called Green Revolution.

The issue of land utilization deserves a fuller discussion. One can cite three possible explanations for the low intensity of cropping in big farms; these explanations are essentially derived from traditional economics. To begin with, a common argument is that the farmer is not interested in income beyond a certain level; that is, his utility function is such that the marginal utility of income approaches zero at a relatively moderate amount of income. If he

TABLE 12

CROPPING INTENSITY IN INDIA

(Per cent)

Farm size, in ascending order	Uttar Pradesh 1966–67	Punjab 1967–68	Orissa 1967–68	Maharashtra 1967–68	Tamilnadu 1968–69	Assam 1968–69	Rajasthan 1971–72 Participant	Rajasthan 1971–72 Non-participant
1	140	151	148	119	170	134	172	132
2	137	143	133	112	165	130	133	124
3	144	138	128	110	172	123	125	102
4	136	120	129	107	167	118	—	—
5	122	—	119	106	135	111	—	—
All farms	135	129	128	111	155	120	134	115

Notes: (*a*) Cropping intensity is measured by the ratio between *gross* cropped area and the *net sown* area.

(*b*) Class intervals of farm sizes differ from state to state as follows: *UP* (Muzaffarnagar district), (1) below 7 acres, (2) 7–11 acres, (3) 11–17 acres, (4) 17–25 acres, (5) above 25 acres; *Punjab*, (1) below 10 acres, (2) 10–17.5 acres, (3) 17.5–25.0 acres, (4) 25 acres and above; *Orissa* (Cuttack district), (1) below 2 acres, (2) 2–3 acres, (3) 3–5 acres, (4) 5–9 acres, (5) 9 acres and above; *Maharashtra* (Ahmednagar district), (1) below 10 acres, (2) 10–17 acres, (3) 17–26 acres, (4) 26–40 acres, (5) above 40 acres; *Tamilnadu* (Thanjavur district), (1) below 2.5 acres, (2) 2.5–5.0 acres, (3) 5.0–7.5 acres, (4) 7.5–14.0 acres, (5) above 14.0 acres; *Assam* (Nowgong district), (1) below 4.5 acres, (2) 4.5–6.0 acres, (3) 6.0–8.0 acres, (4) 8.0–10.0 acres, (5) above 10.0 acres; *Rajasthan* (Udaipur and Chittorgarh districts), (1) below 5 acres, (2) 5.15 acres, (3) above 15 acres.

(*c*) The Rajasthan farms are classified according to whether or not a farm participates in the programme of high-yielding varieties of seeds of wheat and maize which ushered in the so-called Green Revolution.

Source: For the first six states, the *Studies in the Economics of Farm Management*, respectively of the corresponding years. The page references are as follows. UP, p. 63; Punjab, p. 23; Orissa, p. 55; Maharashtra, p. 105; and Assam, p. 57. For Rajasthan, see Acharya (1975).

has enough land then just one crop is adequate to satiate his crav-ings; once the 'bliss' level of income is reached he leaves the land idle. There seems to be a rectangular hyperbola: as the farm size goes up the cropping intensity declines keeping the total in-come of the farmer constant at the 'bliss' level. It is not difficult to see the weakness of this theory. There are plenty of facts to contradict the premise that the farmer aspires for a fixed quantum of income and no more. The rich farmers' lobby, for instance, continuously presses for higher prices. Besides, in a country like India all too often it is the big farmer who also engages in various non-agricultural activities such as usury, trading, or investment in the local transport of bus and truck, in order to augment his in-come. Certainly he is not content with his farm income. Another type of explanation for the inverse relation between farm size and the degree of land utilization runs very much along the lines of a textbook on microeconomics. A big farmer usually supplies a sizable part of the local market; as such he faces a downward sloping demand curve for his product. To that extent he enjoys a sort of monopoly power. And just like the monopolist in the textbook he tends to restrict output. There may be a grain of truth in this proposition, although it is not easy to ascertain it empirically. However, if it were true, at most this hypothesis can explain why the big farmer restricts the output of a *given* crop; but it cannot show why he does not produce the *second* crop. A 'monopolist' farmer may limit the production of rice in the hope of a better price; but why should he not follow up the rice crop with, say, potato?

The third kind of reasoning is that the big farmer may not find multiple cropping profitable.[18] This point can be elaborated as follows. In Figure 5, let AA', BB', and CC' be the curves of marginal productivity of labour in the three consecutive crops respectively, with a given amount of land. The big farmer em-ploys hired labour at wage rate OW. Obviously he would pro-duce only one crop, and make a profit to the extent of AWP; the other two crops are not profitable to him. A small farmer, on the other hand, cultivates land mainly with his own family labour whose effective wage rate is about nil or negligible, say OF in Figure 5. It is clear that he would raise three crops in his land with labour FQ, FR and FS respectively, whereas the big farmer would leave the land idle after the first crop. Now, whether or

CROPPING INTENSITY IN BIG AND SMALL FARMS

Marginal productivity

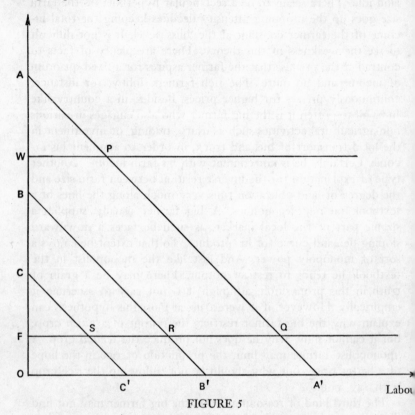

FIGURE 5

not profitability drops to zero after the first crop in a big farm is
an empirical question. However, it seems that the reluctance of
the big farmer to do multiple cropping cannot be fully ascribed
to such a factor. As we know, availability of water is a major
determinant of the productivity of land. Yet, there are indications
that big farmers do not use the land fully even where irrigation
facilities are present. The two main crop seasons in India are
called *kharif*, or *aman* (May to mid-October) and *rabi*, or *boro*
(mid-October to mid-April). In a study of inter-season use of
irrigation water by size group of farms in the Kosi canal area it is
found that the percentage of irrigation during *rabi*, relative to

that during *kharif*, varies inversely with the farm size, even though the irrigation potential remains the same in both the seasons (Table 13). Big farmers curtail the scale of their agricultural activities after the *kharif* cultivation, whereas water being equally available the profitability of agriculture is not likely to diminish very much in the mean time. So the zero or negative profitability of subsequent crops in a big farm does not appear to be factually correct and hence an explanation is required for the decline in cropping intensity as farm size rises.[19]

TABLE 13

INTER-SEASON USE OF IRRIGATION WATER BY SIZE GROUP OF FARMS IN THE KOSI CANAL AREA, INDIA

Kharif irrigation size group (acres)	*Rabi irrigation to Kharif irrigation (per cent)*
0–2	102.43
2–5	66.38
5–10	57.11
10–20	54.29
Over 20	36.50
All sizes	65.88

Source: Prasad (1974).

Having critically reviewed the above-mentioned three conventional arguments, we shall now proceed to suggest a somewhat unorthodox hypothesis. It is our contention that the big farmer has a multiplicity of channels of profit-making. He cultivates land with hired labour; engages in trading in foodgrains and other agricultural products; brings industrial goods from the town to the village market; and lends money to small farmers and agricultural labourers at usurious rates of interest.[20] All these *four* modes of extracting profit are exercised by him throughout the year in a certain 'optimal' sequence; as such the cultivation of land appears on his agenda only for a brief period; at other times of the year his land remains fallow. To elaborate, a year may be conceptually divided into three periods. The big farmer cultivates land in period 1. It is known that small and middle farmers sell their output at a low price after the harvest; the big farmer then finds it worthwhile to buy up the grain at that price, to be sold later in the year with a substantial margin. Even in a country like India where the procurement operations of the government are quite substantial in magnitude, private traders still handle about two-thirds of the marketed surplus. In other countries of the Third World the trade of agricultural produce is entirely in private hands. In period 2 the big farmer invests his money in purchase of the last season's crop. Cultivation of his land now could be profitable, but not as much as trading. Meanwhile, money having flown into the hands of small and middle farmers, the big farmer then seizes the opportunity of selling urban industrial goods to them. Accordingly, in period 3 he engages himself in another kind of trading, namely sale of goods from the town in the rural market. The three different modes of extracting profit are thus resorted to by him in three periods consecutively. As for usury, it could be a year-round exercise for him with seasonal ups and downs. Guided by the criterion of relative profitability the big farmer indeed leaves his land idle in periods 2 and 3. Small and middle farmers however cannot afford to do that, simply because they do not have enough money to invest in trading; they have no other alternative but cultivation of land. It is now understandable why the big farmer raises only one crop in his land. But, one may wonder, why does he not lease out the land in the last two periods of the year? Here a number of factors are involved. First, he may be afraid to lease out much of his land for a part of the year, lest it should be occupied by the tenants for the entire year and then for an indefinite future. That is to say, security considerations may require that the land is kept fallow rather than let out for a few months of the year to small farmers. Besides, there may be even a lack of demand for tenanted land on such a huge 'scale; after all, big farmers own one half of the total cultivated land of the country. Small farmers presumably do not have the complementary wherewithal that is necessary for producing the second and third crops in such wide tracts of agricultural land leased in from big farmers. In sum, the ownership pattern of land and other assets stands in the way of full utilization of resources.

It is significant that the big farmer's four modes of profit-making, as cited above, partly reinforce and partly contradict one another. His usurious loan to small farmers ties up the latter as a seller of agricultural output to the former and also as a purchaser of industrial goods from the same. And yet to the extent the small farmers are impoverished in the process it limits their supply of agricultural products and thereby reduces their demand for industrial commodities. To take another example, should a good harvest lead to a decline in the big farmer's speculative profit from trading in agricultural produce, it may at the same time generate a higher income for small and middle farmers, and thereby improve the market for trade in industrial goods from which the big farmer may now reap a bigger profit. In this complex ensemble of multiple modalities of profit-making by the big farmer, agricultural production cannot but stagnate, or at best grow at a snail's pace. Be that as it may, this much is certain that the view from the Chicago window is distorted; Third World agriculture is a far cry from the neoclassical competitive system of atomistic agents. The market mechanism has not brought about full employment of land and labour, nor has it equilibrated the allocation of resources on any criterion of efficiency. To take yet another striking illustration that runs counter to the Chicago view: even though irrigation is highly remunerative from the standpoint of society as a whole barely one-fifth or so of India's cropped area has been brought under it so far.[21] Table 14 gives the alternative estimates of costs of one additional tonne of wheat under two different strategies, namely, (*i*) irrigating the hitherto un-irrigated area and using the traditional method of production, and (*ii*) intensifying the cultivation in the already irrigated area, with the new high-yielding varieties (HYV) of seeds and other inputs as recommended by the 'New Strategy'. The estimated costs under the former are evidently lower (Table 14). But the expansion of

TABLE 14

Cost per Tonne of Wheat under Two Strategies in India

(*Rupees*)

Strategy	Including direct labour cost	Excluding direct labour cost
1. From traditional non-irrigated to traditional irrigated	337.96	263.39
2. From traditional irrigated to non-traditional 'New Strategy'	349.04	336.45

Source : Sau (1973), p. 92.

output which has taken place in India since 1965 has largely been a product of the second, more expensive strategy, under the aegis of the government. The competitive market mechanism of Schultz has not worked towards the extension of the irrigated area, any more than it has laboured to ensure the full utilization of the existing irrigation network. So much for the efficient capitalism in the Third World as propagated by the Chicago school.

Another species of the same genus of the bourgeois school on the characterization of the Third World is the Lewis theory of *dual* economy—dual because the economy is said to comprise a modern, capitalist sector of industry along with a backward, primitive sector of agriculture that has a practically unlimited supply of labour. With its excessive burden of unproductive labour the agricultural sector obviously cannot afford to play according to the rules of the capitalist game. This much is simple. And now the real story begins. Under the circumstances, according to this theory, State intervention may be necessary only for a well-defined, finite period in order to effect a transition from this dualism to the infinite regime of capitalism. The function of the State would be confined to mobilizing the surplus labour from the backward sector and deploying it in the 'modern', capitalist sector of industry. The excess of the average productivity of labour above the constant real wage rate gives rise to profit which is to be ploughed back into industry to attract another round of surplus labour from agriculture. And so on. Finally a time would come when the marginal productivity of labour in agriculture would become equal to the wage rate, whereby a *turning point* will be reached. The State may then withdraw from the economic scene; since the marginal productivity of labour has risen to the level of the wage rate, the first order conditions of profit maximization come into operation. The market mechanism having been put into forward gear, capitalism now holds sway over agriculture. The entire economy is thus transformed into full-fledged capitalism; thereafter there is very little to worry about.[22]

The third variant of the bourgeois theory finds its fullest expression in the magnum opus of Myrdal.[23] Reviewing the South Asian landscape, particularly its rural segment, Myrdal concludes that it has reached a sort of equilibrium which is unstable but an equilibrium nevertheless. 'The relative stability of the rural scene must also be understood as an equilibrium resulting from the

interplay of diverse interests within the complex rural hierarchy—
a situation that makes it difficult to mobilize support for change.'[24]
His characterization of the rural society is best summarized in the
following words: *'The South Asian village is thus like a complex
molecule among whose parts extreme tensions have been built up.*
Although the tensions crisscross in a manner that maintains equilibrium, it is conceivable that they reorganize in a way that would
explode the molecule. This probably would not happen sponta-
neously, but as the result of a forceful onslaught from outside.'[25]
According to Myrdal, the economic interests of various groups
are so interwoven with mutual conflict and complementarity that
no clear-cut alignment among the groups is possible. So the *status
quo* continues despite the resultant stagnation for all concerned.
As for the way out of this impasse Myrdal is quite clear that it
lies through unhindered capitalism. As he puts it, 'it may be pre-
ferable to make a deliberate policy choice in favour of *capitalist
farming* by allowing and encouraging the progressive cultivator
to reap the full rewards of his enterprise and labour.'[26]

The three shades of bourgeois theories, despite their differences
in characterizing the initial conditions, are unanimous about the
prospects of capitalism in the Third World, and are categorical
about the potentialities of economic development of the Third
World under capitalism. In sharp contrast, the Marxists and the
neo-Marxists, as they are called, are convinced that the Third
World cannot achieve economic development along the capitalist
line; and that competitive capitalism is a thing of the long past. But
here ends their unanimity. They are bitterly divided among themselves in the assessment of the present situation of the Third
World, and in the identification of the next phase of the movement towards the ultimate destination of socialism, and also in the
strategy and tactics to be followed. Certain preliminary remarks
are called for before these formulations can be taken up for discussion. We now turn to the preliminaries.

POLITICAL ECONOMY: SCOPE AND METHOD

The task of political economy is two-fold: *to analyse the prevailing mode of production, and to discern the contours of the new,
emerging mode.* The current abuses of the day, the poverty,
degradation, exploitation and misery, are the direct consequences

of the existing socio-economic formation, and at the same time they are the signs, the indicators, of its approaching dissolution. Political economy has to relate these phenomena in their interconnection and to their source.[27] A socio-economic formation does not collapse on its own, nor does it give way before its possibilities are exhausted. With the accomplishments as well as the shortcomings of today's formation, political economy has to identify and reveal the features of the socio-economic formation that is in the making. A society harbours many a contradiction at all levels: between the classes, between the productive forces and the relations of production, between the economic base and the superstructure. Among them, there is one fundamental, *principal* contradiction which regulates the numerous other major and minor ones, and plays the leading and decisive role. A society acquires its characteristics primarily from the principal contradiction. The mosaic is never stationary though; contradictions change their position. The main contradiction of today may yield place tomorrow to another which is of minor importance at present. For instance, when imperialism carries on its oppression not by war, but by milder means—political, economic and cultural—the ruling classes in semi-colonial countries capitulate to imperialism, and the two form an *alliance* for the joint oppression of the masses of the people. At such a time, this *alliance* assumes the position of principal contradiction against the people. The moment imperialism launches a war of aggression against such a country, the situation changes; at such a time, the contradiction between imperialism and the country concerned becomes the principal one, while all the contradictions among the various classes within the country are relegated to a secondary and subordinate position.

The society moves ahead as a result of the interaction of the contradictions, the change in their relative positions, the resolution of some of them, and the emergence of new ones in the process. Among the numerous major and minor contradictions which are determined or influenced by the fundamental contradiction, some are intensified, some are temporarily or partially resolved or mitigated, and some new ones appear on the scene. Hence the process of development is always marked by *stages*. Through proper analysis, *political economy has to grasp the principal contradiction, and to reveal the dynamics of the various major and minor contradictions whose shift and intensity delineate*

the stages in the development of society. It is important to remember that, in *any* given contradiction, whether principal or
secondary, the two contradictory aspects must *not* be treated as
equal. In any contradiction the development of the contradictory
aspects is *uneven*. Sometimes they seem to be in equilibrium,
which is however only temporary and relative, while unevenness
is basic. Of the two contradictory aspects, one must be principal
and the other secondary. The *principal aspect* is the one that plays
the leading role in the contradiction. The nature of a thing is
determined mainly by the principal aspect of a contradiction, the
aspect which has gained the dominant position. But again the
situation is not static; the principal and the non-principal aspects
of a contradiction transform themselves into each other and the
nature of the thing changes accordingly. In a given process or at
a given stage in the development of a contradiction, *A* is the
principal aspect and *B* is the non-principal aspect; at another stage
or in another process the roles are reversed—a change determined
by the extent of the increase or decrease in the force of each
aspect in its struggle against the other in the course of the development of a thing. To take an example, the bourgeoisie of a
semicolony is in alliance with imperialism; now, from the viewpoint of the bourgeoisie there are favourable as well as unfavour-
able aspects of this alliance. The alliance continues so long as the
favourable aspect outweighs the other. The former therefore is
the *principal aspect* of the contradiction between the bourgeoisie
and imperialism. However, should imperialism launch a war of
aggression the relative position of the two aspects of the contradiction would change.[28]

Abstruse though they may sound, these brief observations are
helpful for an understanding of the complex situation of the Third
World. The full meaning of these terse formulations would become gradually transparent as we proceed. Let it be made clear
that the methodology of our analysis of the Third World's socio-
economic formation draws heavily upon this thesis on dialectics.

The Marxists and neo-Marxists divide themselves into three
schools in terms of their characterization of the prevailing order in
the Third World, which is one of the two tasks of political economy as mentioned above. What is the dominant mode of production in the Third World? The three schools give three separate
answers to this question as follows: (*i*) capitalist, (*ii*) colonial-

postcolonial, and (*iii*) semifeudal-semicolonial. We may now consider this interesting controversy among the Marxists and neo-Marxists.

ON CAPITALIST UNDERDEVELOPMENT

If Marx and Lenin laid more explicit emphasis upon the dynamic and progressive nature of capitalism in the historic specificity of their field of enquiry, soon questions were to be raised with regard to the net effects of the development of world capitalism upon the colonies and semicolonies. In September 1928, Kuusinen introduced 'theses on the revolutionary movement in colonial and semicolonial countries', which rejected the so-called 'decolonization' thesis. A major part of Marx's argument and much of Lenin's tone, if not of his analysis, were incorporated into the notion that capitalism, rather than developing all areas that it touches, can positively 'underdevelop'.[29] This marks the beginning of a new trend in thinking on world capitalism. This notion was taken up by Baran and later by Frank to explain the underdevelopment of some countries as a corollary, as the obverse, or even the cause of the development of others. It perceives a whole hierarchy of exploitation—a chain of metropolis–satellite relationships moving from the world metropolis via nations, capital cities, regional and local centres, large landowners and merchants, small peasants and tenants, right down to the landless labourer at the bottom. Thus surplus is extracted upwards and inwards as it is created, developing some areas at the expense of others.[30]

On the morrow of integration into the world capitalist system four centuries ago, the colonies shredded whatever pre-capitalist features they had, and transformed themselves into a sort of capitalism that was distorted and deformed from the very beginning. But it is capitalism nevertheless which holds sway in these economies. Surplus is extracted by the local agents of the metropolis, and it is ultimately funnelled into the hands of the metropolitan capitalists. According to Frank, thus 'no part of the economy is feudal'.[31] Although his case studies cover Chile and Brazil, his conclusions are claimed to have validity on a much wider scale.[32] It is therefore generalized that the elements of feudalism or semi-fuedalism either never existed in the Third World, or if they at all had existed they disappeared four centuries ago in the face of the onslaught of world capitalism. The class structure in the Third World is then remarkably simple; there are only two classes, the proletariat and the bourgeoisie. Indeed, it is true for the global capitalist system as a whole. 'There is, in fact, only one single capitalist system which embraces most of the world. . . . There are only two classes in the capitalist world today, though there may be all kinds of strata.'[33] Accordingly, the principal contradiction in the world capitalist system is that between the proletariat and the bourgeoisie. At the level of a Third World country however the position of the *principal contradiction* is occupied by *imperialism*, that is, the bourgeoisie of the metropolis of world capitalism, with which the domestic bourgeoisie are linked up in many ways as their subordinate partners.

This thesis of Gunder Frank, which is built upon the works of Baran, has given rise to an extensive debate. Suffice it to say at this stage that Frank's characterization of the mode of production in the Third World primarily relies upon the exchange relations rather than the relations of production. It overemphasizes the aspect of who eventually appropriates the surplus and how the surplus is extracted, to the point of overlooking the very process of the *generation* of the surplus as such. It ignores the conditions under which production takes place; and it concerns itself mainly with the terms under which the output is transacted in the market.[34] To that extent it is a lopsided view.

THE COLONIAL MODE OF PRODUCTION

The colonies have gone through such a subservient process of development that their experiences cannot be summed up in the terminology that is applicable in the history of the metropolis of world capitalism. The feudalism–capitalism conceptual framework which is derived from the European terrain would find very little to illuminate in the soil of the Third World. A distinct new category is therefore called for in order to conceptualize the reality of the Third World. The colonial mode of production as a historical category is a product of this dissatisfaction and the search for a suitable analytical paradigm.

'The concept of internal disarticulation of the colonial economy is crucial for an understanding of the colonial mode of production.'[35] A colonial economy is oriented towards meeting the demands of the metropolis; all its activities are consummated only when the products of these efforts finally reach the factory or the department store in the metropolitan centre. There is very little intercourse among the sectors within the colonial economy itself, as reflected in the presence of wide inter-sectoral variations in productivity, capital intensity and employment. That is to say, the colonial economy is disarticulated internally; it is articulated only externally in the world capitalist market.[36] Production is not stagnant in the colony, nor is it meant for self-consumption, unlike in the feudal mode. But the system of expanded reproduction is of a deformed nature in that 'a substantial part of the surplus generated in the colonial agrarian economy (as well as that generated in colonial industry) is appropriated by the imperialist bourgeoisie and enters into expanded reproduction not directly within the colonial economy but rather at the imperialist centre. Its special characteristic is that the expanded reproduction and the attendant rise in the organic composition of capital benefits the imperialist bourgeoisie rather than the colony from which the surplus is extracted.'[37]

The mode of production in a colony is therefore neither feudalism nor capitalism in the classical sense of the terms; nor can it be a mixture or co-existence of the two. For, 'even if we accept for the moment the suggestion of simultaneous existence of "feudal" and "capitalist" modes, . . . one must point out that these formulations miss an essential problem. That is the problem of the necessary contradiction between modes of production in historical development: A new emergent mode of production stands in contradiction to the old disintegrating mode of production. If that basic Marxist postulate is accepted, there is a necessity, at each stage of historical development, to identify which mode is dominant and, therefore, represents the principal contradiction in the class struggle.'[38] Indeed, 'the issue is not simply whether "capitalist" relations of production *exist*, nor indeed whether they have completely done away with all feudal survivals, but precisely of the relative weight of each, the alignment of classes that represents each mode of production *vis-à-vis* each other.'[39] Having said this, the protagonist of the thesis of the colonial mode of production then proceeds to argue that in point of fact 'there is no conflict between the urban and rural bourgeoisie [in a colony] on the one hand and the landowners on the other'[48]—all of them prosper simultaneously at the expense of the labouring masses, but only as subordinate agents of imperialism. What is more, in the colonial agrarian economy the so-called rural 'capitalist' class cannot even be structurally distinguished from the 'feudal' landlords.[41] But that does not mean that, unlike in the schema of Frank as mentioned above, there is only one ruling class: the world capitalist class; 'the landowners of Brazil, the bourgeoisie of India, and the great imperialist bourgeoisie would [then] all be a single class, the capitalists of the world.' Such a conflation would obscure the mutual structural differentiation of several different classes.

So, the colonial mode of production envisages a hierarchical structure of world capitalism, with the colonial bourgeoisie as junior partners of the big bourgeoisie of the metropolis. 'The imperialist bourgeoisie ... carried through the bourgeois revolution in the colonies. It created a bourgeois State and bourgeois legal and institutional framework to complement the penetration, at the structural level, by metropolitan capital, of the colonial economy. By virtue of the transformation also of feudal relations on the land into capitalist relations, the colonial mode of production, *which is a capitalist mode*, was set into motion.'[42] Thus stated that thesis seems to differ very little, if at all, from the Baran–Frank theory on the mode of production in colonies. Here again, the elimination of feudal elements is no longer on the agenda; it was accomplished long ago.

CO-EXISTENCE BY STALEMATE

In the course of analysing the situation in their countries before liberation, the revolutionaries of China and Vietnam characterized the then prevailing mode of production neither as fully 'capitalist', nor as fully 'colonial' but as *semifeudal-semicolonial*.[43] To project their views on two specific countries into a generalization for the Third World, the penetration of foreign capitalism into a colony in the nineteenth century greatly accelerated the process of disintegration of feudalism and the emergence of capitalism. But at the same time there was another concomitant aspect of the same process, namely, the collusion of imperialism with the feudal forces which in effect did arrest the development of capitalism.

Recall that any contradiction has two aspects, one principal and the other secondary. Such was the dialectics of the imperialist conquest of the colony that on the one hand capitalism in the colony received an impetus; on the other, it was held in check. These two aspects were hardly ever in balance; one was dominant over the other; and they switched their positions from time to time. So the development of capitalism in the colony was uneven over time and space. The indigenous bourgeoisie was not strong enough to oust the feudal remnants; nor was it to the interests of imperialism to see the fuedal elements swept away. The capitalist mode of exploitation was thus superimposed upon the feudal exploitative machinery; and accordingly the colony assumed the character of a semi-feudal mode.

Imperialism used the local feudal remnants and the bourgeoisie as the mediator of its own class interests. The economy was not totally transformed into just another factory or farm for the exclusive benefit of imperialism. Politically the country might be a colony, but its economy remained only semi-colonial. An arrangement had to be worked out whereby the interests of the three classes—the feudal landlords, the indigenous bourgeoisie and the imperialist bourgeoisie—could be duly accommodated. On their own feudal landlords found very little incentive to adopt the capitalist mores. As the surplus was being drained out of the country, the expansion of industrial capitalism could not gather much momentum. On the other hand, the ranks of the displaced artisans and pauperized peasants continued to swell as the commodities from the metropolitan centre eroded the home market of indigenous industries. Under such circumstances semi-feudalism thrived on the poverty of the masses.[44] The bourgeoisie of the colony was born under the conditions of imperialist domination, and it grew within the limits set by imperialism. No doubt, there were contradictions within this triangular alliance of feudalism, capitalism and imperialism; but the internal contradictions among the exploiting classes occupied a secondary position relative to their common contradiction against the toiling people.[45]

The countries of Asia, Africa and Latin America had won political independence; but their economic dependence, their status as a semifeudal-semicolonial adjunct to world capitalism, remains by and large intact in many cases. If capitalism did not develop much during the colonial days, can it flourish now? Can it transform the economy? These are all momentous questions which deserve scientific analysis. We have already studied the answer given by bourgeois theories; and to the above-mentioned two neo-Marxist schools these questions do not arise in the first place simply because the mode of production is assumed to be capitalist, albeit deformed and distorted. However, according to the other school in the Marxist tradition, which holds that the mode of production is semifeudal-semicolonial, the prospects of capitalist development in the Third World are indeed bleak. It is the agricultural sector which still harbours feudal and semi-feudal traits; and capitalism cannot fully sweep them away, as the Kautsky–Lenin laws and limits of agrarian capitalism are in operation. What are the Kautsky–Lenin laws and limits? A sizable part of Lenin's writings is devoted to the agrarian question of Russia. Sifting the data of Europe and the United States of America, Lenin arrived at certain generalizations about agrarian capitalism which were profoundly influenced by the works of Kautsky. Hence we call these broad observations the Kautsky–Lenin laws. Where does the impulse for the origin and growth of agricultural capitalism come from? How is this process of capitalist development sustained? What are the limits to the spread of agricultural capitalism? The Kautsky–Lenin laws are addressed to these issues.

'It is the development of capitalism in the manufacturing industry that is the *main force* which gives rise to, and develops, capitalism in agriculture,' observes Lenin.[48] As another author had put it recently, 'whether there will be meat in the kitchen is never decided in the kitchen. Nor is the fate of agriculture under capitalism ever decided in agriculture. Economic, social, and political processes unfolding outside of agriculture, and in particular the accumulation of capital and the evolution of the capitalist class, while themselves originally largely determined by the processes that have taken place in agriculture, become with the onset of capitalism the prime movers of the historical development.'[47] It should also be kept in view that in agriculture the process of development of capitalism is immeasurably more complex and assumes incomparably more diverse forms than that in industry. In terms of the history of Europe and the USA, there are basically two features in this process of capitalist development: one is the growth of commercial agriculture, and the other is the formation of the agricultural proletariat. With the expansion of industry, the population outside the agricultural sector grows; and in response to the increasing demand therefrom, an extensive development of commodity agriculture takes place. As for the second feature, namely, the rise of an agrarian proletariat, it occurs as a section of the peasantry gets disintegrated into two strata: (*a*) the farmers who regard agriculture as an industry, i.e. the capitalist farmers, and (*b*) wage-workers. This is known as the differentiation of the peasantry.[48] In this formulation of Kautsky–Lenin laws the factors that determine the pace and pattern of agricultural capitalism are partly situated within the agricultural sector and partly outside it. The differentiation of the peasantry is largely an internal matter of the agricultural sector while the stimulus for production for the market comes from outside.

So far as the Kautsky–Lenin 'limits of capitalist agriculture' are concerned, one of them particularly deserves to be highlighted; it is the rigidity of the land market. The monopoly in landed property limits agricultural capitalism. In industry, capital grows as a result of accumulation, as a result of the conversion of surplus value into capital; and centralization, i.e. the amalgamation of several small units of capital into a large unit, plays a lesser role. That is to say, an industrial capitalist can go on increasing the scale of his operation, almost without limit, by more and more investment. In agriculture the situation is different. The whole of the cultivated land is already occupied by different owners. If one wants to enlarge the area of the farm one can do so only by purchasing several plots from others. And herein lies the difficulty, particularly in view of the fact that the small plots are usually occupied by agricultural labourers and small peasants who are masters of the art of maintaining their hold by reducing consumption to an unbelievable minimum. This then draws a line beyond which the capitalist farmer cannot aspire to go.[49] Another pre-capitalist feature of the agricultural sector which may weaken, if not limit, the growth of capitalism is the independent development of merchants' and usurers' capital in the countryside as it retards the differentiation of the peasantry.[50]

The Kautsky–Lenin laws and the limits of agrarian capitalism were conceived in the perspective of European and North American history. How far are they operative in a colony or a semicolony? Imperialism does not permit rapid expansion of the manufacturing industry in a colony; as a result the non-agricultural population remains more or less stagnant. In other words, the impulse emanating from industrial expansion that sets agriculture on the road to capitalist development is weak or even non-existent in a colonial set-up. However, the colonial agriculture is not immune from outside pressure; indeed it is reduced to an adjunct to the economy of the metropolitan country. It may be recalled, for instance, that in India the railway network having been laid in the middle and late nineteenth century, bulk no longer remained a barrier to transport, and the entire composition of Indian exports changed. Foodgrains, raw cotton, jute, oil seeds and tea began to be exported in huge quantities to satiate the hunger of the British economy. Indeed, there was a double shift in Indian agriculture: first, a shift in relative acreage from foodgrains to non-food crops, and second, an enlargement within the acreage under foodgrains of the portion devoted to crops for exports.[51] The resultant 'commercialization' of agriculture under such circumstances of imperialist dominance may or may not be conducive to the growth of capitalist production relations, because much of this commercialization is forced on the peasantry at gunpoint as it were. This is only to emphasize that in a colonial environment there is the possibility of a disjunction between 'commercialization' of agriculture and the growth of agrarian capitalism. As for the second element, namely, the differentiation of the peasantry, there are again certain peculiarities in a colony about the growth of the agricultural proletariat. According to the classical schema, the middle peasantry splits itself into two strata: capitalist farmers and wage workers. In a colony there is yet another process by which a group of agricultural labourers comes into being. The import of manufactured goods from the metropolis into the colony assails a wide range of indigenous industries, and as a result the artisans are displaced and are then forced to join the ranks of the agricultural proletariat. The number of available wage workers in agriculture thus rises even though the basic conditions of production may remain essentially pre-capitalist. Thus here also arises a case of possible disjunction between the growth in the size of the agricultural proletariat and the extent of agrarian capitalism.

All this, however, does not invalidate the Kautsky–Lenin laws of agrarian capitalism in the colonial or semi-colonial context. Still the inducement for increasing production for the market has to come from outside the agricultural sector in the form of industrial demand or demand generated by the wage-and-salary bill of the government. Secondly, still the development of capitalism in agriculture would connote the differentiation of the peasantry, i.e. the emergence of capitalist farmers as well as wage workers from the section of the middle peasantry. What complicates the picture in a colony or semicolony is that sometimes the symptoms such as production for the market and a multitude of agricultural labourers may appear in consequence of a series of historical events other than the growth of capitalist relations in agricultural production. One must not be misled by such surface phenomena into a conclusion about the extent of agrarian capitalism. Now to return to the original question, if the prevailing mode of production is semi-feudal, how far would capitalism succeed in dissolving the elements of semi-feudalism? This question may be tackled step by step. Why does not industrial capital penetrate agriculture and transform the latter in its own capitalist image? This has happened historically in other parts of the world. Capitalism on the continent of Europe, in countries like Germany and France and later Russia, and also in the USA, looked in the direction of what may be termed as the 'internal colonial policy' of industrial capital towards agriculture before its interest in an export market for manufactures had been fully awakened.[52] Or, like the Prussian Junkers why do not the feudal-semifeudal landlords in the Third World turn themselves into capitalist farmers? Similarly, why do not the rich farmers like the English yeomen spearhead the advancement of capitalism in agriculture?

In a way, to a certain extent all this is happening in the Third World. A trickle of industrial capital has lately found its way into 'cowdung capitalism'. The 'gentlemen farmers' from cities—retired businessmen, lawyers, doctors, army officers, and other professionals also—have descended on the villages to engage themselves in farming. In the wake of land reform legislations quite a few big landowners have taken to the cultivation of land, evicting thousands of tenants. And, finally, there are numerous instances where affluent farmers have given up their age-old mores of treating land as only a means of supporting a luxurious, idle life style, and have started looking upon it as an asset that helps produce surplus value. However, the point at issue is: how far will this trend go? In many countries of the Third World a large number of small peasants own tiny fragments of land, scattered all over the place. Since the opportunities of industrial employment are almost non-existent, they hang on to their pieces of land with proverbial tenacity. As such the Kautsky–Lenin limit of the rigidity in land market becomes an important barrier against the spread of agrarian capitalism. Of course, there are quite a few big landowners to whom land is certainly not the limit for expansion along the capitalist line. For them it is the scope of profit-making through a multiplicity of modalities such as usury, trading and tenancy, in a situation of huge unemployment in the countryside, that lures them away from full-fledged capitalist farming.[53] Besides, the independent development of usurers' and merchants' capital further restricts the differentiation of the peasantry as mentioned above.

The new agricultural technology of high-yielding varieties (HYV) of seeds and fertilizers has ushered in the so-called green revolution in many a country of the Third World. Since the mid-sixties it has spread with remarkable speed throughout the continents of Asia, Africa and Latin America. It has stimulated capitalist farming on a wide scale. But even this wave of agrarian capitalism appears to be losing its momentum because of its internal contradictions. The new technology is substantially cash-intensive since large amounts of inputs have to be bought from the market. The cash requirement for cultivation with this technology is eleven times higher than that with the traditional method. Initially the transnational agri-business corporation looked upon it as yet another opportunity to penetrate the countryside. But now it is increasingly realized that the agri-business corporation is not a short cut which can entirely bypass the existing network of local traders. The ESSO Fertiliser Company in the Philippines, for instance, is said to have run into difficulties in recruiting a sufficient number of trained staff to man its local branches. The failure of the Bimas Gotong Rojong programme in Indonesia, under which the foreign companies contracted with the government to supply the farmers with packaged inputs but left it to the government agency to collect the output, is even more instructive. So it is concluded by expert observers that the non-institutional sources of credit, such as the money-lender, the village shop-keeper or the landlord, will continue to play an important part in financing the green revolution.[54] The new technology, instead of dissolving, may actually strengthen the archaic relationships in the villages.

There is yet another feature of the new technology which makes the green revolution susceptible to the realization crisis. An estimate of itemwise expenditure for wheat cultivation under the new technology, as given in Table 15, reveals that chemical fertilizers claim 38.5 per cent of total costs; insecticides, 1.9 per cent; and interest, depreciation and repair charges of machinery and equipment, 29.5 per cent. These three items together thus claim 70 per cent of total costs. All or most of these inputs came from the urban, industrial sector. That is to say, if Rs 100 is spent in cultivation with the new technology two-thirds or more of it flows out of the rural, agricultural sector into the urban, industrial sector. If an equivalent amount of purchasing power does not come back from the latter in the form of demand for the wheat thus produced, there will be a deficiency of demand. Usually, the urban area absorbs one-third of the foodgrains output. Now, with the new technology, it has to double its intake in order to main-

TABLE 15

COST PER ACRE OF WHEAT UNDER THE NEW TECHNOLOGY
OF THE GREEN REVOLUTION

	Rs	Per cent of total costs
A. *Current expenses*		
1. Human labour	54.54	10.7
2. Bullock labour	56.04	10.9
3. Seeds	14.22	2.7
4. Insecticides	10.00	1.9
5. Irrigation	30.00	38.6
6. Fertilizers	195.00	38.6
Total	359.84	70.5
B. *Capital expenses*		
1. Interest on capital, depreciation and other charges on machinery and equipment	150.00	29.5
C. Total costs (A+B)	509.84	100.0

Source : Sau (1973), p. 83.

tain balance in the wheat market. In other words, we come back to the Kautsky–Lenin laws: the industrial population has to expand at a fast rate to sustain agrarian capitalism. The limitations of the new agricultural technology as a vehicle for capitalism having been thus recognized, it must also be understood that agricultural capitalism is not predicated upon any particular type of technology. Let us recall that in the ultimate analysis the growth of capitalism in agriculture is conditioned by the overall class relations in the country. At this level of perception also the future of capitalism in Third World agriculture does not appear to be much different from what its present is. So long as the massive unemployment in the countryside continues, and the expansion of the non-agricultural population remains negligible, the pace of capitalist development in agriculture is bound to be marginal; and the overall capitalist transformation of agriculture would appear to be only a very remote possibility.

The superimposition of capitalist exploitative relations in an otherwise feudal system gives rise to semi-feudalism. If the capitalist force is not strong enough to establish its supremacy the stalemate of semi-feudalism persists despite the enormous tension within the system as the capitalist and feudal elements continuously struggle against each other. On the other hand, to be characterized as semicolony a country need not be under the direct political domination of a foreign power; it is enough if its economy is exploited by the bourgeoisie of another country. The question of feudalism and semi-feudalism has been one of the most debated points among the Marxists. It is interesting to note that the Second Havana Declaration of 1962 recognizes the prevalence of feudal remnants in Latin America, but declares at once that, nonetheless, the path of economic development for Latin America does not lie through further development of capitalism.[55] In general, those who identify the prevailing mode of production in the Third World as essentially semifeudal-semicolonial agree that capitalism can no longer fully develop in the Third World, nor can it be the answer to the aspirations of the peoples of the Third World.

So the debate goes on among the Marxists and neo-Marxists. It emerges from the brief exposition above that the crux of the controversy is related to the extent of the development of capitalism in the Third World. The first two theories argue that capitalism, albeit deformed and distorted, embraced the entire economy from the very beginning of the colonial era; whereas the other school admits only a partial and diluted role for capitalism in the Third World, surrounded as it is by the relics of feudalism and semi-feudalism. At this point one may wonder whether it might not be better to make an attempt to quantify, if possible, the extent of capitalist development in the concrete specificity of a Third World country rather than continue with *a priori* polemic and thereby settle the above debate once for all.

ESSENCE AND MANIFESTATION

Any endeavour to prepare a quantitative index of the development of capitalism in a given historical situation comes up against a whole lot of difficulties. First and foremost, one has to define capitalism as a mode of production, the capitalist as a class, and the proletariat as its alter ego. This is only the beginning. It should be borne in mind that the definition of a thing gives the *necessary and sufficient conditions* for the thing to be what it is. So, having the definition is not enough; because nowhere in the world did pure capitalism ever exist in its pristine glory. In a specific situation therefore one has to look for the *essence*, or the principal features, of the definiendum, in the midst of an admixture of a variety of attributes. When Lenin calls capitalism 'that stage where labour-power itself is a commodity' he is giving the 'essence' of capitalism, rather than the full set of 'necessary and sufficient conditions' thereof. Note that the 'essence' of a thing is but *one or a few* of the major necessary conditions of its being, rather than the complete collection of its necessary and sufficient conditions. Now comes the next layer of hurdles.

The essence as such is one thing, the *manifestation* of the essence is another. When one *measures* the degree of capitalist development in a country what one measures is *not* the essence as such but the extent of the manifestations of the essence of capitalism. The essence—'where labour-power itself is a commodity'—is manifested in the employment of wage-labour. According to Lenin, for example, 'the employment of hired labour is the *principal* manifestation of . . . capitalism'.[56]

'Essence reveals itself both in the mass of phenomena and in the individual, essential phenomenon. . . . Essence is expressed in its many outward manifestations. At the same time essence may not only express itself but also disguise itself in these manifestations.'[57] Indeed, all science would be superfluous if the outward appearance and the essence of things directly coincided. Which particular manifestation of the essence should be measured and how it should be measured in order to appreciate the degree of development of capitalism in a given case depends considerably upon the nature and availability of data as well as upon the specificity of the context. On one occasion, for example, Lenin found that railway statistics provided remarkably exact data on the different rates of growth of capitalism and finance capital in the world economy. He compared the railway mileage between 1890 and 1913 in Europe, the USA and the other parts of the world, and came to the conclusion that capitalism was growing rapidly, more so in the colonies and the overseas countries.[58] If this method is applied mechanically in another set-up, the result is likely to be misleading. Recall that during the period of twenty-five years between 1871 and 1895 the railway mileage in India went up fourfold, from 5,000 miles to nearly 20,000 miles. But then, to seek a correlation of the spurt in railway construction with the growth of capitalism in India at that time would be an exercise in futility.

Following the seminal analysis of Lenin of the development of capitalism in Russia at the turn of the century, the employment of hired labour is quite often taken as the acid test of capitalism. But it is hardly ever noticed that later on Lenin himself realized that the use of wage-labour as the main empirical indicator of capitalism led to '*an overestimation of the degree* of capitalist development in Russian agriculture'. In dialectical materialism, practice is the criterion of truth. And it was, indeed, in the light of the practice during the Russian Revolution of 1905 that Lenin came to realize the limitations of his earlier assessment of capitalism in Russia.[59] One could also *a priori* argue that the employment of wage-labour is the essence of capitalism in the sense of being a major necessary condition; but it is not sufficient for capitalism to emerge and prevail. There are cases where even subsistence farmers do employ hired labour to a significant extent; but they do not produce for realization of surplus value; nor do they accumulate. Thus as an indicator of capitalist development the incidence of wage-labour has an upward bias. Now, obviously capitalism is impossible without the class of capitalists, and vice versa. The strength of the capitalist class, therefore, rather than that of the proletariat, is a more reliable measure of the development of capitalism. While clarifying the issue, this however does not resolve the problem; for one has yet to find a method for identifying and assessing the capitalist class.[60]

Moreover, a conceptual distinction must be made between the *moment* or level of a development, and its *trend* or rate and direction of movement. Perhaps it is in principle easier to discern the trend than to size up the moment of capitalist development. But even here one comes across a series of complications which arise from the *uneven* nature of capitalism. We would like to emphasize here that contrary to the common perception, there are, not one, but two laws of uneven development as propounded by Lenin. One of them may be called the law of uneven development *of* capitalism; and the other, the law of uneven development *under* capitalism. According to the first law: 'In no single capitalist country, in no single branch of economy, is there, or can there be (the market being predominant) an even process of development: capitalism *cannot* develop otherwise than in leaps and zigzags, now rapidly advancing, now dropping temporarily below the previous level.'[61] In other words, in its battle against precapitalist or non-capitalist modes of production, capitalism sometimes wins and moves ahead, and sometimes it is beaten back and is forced to withdraw a step or two. In contrast, the second law of uneven development defines the situation where capitalism already holds full sway. It states that 'the uneven and spasmodic development of individual enterprises, individual branches of industry and individual countries is inevitable under the capitalist system'.[62] What is of immediate relevance to us here is that in view of the first law, the law of uneven development of capitalism, only a study of a given country over a fairly long period of time can reveal the true moment and trend of the development of capitalism. To put it differently, the cross-section over a brief period of time would show advancement or retardation of capitalism depending upon in what phase of the cycle of capitalism that period is situated; and as such it cannot provide a basis for generalization.

Definition, essence, manifestations, railway mileage, wage-labour, moment and trend, uneven development, a mere recollection of these words of the above discussion would lead the reader to the conclusion that the dispute over the extent of capitalism in the Third World can hardly be resolved by resorting to a direct empirical estimation as such. There is one more reason why it is so. Feudalism and capitalism do not add up to a constant arithmetic number so that the rise in one can be construed as a measure of the erosion of the other. For imperialism can, and did on occasion, strengthen the feudal grip and at the same time encourage the growth of capitalism. It will be our endeavour here, therefore, to propose an alternative approach to the question of the mode of production in the Third World. To anticipate what follows below, the class relations can be analytically projected in a matrix of contradictions, with due regard to the positive and negative aspects of each contradiction, and one of them having the place of *principal contradiction*. And it is the ensemble of these contradictions which will determine the laws of motion of the system as a whole.

CONTRADICTION, ALLIANCE AND THE LAWS OF MOTION

The controversy on the characterization of the Third World is particularly acute due to the fact that there the process of surplus generation and appropriation is immensely complex. The contradictory nature of imperialism in relation to the internal class structure of a semicolony generates a complicated mosaic of production relations which does not fall neatly into any preconceived notion of classification derived from the European records. In Marx's model of capitalism the scenario is rather simple. There are two classes; one class exploits the other; labour produces surplus value that is expropriated by capital. And the line of demarcation between the exploiter and the exploited is neatly drawn. Now consider the following description of the Third World within the network of world capitalism as given by Frank: The exploitative relation 'in chain-like fashion extends the ... link between the capitalist world and national metropolises to the regional centres (part of whose surplus they appropriate), and from those to local centres, and so on to large landowners or merchants who expropriate surplus from small peasants or tenants, and sometimes these latter to landless labourers exploited by them in turn.'[63] In this scheme of surplus expropriation, the expropriators are arrayed in a hierarchical fashion. At each step along the way, the relatively

9

few capitalists above exercise monopoly power over the many below, expropriating some or all of their economic surplus and, to the extent they are not expropriated in turn by the still fewer above them, appropriating it for their own use. Thus at each point, the international, national, and local capitalist system generates economic development for the few and underdevelopment for the many.[64] The layout of surplus extraction as depicted by Frank is certainly quite different from that in the model of Marx. It is worthwhile to dwell on this matter a little more.

For conceptual clarity one may classify the various possible patterns of surplus expropriation under two heads; and in the absence of a better terminology, call them respectively (*a*) *horizontal* or *unilateral*, and (*b*) *vertical* or *hierarchical*. For convenience of analysis let 'exploitation' be the short-hand expression for the expropriation of surplus. Now, if the line of demarcation between the exploiting and the exploited classes is absolute and distinct so that it is possible to identify that class *A* exploits class *P*, class *B* exploits class *Q*, class *C* exploits class *R*, and so on, and classes *A*, *B* and *C* are not exploited by anybody else in turn, then we call it a case of *horizontal* or *unilateral* exploitation. Marx's model of capitalism is an example of this type, with two classes. Frank also visualizes only two classes in his analysis of world capitalism; but within the world capitalist class he postulates a multiplicity of strata, each exploiting the lower stratum and at the same time being exploited by the one above. If the situation is such that class *A* is exploited by class *B*; in turn class *B* by class *C*; again *C* by *D* and so on; it would be an instance of *vertical* or *hierarchical* exploitation[65] in our nomenclature. It goes on in the shape of a pyramid; exploiters in the lower rung are exploited by the ones higher up; and imperialism sits at the top, while the toiling masses man the bottom. This is how even a small farmer in a remote village of Asia, Africa or Latin America is linked up, through a continuous chain of exploiters, with the headquarters of imperialism in London, Paris, Bonn, Tokyo, Rome or New York.

The two patterns of exploitation as mentioned above are the two extreme cases; what obtains in a Third World country today is a complex combination of the two, which has evolved through the centuries of colonialism. How can such a complicated, intertwined layout of class structure be analytically perceived? Certainly a one-dimensional measurement of the development of capitalism is not enough if at all that is possible. Nor is it valid to claim *a priori* that feudalism has totally disappeared from the scene, especially when the lessons of pre-revolution Russia, China and Vietnam point to the contrary, and the Second Havana Declaration agrees with the latter in this respect. If practice is the criterion of truth let us recall that Lenin realized in the light of the first Russian Revolution of 1905 that he had earlier *over-estimated* the degree of the development of capitalism in Russia, even though he had conceded the simultaneous existence of feudal and semi-feudal elements. It is therefore necessary to devise an analytical framework where feudalism is not ruled out from the beginning by assumption, nor is the totality of capitalism–feudalism co-existence mechanically conceived as a two-person constant-sum game such that the growth of capitalism is *ipso facto* taken as the indicator of the proportional decline of feudalism. Let us remember that historically imperialism has accelerated as well as retarded the growth of capitalism; it has paved the way for the emergence of the bourgeoisie on the one hand, and on the other it has relied on feudalism as its mainstay. It is therefore proposed here that for a better understanding of class relations it may be worthwhile to conceptualize the economy in terms of a matrix where the positive and negative aspects of the contradiction between every pair of classes, during a given period of time, are arranged in a certain order. Much of the current debate on the mode of production in the Third World can then be conducted in a more enlightened perspective. For, then, it would be possible to analyse all the relevant contradictions, and to identify the major ones. The semantic quibblings would be cut down to size, and the fundamental task of discerning the laws of motion would be facilitated.

To proceed, consider Table 16 which takes into account seven classes, for illustration. A typical element of the matrix, x_{ij} $(i, j = 1, 2, \ldots 7)$, represents the inter-relationship between classes i and j. Elements x_{ij} and x_{ji} may appear to stand for the same thing; that is, the matrix may appear to be symmetrical. However, as we know, every contradiction has two aspects, one positive and the other negative, which are usually uneven in strength and rarely in balance; one is the principal aspect of the contradiction, and the other is secondary. Today the positive component may dominate, tomorrow the negative. It may be convenient to place all the positive aspects of class relations above the diagonal of the matrix, and all the negative aspects below the diagonal. In some spheres the interests of a pair of classes are mutually consistent and even reinforcing; these are incorporated in x_{ij}, with j greater than i, which is placed above the diagonal. The areas of conflict, then, are taken note of in element x_{ji}, with i greater than j, which is situated below the diagonal. Both x_{12} and x_{21} in Table 16, for instance, depict the inter-relationship between feudal landlords and capitalist farmers. According to our scheme, x_{12} indicates where and how their class interests are consistent, identical, or mutually complementary; while x_{21} gives the points of their conflicts. Indeed, as in the above-mentioned case of measuring the degree of capitalist development, here also the problems of identifying the feudal landlords to be distinguished from capitalist farmers do remain; but they are now articulated in the overall perspective of the entire matrix rather than in isolation. Should (x_{12}, x_{21}) turn out to be a relatively minor contradiction in the context of the total matrix then both the categories of classes can be combined into one, and called feudal or capitalist depending upon the dominant characteristics of the class as a whole. As for ascertaining and verifying the strength of (x_{12}, x_{21}) or any such class relation, Lenin's method of analysing the behaviour of the classes during the critical twists and turns of history remains the supreme example of the application of dialectics. That is to say, one has to examine the evolution of this matrix through different phases of history in order to grasp the strength of various classes.

Table 16 is an analytical abstraction of the complexity that obtains in the Third World; it will be used in part to analyse concretely the class relations in the Third World, in the following chapter. Meanwhile let it be noted that the *principal contradiction* may not reside in one particular pair of (x_{ij}, x_{ji}) as of Table 16; it may rather be in the form of an *alliance* of certain classes, particularly when imperialism conducts its business through milder means of political, economic and cultural domination rather than by military aggression. There are two types of grounds for class alliance, which may be again called positive and negative, respectively. To understand this, note that the process of exploitation has two essential phases, namely, production and circulation. Marx shows that surplus value originates in the sphere of production, not circulation, under competitive capitalism;

TABLE 16
AN ANALYTICAL FRAMEWORK OF CLASS RELATIONS

Classes	1 Feudal landlords	2 Capitalist farmers	3 Industrial bourgeoisie	4 Petty bourgeoisie	5 Industrial proletariat	6 Peasants	7 Foreign capitalists
1. Feudal landlords	x_{11}	x_{12}	x_{13}	x_{14}	x_{15}	x_{16}	x_{17}
2. Capitalist farmers	x_{21}	x_{22}	x_{23}	x_{24}	x_{25}	x_{26}	x_{27}
3. Industrial bourgeoisie	x_{31}	x_{32}	x_{33}	x_{34}	x_{35}	x_{36}	x_{37}
4. Petty bourgeoisie	x_{41}	x_{42}	x_{43}	x_{44}	x_{45}	x_{46}	x_{47}
5. Industrial proletariat	x_{51}	x_{52}	x_{53}	x_{54}	x_{55}	x_{56}	x_{57}
6. Peasants	x_{61}	x_{62}	x_{63}	x_{64}	x_{65}	x_{66}	x_{67}
7. Foreign capitalists	x_{71}	x_{72}	x_{73}	x_{74}	x_{75}	x_{76}	x_{77}

nevertheless, circulation is an integral part of the total process, for it is in circulation that surplus value is realized. The *positive* ground for alliance among exploiting classes may arise if they help each other in achieving their respective class interests either in the sphere of production or in that of circulation. During the colonial days, imperialism came to the assistance of landlords in keeping the latter's hold over production of agricultural crops; and then in the sphere of circulation, the imperialist bourgeoisie was the major purchaser. After independence, the role of imperialism in the former area has been reduced but that in the other area continues unabated. This is an example of 'positive' ground for alliance between feudalism and imperialism. Concrete instances will be cited in the following chapter. On the other hand, the *negative* reason for class alliance may be found when the exploiting classes face a common enemy; in that case they would bind themselves in an alliance for the sake of survival. To return to the main theme, the *principal contradiction* of a system therefore may assume the shape of a bloc of elements rather than a pair or a single element as in Table 15. The importance of these concepts would become clear as we examine the alliance for underdevelopment in the next chapter.[66]

We have not yet provided any clear-cut answer to the question of characterizing the prevailing mode of production in the Third World; we have only made some preliminary theoretical remarks, pending the concrete analysis in the following chapter. Now we shall consider the other task of political economy, namely, discerning the emerging mode of socio-economic formation and identifying its main features. This is not an exercise in forecasting, nor is it a subscription to the thesis of historical determinism, or spontaneity. Rather it is an endeavour to work out the order of the day keeping in view the specificities of the current historical juncture.

NON–CAPITALIST PATH?

Those Marxists and neo-Marxists who hold the view that capitalism has not yet fully developed in the Third World are unanimous that economic development of the Third World cannot be achieved along the path of full-fledged capitalism. Among them, however, there is a group which makes out a case for some further development of capitalism in a limited and well-demarcated sphere of the economy with certain restraints, especially in those countries of Asia and Africa where capitalism has hardly asserted itself so far. It is argued that a strong and growing public sector should come into existence, and under its dynamic influence a progressive, middle bourgeoisie would take shape. The availability of credits from socialist countries would facilitate independent economic development—independent from the clutches of imperialism—and would strengthen the middle bourgeoisie who would spearhead the transition towards socialism. That would be a path of development, though containing some restrained expansion of capitalism, which would bypass the phase of capitalist transformation of the economy and lead directly towards socialism. This is called the *non-capitalist path* of development.

The non-capitalist path of development visualizes that the *leadership* will lie with the middle, intermediate strata of the bourgeoisie, and it would have the *support* of the working people. The middle bourgeoisie would lead the anti-imperialist, anti-feudal and anti-big-bourgeoisie struggle, and thus prepare the material foundation for the transition to socialism. The political counterpart of the non-capitalist path is known as *national democracy*. In the words of one of its most vigorous protagonists:

It would be correct, as hitherto, to characterize states embarking on the *non-capitalist path* or states of *national democracy* as the political power of a broad social bloc of the working people, including also the growing proletariat, petty-bourgeois strata of town and country and elements of the national bourgeoisie which stand for progressive social development from anti-imperialist positions.... With inadequate political organization of the working people and insufficient influence of the working class the prospects of the non-capitalist development largely depend on the *radical petty-bourgeois intellectuals who stand at the helm.*[67]

Again, 'national-democratic revolution is no longer a bourgeois revolution because it is *led* by middle, intermediate strata, with the *support* of the working people.'[68]

The crux of the matter here lies in the class character of the middle and petty bourgeoisie who are assigned the role of leadership in the regime of national democracy and non-capitalist path of development. Are they in a position to launch an anti-imperialist struggle? Can they afford to take an anti-feudal and anti-big-bourgeoisie stand? Our analysis of the data about the penetration of foreign capital and technology into various layers of the bourgeoisie would cast doubts on the capability of the middle bourgeoisie to assume such a role. It may be recalled that the overwhelming proportion of technology imports are ascribed to small firms which are presumably owned by the middle bourgeoisie. The availability of credits from socialist countries does not mitigate to any considerable extent the preponderance of imperialist capital in the Third World. Of the total external resources received by Third World countries the bulk comes from the advanced capitalist countries, and less than ten per cent from the socialist countries. Besides, the socialist credits do not always strengthen the middle and petty bourgeoisie *vis-à-vis* the big bourgeoisie.[69]

The question of leadership in the anti-imperialist struggle is very important. The lessons from the history of China and Vietnam in the late thirties or early forties are quite relevant in this context.[70] It remains a moot question then whether transition to socialism can at all be effected without the leadership of the working class; and whether with the leadership of the petty and middle bourgeoisie the so-called non-capitalist path would not lead to a blind alley, or worse, to a position of perpetual capitalist underdevelopment.[71]

It is indeed hazardous to generalize for the entire Third World about the future prospects of this or that path of development in precise terms. The protagonists of the non-capitalist path themselves are aware of it. The idea of non-capitalist development has been applied and has become a promising political trend mainly in the African countries and partly in Asia. Here non-capitalist development has a great future and more and more new countries will take this path. As for Asian countries which are approaching the average level of capitalist development and, even more so, Latin America, where many countries have already reached that level, the idea of non-capitalist development is hardly if ever advocated and, as a rule, has quite a different connotation.[72] Of the ten countries which were claimed to have set out on the road of non-capitalist development by 1972, six were in Africa and four in Asia. These are the Arab Republic of Egypt, Algeria, Guinea, Tanzania, the People's Republic of Congo, Syria, Iraq, Somalia, the People's Democratic Republic of Yemen and Burma.[73] As we have said above *a priori*, there is grave doubt whether the petty and middle bourgeoisie can accomplish the task of leading the anti-imperialist, anti-feudal and anti-capitalist struggle. However, it would be interesting to see how the ten countries, which are allegedly on the path of non-capitalist development, steer their course in the days ahead.

While the idea of a non-capitalist path has been traced back to some isolated remarks of Marx and Lenin, a more precise formulation of it was first given in 1960. About that time, in 1964, Kalecki propounded a thesis that appears to be very close to that of national democracy and the non-capitalist path, but which presumably has a wider significance. Kalecki's category of *intermediate regime* as it is called is a conceptualization of the prevailing situation in many a country of the Third World.[74] The petty bourgeoisie—consisting of two classes, namely, the lower middle class and the rich peasantry—are numerically very large. On the morrow of political independence the reins of government have fallen into their hands. In the past, whenever social upheavals did enable the representatives of these two classes to rise to power, they invariably served the interests of the big bourgeoisie who are often allied with the remnants of the feudal system, despite the fact that there is a basic conflict between the interests of the lower-middle class and big business. But now, according to Kalecki, there is a fundamental difference in the scene which confers a certain degree of autonomy to the class of the petty bourgeoisie. Three peculiarities of the present epoch tend to enable the ruling class of the petty bourgeoisie to maintain a distance from big business and feudal remnants as well as from imperialism. These are: (*i*) the numerical strength of the lower-middle class, (*ii*) the extensive intervention of the state in the economic sphere, and (*iii*) the possibility of economic assistance from the socialist countries. However, the antagonists of this regime are: from *above*, the big bourgeoisie, foreign capital and feudal landowners; from *below*, the small landholders and landless peasants as well as the poor urban population. Kalecki argues that such a regime not only can, but must, follow a policy of autonomy, for its own survival. As he puts it, 'to keep in power they [the ruling lower-middle class and rich peasantry] must:

(*a*) achieve not only political but also economic emancipation, i.e. gain a measure of independence from foreign capital;

(*b*) carry out a land reform;

(c) assure continuous economic growth; this last point is closely connected with the other two.'[75]

The regime performs the trick of tight-rope walking between the two contending blocs, i.e. capitalist and socialist; and receives financial support from both.

Kalecki thus demonstrates the feasibility and viability of the intermediate regime. Others have joined him to prove, moreover, its efficiency. They have fitted the Cobb–Douglas production function to show that constant returns to scale is the rule which governs agriculture and industry. So, scale does not matter; a small firm can be as productive as a big one. Furthermore, such is the nature of the modern technology that its benefits are divisible, and hence can be brought to the door of even a small or medium enterprise as well. The petty capitalist entrepreneur, it is observed, is quite willing to adopt relatively modern techniques; the same is true for the capitalist farmer involved in the green revolution, though not to the same extent. Under the circumstances the government support of petty capitalist enterprise will raise the national level of labour productivity, boost the domestic demand for producer goods and widen the opportunities for industrial development. Undoubtedly, this will be better for national economic development.[76]

A decade has passed since 1964 when Kalecki first introduced his thesis on the intermediate regime. How has the regime fared in the Third World in the meantime? Only a few brief observations can be made in the light of the past ten years' experience. The momentum of the agricultural sector soon gets exhausted as the scope for further expansion of cropping area is not boundless. Import-substituting industrialization of mainly consumer durables and a few capital goods soon reaches its limit. The 'ruling class' of the petty bourgeoisie comes to realize that its hold over the economic base is not commensurate with its control over the political superstructure. State capitalism is fostered as a means of closing this hiatus. But the public sector cannot grow fast enough to absorb the swelling ranks of educated unemployed, the children of the families of the 'ruling class'. The soaring ambitions and the demands of the petty bourgeoisie can no longer be accommodated within the frail economic structure. As the crisis deepens the big bourgeoisie springs into action to change the balance of power. In the name of humanitarianism, the big bourgeoisie loudly pro-

claims its sympathy for the downtrodden, wretched of the earth.
Bypassing the middle segment, a direct channel of communication is established between the two polar extremes of the class
spectrum, the two antagonists of the intermediate regime. While
this dénouement does not necessarily mark the beginning of the
end of the intermediate regime, certainly it takes the regime to
a new, uncertain phase, the dynamics of which yet remains to be
unfolded.[77]

In contrast with the thesis of national democracy and the non-
capitalist path which is in the nature of an action programme,
Kalecki's idea of the intermediate regime is more of a description
of the present-day reality conceptualized in a theoretical plane;
and yet it may give the impression of being a variant of national
democracy, which it is not. Be that as it may, the transition of a
Third World country to socialism is an area of investigation in
political economy which has attracted very little analysis so far.
Detailed generalization for all the three continents is neither
feasible nor warranted. The matrix of class relations of every
country has its own special features; and only an analysis of this
matrix can throw light on the contours of the emerging socio-
economic formation. However, certain broad generalizations are
possible for the Third World as a whole, which are to be duly
moderated and complemented with further specifications for
grasping the political economy of a given country. Having recognized this, the next chapter then makes an attempt to grapple
with the political economy of the Third World.

6

ALLIANCE FOR
UNDERDEVELOPMENT

IF unequal exchange between the centre and the periphery is a
phenomenon centuries old, how could it go on for so long on
such a scale? If the surplus is being extracted through various
means, from the vast outer periphery to the metropolitan centre
of world capitalism, what sort of internal alignment within the
periphery makes it feasible? If the development of one part of the
world has been, and continues to be, at the expense of the underdevelopment of another, much larger part, why and how did the
latter concede to this arrangement? The superior military power
of imperialism is not the explanation for something that has been
going on for four centuries. The clue lies elsewhere; on which
certain broad generalizations can be made for the Third World
as a whole. Here we shall not delve much into the past history,
since we are primarily concerned with the post-war period of
neo-colonialism.

It is worthwhile to note that the underdevelopment of a country does not always mean its stagnation or total retardation.
Underdevelopment is an on-going process of continuity with
change, with the distinguishing property that the change, its
magnitude and direction, is inconsistent with, and even detri-
mental to, the realization of the potentialities of the resources,
human as well as natural. In this sense the Third World is underdeveloped, since its level of actual economic accomplishment is
far below what is possible with its resources. By the same token
the advanced capitalist countries are developed as their productive
forces have made rapid strides relative to the basic endowments.
The Third World is kept in the limbo of underdevelopment in
two ways. First, a large volume of surplus is being drained away,
as a result of which the poor country cannot accumulate enough

to make effective use of whatever potentialities it has in terms of human and natural productive factors. Second, and related to the point above, the Third World economy is being continuously distorted, as it is reduced to a mere apparatus for supplying raw materials and for absorbing the obsolete products and technology of the advanced capitalist countries. Of necessity, the Third World therefore cannot remain static or even economically backward-sliding. Not static, because if the metropolitan centre has to live off the pillage of the Third World there must be something made available in the Third World which can be seized; that is to say, something has to be reproduced there continually so that it can be plundered. Not backward-sliding economically, because then the products and technology of the centre would soon fail to find a place there. So with the development of world capitalism the Third World also moves on, but the direction of the movement is such that it cannot escape the penumbra of neo-colonialism and the consequent underdevelopment. In course of this distorted motion the economy produces a surplus that is shared among the ruling classes. For the people of the Third World the net result is underdevelopment, but in so far as the ruling classes are concerned it is by no means so; rather it is a grand arrangement for realizing and promoting their respective interests. We shall now look into the working of this arrangement.

When a Third World country was a direct colony it is understandable how feudalism came to be an ally, or even the mainstay, of imperialism. The foreign exploiter relied upon, and protected, the then prevailing order so long as it could be used to extract surplus. And the feudal landlords acquiesced in the arrangement so long as their survival and prosperity were assured, albeit at a high price. But in the post-colonial era the grounds for alliance between feudalism and imperialism are not all that clear. The triangular alliance among feudalism, the domestic bourgeoisie, and the foreign imperialist bourgeoisie is to be understood in its dialectical unity. There are areas where their class interests converge, and also areas where they clash. However, the contradictions among these ruling classes may be major or minor ones, but they are not the principal contradictions of the Third World.[1] Yet it is no less important to be aware of the contradictions of the ruling classes. In what follows we shall begin with the interrelationship between feudalism and the bourgeoisie; then we shall pass on to that between the bourgeoisie and imperialism; and finally to feudalism and imperialism. And thus we shall see how the triangle of alliance is completed, perpetuating unequal exchange, among many other evils. Here, by the bourgeoisie we only mean the industrial bourgeoisie of the big and middle strata. The agricultural bourgeoisie is left out of specific consideration partly because the observations with regard to the industrial bourgeoisie by and large hold in its case as well, and partly because in our view it has yet to emerge as a distinct class over and above the feudal or semi-feudal elements in the agrarian economy. This is by no means to deny the existence of capitalism in Third World agriculture, nor is it intended to belittle its importance today or in the near future. However, for the problem at hand, namely unequal exchange between centre and periphery, we may be permitted to indulge in this abstraction. In our stylized version of the Third World, feudalism or semi-feudalism (which is defined as the superimposition of a capitalist mode of exploitation on the feudal mode) prevails in the agrarian sector.

FEUDALISM/BOURGEOISIE

In terms of Table 16, we are now going to examine elements x_{13} and x_{31}. By our simplifying assumption, we are mainly concerned with the grounds for alliance among feudalism, industrial capitalism, and imperialism. Agriculture occupies a key place in the Third World economy. It produces the bulk of the gross national product, and accounts for the lion's share of export earnings; besides, whatever industry is there is largely based on agriculture for its supply of inputs. The bourgeoisie controls industry as well as foreign trade. The bourgeoisie therefore is the major, if not the sole, purchaser of agricultural products, which are partly used up in domestic industry and partly exported as such. The circuit of exchange of the products expropriated by feudal landlords from primary producers is completed through the mediation of the bourgeoisie.

Feudal landlords exploit the peasants and agricultural labourers; the bourgeoisie, the industrial proletariat. Thanks to the feudal oppression in agriculture, industry is assured of a steady supply of cheap labour at a constant real wage rate. The bourgeoisie is certainly grateful to the feudal landlords for this indirect service.

There are more direct reasons also. Who are the major consumers of the industrial goods of the bourgeoisie? In a country like India the rural market for industrial consumer goods is estimated to be two and a half times the size of the urban market. In 1952–53, for instance, rural India absorbed industrial consumer goods worth Rs 31 billion at current prices as against the urban consumption of Rs 12 billion; in 1968–69 these figures were respectively Rs 58 billion and Rs 25 billion.[2] Under such circumstances, no wonder the bourgeoisie would keep an eager, affectionate eye on the rural scene.

Now, who are the major customers of industrial goods in the rural market? If the Indian data can be taken as a basis for generalization, it can be said that what only the top ten per cent of the rural consumers devour comes very close to the total consumption of industrial goods by all the urban population put together. Should this top ten per cent be identified with the feudal remnants and their associates in villages it is this group which is the strongest pillar that supports the market for industrial production, its share in the rural market being as much as one-third or so (Table 17). The circuit of exchange of industrial products of the bourgeoisie is thus mediated through the significant assistance of the feudal and semi-feudal classes which rule over the agrarian economy.

Finally, one may observe that the class interests of the bourgeoisie are served in another way by the feudal-semifeudal remnants. If the supply curve of foodgrains is downward sloping with reference to the relative price *vis-à-vis* industrial goods, either because the foodgrain suppliers aim at a more or less fixed amount of industrial goods at any given period, or because of any other reason, then it follows that the share of wages in industrial output would decline with the rise in industrial employment. Elsewhere we have presented this theory of income distribution as an explanation for the observed downward trend in the share of wages in the output of India's industrial sector. It is demonstrated that:

With downward sloping marketed surplus curve of foodgrains, the share of wages in industrial output tends to fall as employment rises, if the above-mentioned curve remains stable or shifts up rather moderately, provided that the average product of labour does not decline. On the other hand, in case the marketed surplus curve shifts up substantially so that the equilibrium terms of trade turn in favour of agriculture the share of wages in industrial output would fall, remain the same, or go up, as the average productivity of labour rises more than, equal to or less than, the proportion of improvement of the terms of trade in favour of agriculture.[a]

The essential logic of the argument is as follows. Suppose that the wage rate is fixed in terms of foodgrains. Now, the employment of one more person in industry would require a certain amount of marketed surplus of foodgrains. The supply curve being downward sloping in terms of the relative price *vis-à-vis* industrial goods, in order to bring forth the additional supply of foodgrains for the newly employed worker the terms of trade have to be depressed; that is to say, the relative price of industrial goods has to rise, or that of agricultural goods to fall. Should the average industrial output per worker remain the same, the bourgeoisie now can pay the entire wage bill with much less of industrial goods, since the relative price has gone in their favour, and thus it can make more profit both absolutely and relatively. Here is another instance of the interests of feudalism and industrial capitalism nicely converging. So much about the positive aspect of this contradiction.

The negative aspect of the contradiction between feudalism and industrial capitalism emerges from the very fact that the feudal and semi-feudal classes and their associates are the major component of the home market of industry. Indeed, capitalist production can expand on the strength of the rising demand for capital goods rather than that for consumer goods. However, so far as a Third World country is concerned, most of its capital goods are either imported from the metropolitan centre or produced in the public sector under the aegis of the government. The bourgeoisie is involved mainly in the production of industrial consumer goods; and it is precisely here that the existence of the feudal-semifeudal agrarian structure comes in as an obstacle to expansion. To the extent feudalism-semifeudalism is a fetter on agriculture, the home market for industry suffers in consequence. Table 17 gives data about the share of consumption of industrial goods of various fractile groups in India. The primary source of these data is the National Sample Survey (NSS), which is well-known for its inherently increasing bias towards underestimating the expenditure on consumer durables and other items consumed by the affluent section. It is evident that the distribution of con-

TABLE 17

SHARE OF CONSUMPTION OF INDUSTRIAL GOODS IN INDIA

(Per cent)

Population fractile	1952–53	1953–54	1954–55	1955–56	1956–57	1957–58	1958–59	1959–60	1960–61	1961–62	1963–64	1964–65	1965–66	1967–68	1968–69
Rural															
0–50	23.00	20.07	18.91	19.20	20.32	20.34	20.46	22.96	19.88	19.88	22.29	21.16	20.36	22.78	21.92
50–70	17.20	16.12	15.49	16.66	15.55	15.94	16.00	16.47	15.95	16.96	17.62	16.98	15.33	16.56	16.72
70–90	25.62	28.21	27.54	28.50	26.57	27.06	27.02	26.52	26.47	30.03	28.24	28.45	25.55	27.02	23.72
90–100	34.18	35.60	38.06	35.64	37.56	36.66	36.52	34.05	37.70	33.13	31.85	33.41	38.76	33.64	37.64
Total	100.00	100.00	100.00	100.00	100.00	100.00	100.00	100.00	100.00	100.00	100.00	100.00	100.00	100.00	100.00
Urban															
0–50	19.20	18.57	17.38	18.91	16.80	18.41	20.25	19.63	16.78	18.91	18.18	18.28	16.80	17.90	20.83
50–70	16.06	15.81	15.02	16.51	14.48	15.89	16.11	15.85	13.41	15.75	15.18	14.24	15.62	14.82	15.00
70–90	27.47	28.49	27.17	28.12	25.07	25.55	26.18	27.56	23.76	26.99	27.88	25.02	30.14	28.78	31.02
90–100	37.27	37.13	40.43	36.46	43.65	40.15	37.46	36.66	46.01	38.35	38.76	42.46	37.44	38.50	32.16
Total	100.00	100.00	100.00	100.00	100.00	100.00	100.00	100.00	100.00	100.00	100.00	100.00	100.00	100.00	100.00

Source: Sau (1975c and 1975g).

sumption is becoming more and more skewed over time. Further-more, Tables 18 and 19 indicate that the home market for indus-trial consumer goods is narrowing in the sense that *an average consumer spends less and less of his budget on industrial goods.* In 1952–53, for example, a rural consumer set aside 41.19 per cent of his total expenditure for industrial products; by 1967–68 the ratio declined to as little as 31.34 per cent (Table 18). The corres-ponding figures for an urban consumer are 58.53 per cent and 43.90 per cent (Table 19). The decline is sharpest for the poorer strata of the consumers. Briefly, the home market for industry instead of expanding actually declines, presumably in view of the feudal-semifeudal exploitation in the agrarian sector which is by far the bigger market. A Third World country does not have a colony to dispose of its industrial output; if on top of that the domestic market fails to respond, capitalist production cannot but get stifled. And herein lies the conflict between the interests of agrarian feudalism and industrial capitalism.

BOURGEOISIE/IMPERIALISM

The bourgeoisie as a class is united in defence of its interests in general; but at the same time it is a class that is riddled with inter-nal strife. For centralization and concentration of capital is a basic tendency that prevails in the capitalist mode of production. Big capital swallows up smaller capital; medium capital either grows up to join the top echelon, or simply dissolves into small units to be ultimately engulfed by big capital. This is known as the process of differentiation of the bourgeoisie. Imperialism takes full advant-age of the squabbles among the bourgeoisie of the Third World, as the warring factions run to it for shelter, protection and nourishment.[4]

Imperialism also is in urgent need of an alliance with the Third World bourgeoisie. The tendency of the rate of profit to fall in mature capitalist countries is sought to be neutralized through rapid technological progress. The advancement of technology renders huge stocks of machinery and equipment obsolete; and unless these out of date stockpiles can be profitably jettisoned somewhere this escape route of advanced capitalism from its own crisis would be sealed. We have already given in Chapter 4 an indication of the extent of obsolete plant and equipment in the

TABLE 18

PERCENTAGE OF PER CAPITA CONSUMER EXPENDITURE SPENT ON INDUSTRIAL GOODS

Rural India

(Per cent)

Population fractile	1952–53	1953–54	1954–55	1955–56	1956–57	1957–58	1958–59	1959–60	1960–61	1961–62	1963–64	1964–65	1965–66	1967–68	1968–69
0–5	33.62	25.66	28.91	29.36	25.21	25.13	25.55	24.48	25.30	24.10	24.50	23.26	22.92	24.00	24.18
5–10	33.62	25.66	28.91	29.36	25.21	25.13	25.55	26.87	25.66	24.43	24.47	22.10	22.87	22.83	23.78
10–20	33.00	31.05	28.91	29.36	26.41	25.80	26.94	29.26	26.03	24.76	25.19	24.25	24.07	23.85	24.46
20–30	34.29	31.05	29.89	31.34	26.41	26.47	26.82	29.20	27.16	27.00	26.51	24.68	25.75	24.53	25.04
30–40	36.07	27.58	30.86	31.34	27.22	29.39	28.84	29.22	29.64	27.56	28.84	26.39	26.03	25.67	26.22
40–50	33.66	32.13	32.64	31.63	28.06	29.93	29.49	29.90	30.67	31.40	30.60	26.79	28.08	26.37	27.80
50–60	35.99	34.51	34.60	35.00	30.33	31.18	31.70	30.59	33.93	31.20	31.72	28.40	29.20	27.32	29.02
60–70	38.18	36.03	36.61	36.42	31.77	33.44	33.78	34.77	35.50	36.59	33.89	31.81	31.00	28.54	30.95
70–80	39.50	38.55	42.46	40.28	33.72	35.45	35.59	36.69	39.28	40.98	36.42	34.63	33.33	30.81	32.87
80–90	37.92	45.89	42.32	43.02	40.79	41.49	41.26	38.36	42.08	43.98	40.06	38.26	38.19	33.98	34.67
90–95	47.74	50.20	48.45	49.93	41.92	44.34	43.92	43.91	48.66	48.56	46.04	44.65	42.25	37.34	41.73
95–100	57.07	57.55	60.38	56.70	59.82	57.63	55.41	57.99	64.04	60.03	58.55	57.79	60.35	47.90	57.05
0–100	41.19	40.31	40.87	40.89	37.17	38.47	38.65	39.58	40.14	39.31	36.60	35.70	34.95	31.34	35.22

Source: Sau (1975c and 1975g).

TABLE 19

PERCENTAGE OF PER CAPITA CONSUMER EXPENDITURE SPENT ON INDUSTRIAL GOODS

Urban India

(Per cent)

Population fractile	1952-53	1953-54	1954-55	1955-56	1956-57	1957-58	1958-59	1959-60	1960-61	1961-62	1963-64	1964-65	1965-66	1967-68	1968-69
0-5	34.36	27.49	31.44	30.06	28.41	25.13	29.55	30.51	26.31	29.45	26.59	30.03	30.14	29.08	32.95
5-10	35.33	30.49	31.44	31.96	28.90	26.65	29.80	30.06	30.29	29.57	29.60	30.16	31.82	30.67	31.39
10-20	39.65	33.48	32.21	34.06	30.47	27.93	32.16	31.62	34.14	32.93	30.07	31.30	33.91	31.51	31.86
20-30	42.42	33.54	38.14	36.16	32.52	33.25	36.96	34.60	35.88	34.97	33.97	33.24	35.57	32.55	34.52
30-40	44.63	35.39	38.22	37.91	33.47	36.29	37.56	36.55	37.86	36.50	34.86	34.18	38.14	33.53	35.04
40-50	46.51	36.68	39.87	40.02	38.04	38.95	38.87	38.53	38.79	39.39	37.52	36.90	42.15	36.60	37.02
50-60	47.01	39.38	40.00	42.92	39.00	40.82	40.98	40.95	41.49	41.70	41.15	38.21	44.77	38.24	39.00
60-70	49.63	42.12	46.27	46.47	41.80	41.90	44.09	41.86	43.21	44.70	43.27	39.51	49.28	37.14	39.78
70-80	51.28	42.07	49.12	48.95	42.99	41.73	45.78	45.43	46.84	47.85	45.10	41.98	52.65	45.20	43.19
80-90	58.54	50.14	51.20	50.39	48.53	49.19	48.39	49.54	51.05	51.76	52.63	48.81	62.18	46.96	51.86
90-95	60.32	56.20	61.88	59.49	60.99	58.93	60.00	56.69	56.58	57.34	61.58	55.00	66.91	54.65	57.80
95-100	70.00	60.37	70.00	65.00	69.73	67.06	65.00	65.00	70.00	69.18	66.78	70.00	73.25	63.67	57.80
0-100	53.53	47.10	51.56	50.56	50.00	49.35	48.68	47.50	48.97	49.73	48.36	47.25	50.72	43.90	45.15

Source: Sau (1975c and 1975g).

American and British industries. Here is another estimate, as given in a report of the United Nations: 64 per cent of the machine tools in the United States in 1963 were ten years old or older. Comparable figures for that same year were: 59 per cent for the United Kingdom, 58 per cent for France, 57 per cent for Italy, 55 per cent for the Federal Republic of Germany, and about 50 per cent for the USSR.[5] Furthermore, the report goes on to add that, according to expert opinions, industrial equipment on the average ten years old should be replaced by new (or reconditioned) equipment in order not to slow down increases in productivity and not to increase production costs.[6] On the basis of such a criterion, in 1965 there were about 1,300,000 metal-working machines already marked for replacement in the United States alone. Thus there is a huge surplus of second-hand equipment; and with it, the production facilities for producing such equipment also are simultaneously found to be outmoded. In a word, the advanced capitalist countries are always burdened with a stock of new, as well as old, obsolete plant and equipment, which has to be disposed of profitably; otherwise technological progress would be choked off. To be sure, most of the commercial transactions in second-hand equipment are within the industrialized countries themselves. Export sales represent only a small fraction of the total sales. For instance, the United States Machinery Dealers National Association reports that export sales for its members in 1964 represented only $22.4 million or 5.5 per cent of the total sales figures.[7] This need not be surprising; after all, the Third World accounts for about 7 per cent of the total industrial production of the world as a whole.

Earlier, in Chapter 4, we have argued that there are two major flows of technology and equipment within the world capitalist system: one is directly from the United States to various other countries including those in the Third World; the other originates in the United States and then, filtering through the countries at different levels of technological maturity, reaches in the end the least developed ones. These two patterns also can be traced in the case of second-hand machinery. The United States is the largest source of used machinery, followed far behind by Great Britain with one-fifth the size of the US second-hand market. It is observed that much of the second-hand equipment in Great Britain is exported to the countries of the Commonwealth.[8] The UN report cites a particularly interesting example which lends further support to our hypothesis of the *filtering* flow of technology and equipment. It narrates how textile machinery built in the United States in the 1890s was first used in Europe, then in one country of Central America, and finally was installed in another Central American country during World War II for the production of coarse cloth.[9] No doubt, quantitatively much of the international movements of commodities, capital and technology are within the advanced capitalist countries themselves. The flows towards the Third World may be quantitatively small; but in the world capitalist system they play a very crucial role. These latter flows are organically related to those within the advanced capitalist countries. In case the shipment of second-hand equipment from England to Kenya, for example, is interrupted the impact would immediately be felt by the US multinational corporation which was about to despatch a batch of modern machines to England. As the rate of technological progress accelerates, it is plausible that the advanced capitalist countries will trade more and more among themselves in commodities, capital and technology; and in view of the underdevelopment in the periphery relative to the metropolitan centre the flow towards the periphery may diminish in the arithmetic sense; but like the umbilical cord, slender though it may look, it would continue to play a vital role in the world capitalist system. Snap this cord, and world capitalism would run into a serious crisis.

Why does the Third World bourgeoisie acquiesce in the flow of second, third, or *n*-th degree obsolete technology and equipment? Their industrial production is aimed at meeting the demands of the richest section of the population, for which the foreign technology that is meanwhile rendered obsolete in its own home country is quite suitable. After all, the fashions of New York, London and Paris take a little time to reach Bombay, Sao Paulo, and Cairo.

However, the relationship between the Third World bourgeoisie and imperialism is not all that sweet; there are indeed areas of conflict. Many of the branches or subsidiaries of foreign companies operating in the Third World are not even 2 or 3 per cent the size of the parent corporations, although they might be giants by local standards.[10] This enhances the bargaining power of foreign capital on the soil of the Third World. Besides, the ambitions of the local bourgeoisie are occasionally thwarted by the designs of world monopoly capital. The recourse to State capitalism in many parts of the Third World in fact is intended to protect and foster the interests of the domestic bourgeoisie against the powerful onslaught of foreign capital. If this is the negative aspect of the bourgeoisie/imperialism contradiction, it is all too often overshadowed by the positive aspect, i.e. the homogeneity of their class interests.

FEUDALISM/IMPERIALISM

This is the least-explored aspect of the triangular alliance which holds the Third World in its grip. Again, in the days of direct colonialism the *raison d'être* of the feudalism/imperialism collaboration is somewhat clear. But when a country is politically independent, what does feudalism have to offer to imperialism, and vice versa? In short, the relation of feudalism with imperialism is much the same as it is with the domestic bourgeoisie.

In recent years foreign capital in the Third World is getting more inclined towards manufacturing and chemical industries rather than the traditional extractive industries which were destined mainly for exports. The home market in the Third World is thus becoming more important for absorbing the products and technology of the advanced capitalist countries. Let us recall here that it is the feudal and semi-feudal landlords and their agents who in the ultimate analysis constitute the bulk of the market for industrial goods. On this account, the bourgeoisie, both domestic and foreign, seek and cultivate the alliance with these exploiters of the agrarian sector. What does imperialism have to offer, in return, to feudal and semi-feudal landlords? In league with the local bourgeoisie the imperialist bourgeoisie consummates the exchange of the agricultural products for industrial use within the Third World or for export abroad. Besides, in countries where merchant capital keeps the peasants in bondage, usually foreign banking capital is at the top of the credit pyramid; and the local landlords are the main intermediary between the export house and the impoverished peasants. For a price, the imperialist capital thus gives the feudal and semi-feudal landlords the wherewithal for exploiting the peasants through usury.

The links between feudalism and imperialism thus appear to be somewhat tenuous. But in a country of fragile bourgeoisie the feudal class may turn out to be the main defender of the prevailing order; and on that ground so much more solid would be the alliance between feudalism and imperialism. The three sides of the triangle of the feudalism/capitalism/imperialism alliance are not equal in strength; but as a whole it is a formidable confluence, with imperialism usually the dominant partner. The whole is far stronger than the sum total of individual parts, especially when the Third World society is 'pregnant with two revolutions', because of which none of the partners dares upset the arrangement.

ALLIANCE, UNDERDEVELOPMENT AND THE UNEQUAL EXCHANGE

Neither the alleged lack of entrepreneurship on the part of the Third World bourgeoisie, nor the 'isolation paradox' of individual savers and investors, nor the dearth of so-called 'non-traditional' inputs, let alone the so-called savings gap, can be taken singly or jointly as the root cause of the underdevelopment of the Third World. To grasp its fundamental drawback one has to understand how the economic system works with all its complexity and conflicts. It is not a neoclassical competitive model; nor is it a classical prototype heading towards a Ricardian stationary state. Even Keynes would find a Third World economy a foreign territory. His multiplier would founder on the rock of unresponsive output supply. In the vast agrarian sector, his schedule of marginal efficiency of capital would go unrecognized by the semifeudal landowner as well as the tenant farmer, as a guide for investment decision. The Keynesian investor did not have multiple modalities of profiteering, in addition to that of production; nor was he subject to exploitation by the landlord. In short, the classical, neoclassical, and Keynesian models visualize a pure, competitive capitalist system; and as such they are all incapable of revealing the dynamics of an economy that is semifeudal-semicolonial. The Third World economy, even in its utmost abstraction, is not akin to a competitive capitalist model; and as we have argued above, it is not tending to be so over time. The 'macroeconomics' of the Third World yet remains to be written.

The contradictions among the ruling classes which have been described so far in this chapter can be the basic elements of a macroeconomics of the Third World. We may now put them together in the sketch of a theory. The semi-feudal landowners cultivate land with hired labour; lease out land to tenant farmers; engage in trading in agricultural and industrial products; and practise usury. A multitude of small farmers and agricultural labourers are tied to them in a thousand ways. Middle farmers also are kept in bondage by merchant capital, so much so that the differentiation of the peasantry is retarded. The market for agricultural goods expands more in response to the purchasing power of the tertiary sector generated by government expenditure than by the demand originating from industrial growth. The foreign technology adopted by the industrial sector is not labour intensive in any case; and partly due to this factor, industrial employment rises very slowly. Whatever little impulse to agrarian capitalism thus comes from outside is to a large extent swamped by the archaic relations prevailing within the agricultural sector. The new agricultural technology with HYV seeds and other associated resources indeed created a stir in the countryside; but even this new wave of agrarian capitalism is likely to subside sooner or later. The productivity of land is low as well as fluctuating; under such circumstances the crop, rather than the land, attracts investment. Merchant capital thrives. Rich farmers, armed as they are with several modes of profiteering, do not work towards the further development of productive forces in agriculture; and so the tendency of stagnation persists. On the other hand, industry produces for a tiny fraction of the population and for export abroad. The investment decision of the private industrial capitalist is moulded by the nature of obsolescence in the metropolitan centre of world capitalism. Quantitatively, foreign technology and capital may not be much on the whole; but all too often they occupy strong positions in the strategic areas of the economy such as power generation, transport, manufacturing and chemical industries, and export. For reasons mentioned at the outset, the scale of industrial production rises, its output-mix changes with time, and a semblance of economic development takes place. But its locus is largely determined by the requirements of the metropolis of world capitalism; indeed, we have seen that the domestic bourgeoisie and the foreign imperialist both gain in this process. The ambitions of the bourgeoisie occasionally press against this two-fold barrier of semi-feudalism on the one hand and imperialism on the other. Tensions are created; certain contradictions get resolved; and others are intensified. And so the economy moves on. The three sides of the triangle of alliance that rules over the Third World are hardly in balance; and as a result the Third World economy continually goes through a process of uneven development, or more accurately, uneven underdevelopment.[11]

Among the *trimurthi*, the triumvirate, of ruling classes, imperialism is by far the strongest partner even though the degree of its influence and the mode of its operation vary from time to time and place to place. Imperialism is deeply entrenched in many a Third World country through diverse means. From the smallest peasant to the biggest of the capitalists of a Third World country everyone may be enthralled at its altar, sometimes knowingly, more often in ignorance. Unequal exchange between the Third World and the advanced capitalist centre therefore is built into the system right from the very beginning when the seeds germinate in the paddy field or the foundation stone of a factory is laid in the Third World. Unequal exchange and underdevelopment are the joint manifestations of a single unified process of imperialist exploitation in the Third World: that which makes imperialism possible also makes unequal exchange and underdevelopment inevitable.

Now, as soon as we compare the underlying class alignment the contrast between our formulation of the theory of unequal exchange and that of Emmanuel and his followers comes out in bold relief. Emmanuel's theory implies that the working class and the bourgeoisie of the Third World are joint victims of an unequal exchange which is thrust upon them by imperialism. When the Third World economy is integrated into world capitalism the profit rate there declines so as to be equalized with the overall rate that would prevail in the entire system. This is illustrated in Table 5 above (case 5.2), where the profit rate in the Third World, producing commodity 2, is 100 per cent before trade, but only 66.66 per cent in the wake of trade. Furthermore, it is argued that the wage rate in the Third World is inversely related with that in advanced capitalist countries, as epitomized in the four theorems of Braun drawn from the two-country Sraffa-type model, as mentioned in Chapter 3 above. The conclusion is therefore unavoidable that, as Emmanuel continues, the proletariat and the bourgeoisie of the Third World would make common cause between themselves, and put up a joint front against imperialism

—not just imperialism as such, but against both the working class and the bourgeoisie of the advanced capitalist countries, to be precise; against the metropolitan working class, because this class also gets a share of the plunder of the Third World through unequal exchange, and therefore it supports the exploitation. So here is also the end of proletarian internationalism, as the interests of the working class of the Third World stand in antagonism against those of the metropolis of world capitalism. What is more, the Emmanuel theory casts the Third World bourgeoisie into a heroic role, as the defender of the national economy against the machinations of imperialism. Suffice it to say that if the Third World bourgeoisie were really so heroic and nationalistic as Emmanuel depicts them, world capitalism would have long ceased to be what it is today.

In the historic *Manifesto* of 1848 Marx and Engels observed: 'The bourgeoisie finds itself involved in a constant battle. At first with aristocracy; later on, with those portions of the bourgeoisie itself, whose interests have become antagonistic to the progress of industry; [and] at all times, with the bourgeoisie of foreign countries.'[12] In our perception the Third World bourgeoisie and imperialism are dialectically related; there are areas of conflict but the predominant aspect of their inter-relationship now is one of complementarity and reciprocity. It is our contention that an alliance of feudalism, local capitalism and imperialism holds sway over the Third World; and herein lies the root of unequal exchange. It is this triangular arrangement which permits the multinational corporations to fleece the Third World through transfer pricing and all that; and indeed it is this class nexus which prevents fuller development of productive forces so that even under competitive conditions the Third World gives out more in exports than it gets back in return as imports. Our assessment of the Third World bourgeoisie, as indicated by the relevant data presented above, is that, while retaining some room for manoeuvre, they have by and large got themselves entangled with the imperialist bourgeoisie; this is true not only of the top section but of the lower sections as well. And this is why we have reservations about the so-called non-capitalist path and national democracy so long as its leadership is with the 'middle stratum', and not the working class. The middle bourgeoisie and the 'radical petty-bourgeois intellectuals who stand at the helm' of the Third World have already revealed their true colours, or will do so soon. In any case, it is idle to think of the non-capitalist path of development under the leadership of the middle stratum of the bourgeoisie and radical petty bourgeoisie as an escape route for the Third World from underdevelopment and unequal exchange.

And yet we maintain that it is a gross over-simplification to characterize the Third World bourgeoisie as *lumpenbourgeoisie*, or the class which is 'no more than the passive tool of foreign industry and commerce', and 'the class which is deeply interested in keeping us in a state of wretched backwardness from which foreign commerce derives all the advantages'.[13] We emphasize that it is undialectical to overlook the negative aspect of the contradiction between the Third World bourgeoisie and imperialism. True, the local bourgeoisie mediates the interests of imperialism in the Third World, but it does so because thereby it accomplishes its own ambitions in the process. Similarly the feudal-semifeudal landlords also are a party in the coalition. The three classes are the *joint* exploiters of the people of the Third World; and this is what sustains neo-colonialism today. If the local bourgeoisie depends upon imperialism, so does imperialism upon the local bourgeoisie; they are mutually dependent in extracting surplus. And of course, there are also certain spheres where the interests of the members of the ruling alliance tend to diverge. Under such circumstances the State plays an important role.

In a society where no single class is in command, but an alliance of classes wields power, the State is vested with a measure of autonomy; and it is called upon to reconcile the conflicts of the ruling classes. State intervention in the economy is largely a reflection of this function that has devolved upon it in the Third World. A growing public sector is all too often a composite device to protect the local bourgeoisie here, to promote the interests of imperialism there, and to subserve the alliance on the whole everywhere. State capitalism that has been the hallmark in many a country of the Third World hardly strengthens the middle bourgeoisie, and still less does it pave the way for transition to socialism. But what it unmistakably does is to accommodate the conflicting demands of the feudal-semifeudal landlords, the local bourgeoisie and imperialism. It performs a balancing act all the time; and if as a result the economy moves ahead it is just a coincidence. The local bourgeoisie craves for a bigger market for its products; the imperialists insist on an assured supply of raw materials for their industry and a market for their obsolete plant and equipment; and the feudal-semifeudal landlords maintain their hold on the agrarian economy. A certain degree of congruence notwithstanding, these demands generate considerable frictions, and the State has to preside over their reconciliation. Thus the scale of activity in the economy expands but it is not development; rather it is underdevelopment of the economy.[14]

7

CONCLUSION

The outward thrust of European commerce at the turn of the fifteenth century was carried by its merchant navy, fortified by the men-of-war. The Americas were opened up with the far superior destructive power of European cannon and European diseases. In the east, though, the sailing was not quite so smooth. Trade with and between countries outside Europe was controlled by Asians and Africans who had a well-developed complex of shipping, trade and authority. Here the Europeans had nothing to offer in either superiority of goods, finance or trading ability which could enable them to break into the traditional trade. They did have one decisive advantage, however—the great superiority of European ships of war. Sailing ships strong enough to mount cannon provided sufficient destructive power to force the issue: to cripple the ships of other nations, transfer the trade into European hands and establish forts for control of the seas. The relatively undeveloped means of production and the consequently small economic surplus left direct robbery, whenever practicable, as one of the most effective means of accumulating wealth. Hence, looting, plunder and piracy were the primary means of redistribution and new concentration of wealth.[1] Thus began the high tragedy of unequal exchange between Asia, Africa and Latin America on the one hand, and what would one day become the metropolitan centre of world capitalism on the other. Thus was sown the seed from which in due course modern imperialism was to sprout.

Unequal exchange between the periphery and the centre of world capitalism has been going on for centuries. The *modus operandi* has varied from place to place, and changed over time, but in essence the continuity is maintained. Rosa Luxemburg even goes to the extent of theorizing that it had to be so. She argues that the realization of surplus value under expanded production necessarily calls for non-equivalent exchange between the capitalist centre and the pre-capitalist periphery.[2] Theory or no theory, the facts are indisputable.

THE CRISIS AT THE CENTRE

European mercantilism shaded off into competitive capitalism in the wake of the first Industrial Revolution in England during the late eighteenth century. Within one hundred years thereafter capitalism entered its monopoly phase; and in the next hundred years monopoly capitalism had come of age. Now a rising stream of surplus is being sucked into the centre of world capitalism from the periphery, to supplement the enormous pool of surplus at home. As the investment outlets dry up the rate of profit tends to slide down. Product and process innovations could in principle open up avenues of investment and production; but the monopolist naturally hesitates to take this course, since as a result his already committed plant and equipment would suffer a loss of value. Whatever technological changes he ultimately introduces are bound to be labour-displacing in effect, for two reasons. First, the monopolist would pace and design the changes in such a manner that his existing plant and equipment are put to maximum use, and the least is spent on wages and new capital goods. Secondly, unlike in the case of the classical competitive models of Smith and Ricardo, the fruits of technological progress under monopoly capitalism are concentrated in a few pockets instead of being distributed evenly throughout the system. To the extent that the savings out of the additional profit thus created are not matched by an equal rise in *ex ante* investment demand, the consequent economic expansion may not be able to reabsorb the workers who have been dislodged at the advent of technological change in the first place. On balance, therefore, technological progress under monopoly capitalism has an inherent bias to be labour-saving in nature.

The growing might of the socialist countries has thrown up a fresh challenge to world capitalism, from outside as well as inside. The State in the advanced capitalist country now invests large sums of money in research and development for military preparation in order to meet this growing threat. The monopoly capitalist meanwhile draws upon the scientific and technological findings thus produced at the behest of the merchants of war. Despite all his natural inhibitions the capitalist does embark upon innovations for his own survival and aggrandisement; after all, his rival is waiting in the wings to outwit him in the bid for capturing the consumer's dollars, with the help of government-sponsored scientific and technological breakthroughs. Apart from making weapons and destroying them to keep up the profit rate, the launching of short-lived consumer goods is an effective means of keeping the investment outlets clear.

The rapid pace of technological change takes its toll in terms of equally rapid obsolescence of plant and equipment. The metropolis of world capitalism always finds itself burdened with a huge stock of obsolete machinery—old and new. This is an important dimension of the crisis that besets the metropolis; of course, it is but a manifestation of the basic problem of the falling tendency of the rate of profit in monopoly capitalism.

True to the requirements of their profession, bourgeois economists do search for solutions to the problems of the capitalist system. With an interesting twist in the definition of exploitation, they construct theoretical models of allegedly perpetual capitalism where, we are told, there would be no exploitation of man by man. Strangely enough, in these models of capitalism the class of capitalists is nowhere in sight. In the name of scientific abstraction, the science of economics has been done away with. At any rate, these models of the so-called exploitationless 'golden age' capitalism are such that the capitalists, in case they exist, are not allowed to eat. For if the capitalists' propensity to save is not numerically equal to one, the 'golden age' cannot be seen on this capitalist earth.

Monopoly capitalists are far smarter than their economists. They have still successfully retained a large part of the globe in their domain, and without caring for the niceties of the definition of exploitation they are running the empire in a new style. With the promise of consummating the grand marriage between the economies of large scale production and the Hecksher–Ohlin theorem on factor endowment the multinational corporations have made inroads into every nook and corner of the Third World. They sell commodities, invest capital, and transfer technology or even entire production facilities, lock, stock and barrel.

Lately, they are launching so-called 'joint ventures'. In return, they exploit the two types of invaluable resources of the Third World—human resources and natural resources. The exchange is unequal, much more unequal than what may be conveyed by the malpractice of transfer pricing as such. The crisis in the metropolitan centre of world capitalism further deepens; as more surplus pours in from the periphery, the volume of investible funds strains the profitability of the outlets. And the cycle repeats itself all over again.

FILTERING OF TECHNOLOGY

The technology that reaches the Third World is an organic part of a long trail that winds through the developed countries. The economic distance between rich and poor countries as measured by, say, per capita income or per capita consumption of steel, is enormous; that in terms of overall technological sophistication is also no less glaring. The most modern processes of production in the American industry, for instance, would fit better in the British, French, German or Japanese milieu than in the rather primitive set-up of a country like Liberia or Peru. The bulk of the international movement of technology therefore takes place within the advanced capitalist countries. Chronologically also, it tends to move down along the countries with less and less of technological accomplishment. Given the size and nature of the market in a Third World country, the sort of technology which reaches it is usually assembled by the seller by 'cutting and taping together' bits of knowledge which have been in circulation in the advanced capitalist countries for long. Accordingly, most of the technology supplied to the Third World comes not from the original producer of the product or process but from the 'followers' and from engineering firms.

If there is a major current of technological flow moving from the United States, then to the West European countries and Japan, and onwards to the countries of the Third World in a descending order, side by side there is another major current which carries the American technology, often after obsolescence there, directly to the Third World. With rising wage costs at home, the US transnational corporations find it much more profitable to ship the plant and locate it, say, in Brazil, Taiwan or the Philippines.

11

Either way the rhythm of technological progress in the Third World is dictated primarily by the pace and pattern of obsolescence in the advanced capitalist countries. It is difficult to come out of this dependence. For technology is a peculiar commodity, the marginal cost of whose production or use, once having been developed, is practically zero from the viewpoint of its owner. Besides, the purchaser would not know what he is bargaining for. The seller is in a position to impose tie-in clauses compelling purchase of intermediate products at inflated prices; restrictive clauses with regard to export of the product; and a high rate of royalty. The market can be segmented, and each purchaser squeezed to the utmost.

And yet the flow of plant, equipment and technology to the Third World, though small in comparison with that within the capitalist countries themselves, is a vital link in the total network. Any disruption here would set a chain reaction throughout the system, ultimately affecting the technological progress in the latter group of countries, and thus impinging upon the rate of profit there.

THE NEXUS IN THE THIRD WORLD

To understand what makes unequal exchange a feasible proposition today, one has to examine the nexus of ruling classes in the Third World. No longer is unequal exchange carried on with brute force or by way of ill-concealed fraud; it has been now elevated by imperialism to the level of a fine art, as it were. Class interests of the local ruling classes are protected by giving them a part of the surplus, at the same time robbing them of the other part, and thus making them an instrument for keeping the economy in the permanent limbo of underdevelopment.

Political economy has two main spheres of exploration—the prevailing mode of production and the new emerging mode of production. While the latter has attracted very little attention from political economists, the former has aroused considerable interest among them. Quite a bit of the enthusiasm of Marxists and neo-Marxists, however, has been spent in the pursuit of a quantitative measurement of the development of capitalism using a somewhat obscure methodology.[3] And it appears that the feudalism–capitalism constellation has been taken as a constant arithmetic sum, so to speak, and the rise of capitalism is considered tantamount to a corresponding decline in feudalism. Such a mechanistic approach is discredited by the lessons of history; imperialism evidently props up feudalism as its mainstay on the one hand, and stimulates the development of capitalism on the other—such are the historical records in China, Vietnam, India, among others. Classes are interrelated dialectically; there are positive and negative aspects of the contradiction between any two classes. It is the ensemble of class contradictions which determines the law of motion of the system. That is to say, the class relations can be conceptualized in the perspective of a matrix of class contradictions; the principal and the major contradictions can be identified by an analysis of the matrix; and therefrom the dynamics of the system can be discerned. We have followed this methodology here.

At a certain level the class interests of feudal-semifeudal landlords, the local bourgeoisie and imperialism clearly mesh together. Imperialism perpetrates its exploitation with the other two classes as intermediaries. As it is, the local bourgeoisie finds in the feudal-semifeudal landlords the major customer for industrial goods, and the sole supplier of the agricultural raw materials for industry. Imperialism similarly finds in this bourgeoisie the market for obsolete plant and equipment, old and new; and in the feudal-semifeudal landlords the source for agricultural goods. These three classes thus help each other in realizing their respective class interests, notwithstanding the negative features of their contradictions which simultaneously exist with the positive ones.

There is no consensus among Marxists and neo-Marxists in respect of the above view. There is one school, in particular, which totally denies the prevalence of any traits of feudalism in the Third World. The Third World is conceived as fully capitalistic, having been integrated into the world capitalist system four hundred years ago. We have not debated this issue by quantitatively measuring the degree of feudalism in the world; we have rather pointed out that if the history of China, Vietnam and India is any guide it is a fair approximation to characterize the socioeconomic formation in the Third World as semifeudal-semicolonial, rather than 'capitalistic', or 'colonial-postcolonial'. It is not just quibbling over semantics. Our characterization correctly reflects the fact that world capitalism is no longer a monolithic hierarchical machine of surplus extraction; the local bourgeoisie does retain substantial room for manoeuvre; and the feudal-semifeudal landlords are equally aware of their degree of freedom—thanks to the dialectical nature of class contradiction. We have demonstrated how the coexistence of feudalism-semifeudalism with capitalism is conceivable; and why one mode need not inevitably oust the other; that is to say, how the triangle of alliance of the ruling classes works under the heavy weight of imperialism.

UNEQUAL EXCHANGE

It is this triangle which makes unequal exchange not only possible but inevitable. In a Third World country, imperialism is distinctly the most powerful among the three classes who form the ruling coalition. The scale of economic activity of imperialism in any one country is a small fraction of its global totality; what it might lose in, say, Uruguay, can be amply recouped in Indonesia, for example. Its bargaining power is thus well beyond the proportion of its stake in the country concerned. Investible surplus is drained away, the industrial structure is distorted, and the mineral resources exhausted—and, in consequence, the Third World economy continues to be underdeveloped, notwithstanding the expansion in certain branches of agriculture and industry. Weak and precarious, the feudal-semifeudal landlords and the local bourgeoisie enter into an unequal exchange with imperialism which has penetrated deep into various stages of production in the Third World in addition to its dominance in the sphere of circulation. Unequal exchange has its roots not merely in the area of circulation but more fundamentally in the domain of production relations.

Even if perfectly competitive conditions prevailed in the sphere of circulation, the exchange between centre and periphery is bound to be unequal in terms of the labour contents of the traded commodities. *Prima facie*, this happens due to the wage differential; the wage rate is much higher in the advanced capitalist countries than in the poor countries of the Third World. The price of a commodity in a competitive market is equal to the wage rate times the total labour content duly compounded at the prevailing profit rate. Now, assuming that the balance of trade between two countries is in balance, the total prices of the two bundles of traded commodities are equal. Hence, if the wage rate in one country is higher, the labour content of its exported commodities must be proportionately lower; otherwise the balance cannot be maintained. This simple but decisive formulation of ours does not suffer from the limitations of the models of unequal exchange as constructed by Emmanuel and the subsequent writers after him. Our model also points out that the intensity of unequal exchange would be accentuated over time as labour-saving innovations occur in the advanced capitalist countries. With the rising inequality in exchange, more and more surplus would be extracted by imperialism from the Third World, thereby reducing the latter's ability to develop productive forces through stepped-up accumulation. As the economy thus lingers in underdevelopment, unequal exchange would be further reinforced.

The Third World's two most important endowments—human resources and mineral resources—are given out in unequal exchange with imperialism. The imports from the Third World into the advanced capitalist countries may be arithmetically small; the stream of profits, royalty and dividend may not be proportionately on a par with what it was a century ago; the Third World may be a fraction of the global market for the industrial products of the advanced capitalist countries. Besides, all these figures may have to be drastically altered in the event correction is made for the relative undervaluation of the Third World's exports which obtains under the regime of unequal exchange. The organic link between the Third World and the centre of imperialism is not to be found so much in these statistical exercises as in the fact that the flows running between the two are vital parts of a long chain.

Unequal exchange by itself does not reflect that imperialism is necessarily the main contradiction in a Third World country. After all, imperialism perpetrates its design through a certain medium of internal class collaboration. So long as the Third World remains within the ambit of world capitalism, the triangle of alliance among feudalism, local capitalism and imperialism would persist, and unequal exchange which is but an aspect of underdevelopment would continue with increasing intensity.

NOTES

CHAPTER 1

1. Toynbee (1965); Manfred (1974).
2. Brown (1972), p. 63; and Habib (1971).
3. Magdoff (1974).
4. Cf. 'It is fashionable to talk knowingly today of "Twenty Latin Americas" [title of a book by Marcel Niedergang, first published in France by Plon in 1962; then in Britain by Penguin in 1971]. Anyone who travels from Bolivia to Argentina, or even from Salta in the north of Argentina to Buenos Aires, or from Lima to Cuzco, has the impression of moving from one world and one century to another. But this is only a superficial, geographical impression. Is not underdevelopment and colonial distortion precisely the inequality of economic and social development within one country, between the countryside and the capital? Or rather, is it not the superimposition of different levels of development, an enclave of capitalist and mercantile penetration combined with an interior of *feudal* mono-production? Does not this misery condition those riches, and vice versa? *If underdevelopment is not in its turn a natural product but the result of a history, then South America draws its unity from its history*' (Debray (1967), p. 141; emphasis added).
5. Ho (1973), p. 25.
6. *Ibid.* p. 33. A brief sketch of the colonization of the Indian economy by British imperialism will be given below in Chapter 3.
7. Frank (1972), p. 19.
8. Jalée (1968), p. 5.
9. Servan-Schreiber (1969); Mandel (1970).
10. Lenin in Bukharin (1973), pp. 12–13.
11. Frank (1975), p. 52.
12. Magdoff (1974), p. 1.
13. *Ibid.* p. 7.
14. See Brown (1974; 1974a); Blaug (1968); Kemp (1967; 1972); and Braun (1972).
15. Braun (1972); Emmanuel (1972).
16. Marx (1867), p. 8.
17. *Ibid.*
18. Engels' Preface in Marx (1894), p. 13.
19. *Ibid.* pp. 13–14.

CHAPTER 2

1. Thomson (1966).
2. Sau (1974).
3. Keynes (1936).
4. Harrod (1939); Domar (1946).
5. Harrod indeed emphasizes the instability of capitalist growth; he argues that the market in disequilibrium typically engenders 'perverse' signals and heightens the disequilibrium. All the same, he demonstrates the theoretical possibility of a steady, continuous growth of the capitalist system. Kalecki (1962) observes as follows: 'The "Harrodian" rate of growth is ephemeral in the sense that any deviation from the path determined by it renders the system stationary—i.e. subject to cyclical fluctuation but no trend.' Kalecki continues: 'The antinomy of the capitalist economy is in fact more far-reaching: the system cannot break the impasse of fluctuations around a static position unless economic growth is generated by the impact of semi-exogenous factors such as the effect of innovations upon investment. It is only in such a case that cyclical fluctuations do occur around the ascending trend line.'
6. Robinson, J. (1969), p. 99. Emphasis added.
7. *Ibid*. Given the assumption of Mrs Robinson that workers save nothing and capitalists save everything they earn, we get the 'von Neumann theorem' of rate of profit being equal to the rate of accumulation in equilibrium. In this context see Findlay (1963) and also Robinson, J. (1963).
8. The *steady state* is a state of the economy such that 'all economic quantities grow in time at the same proportional rate of growth, so that all ratios among them (investment to income, savings to income, rate of profits, etc.) remain constant' (Pasinetti (1962), p. 93). An economy may have a number of alternative steady states depending upon the specific values of the relevant parameters. Of all such possible steady states, there is one in which full employment is maintained throughout, the growth rate of population being exogenously given. In the event of Harrod-neutral technical progress taking place, the rise in labour productivity is also to be duly taken into account. Such a special steady state is known as the *Golden Age*. Under it, therefore, profit rate is equalized with the (uniform) growth rate of income, of capital stock, and of employment, the last one being measured with a suitable efficiency unit having regard to the Harrod-neutral technical progress (Weizsäcker–Samuelson (1971), p. 1193). We shall, in the text below, demonstrate these features of the golden age step by step; full employment will be introduced at the end. See also Phelps (1961).
9. Pasinetti (1962). When all wages are consumed and all profits saved, equation (9) is satisfied, of course.
10. Weizsäcker–Samuelson (1971).
11. Keynes certainly did not visualize a steady state golden age of capital-

ism; nor could the golden age of Joan Robinson be equated with that of the neoclassical writers. As Findlay (1963) puts it, behind Harrod–Domar is Keynes and behind the neoclassical writers is Wicksell. Mrs Robinson claims that her model is inspired by Marx, Keynes, Wicksell and Kalecki.

12. The duality does not depend upon the timing of wage payment as it might appear to be otherwise from equation (12). Consider a steady state. Let y be income, c consumption, i investment, k capital, f profit, and w wage, all reckoned on per capita basis. Then:

$$y = c + i = w + f. \tag{i}$$

If K denotes total capital and L population, then:

$$i = (\Delta K/K)(K/L)$$
$$\text{or, } i = gk \tag{ii}$$

where g is the growth rate of capital. On the other hand,

$$f = (fL/K)(K/L)$$
$$\text{or, } f = rk \tag{iii}$$

where r is the rate of profit. In view of (ii) and (iii), equation (i) can be rewritten as:

$$y = c + gk = w + rk. \tag{iv}$$

This resembles equations (12) and (14) in the text above. I am grateful to Amitava Bose for pointing it out to me in this form.

For each technique there would be a pair of lines: wage/profit line and the growth rate/per capita consumption line. The envelope of the wage/profit lines, when there are many alternative techniques, constitutes the so-called Factory Price Frontier (FPF). The analysis of the text could be done in terms of such envelopes as well, with a much more complicated time profile of labour inputs which could make the envelope non-linear with multiple twists and turns as in Nuti (1970a). However, the essence of the problem is well captured with our simplifying assumptions. See also Weizsäcker (1971 and 1973).

13. Weizsäcker (1971 and 1973); Sau (1974). Weizsäcker considers an n-sector model with m groups of workers. His basic idea is presented here in a much simpler one-commodity–one-labour-group model. This however raises a conceptual problem. In case there is only one homogeneous group of workers, how can this group exploit somebody else? There is simply nobody else to be exploited. To repeat, Weizsäcker considers m groups. When r exceeds g in his model, one group exploits others; and if these two variables switch their places, the same group turns out to be a victim of exploitation. Thus he reduces exploitation to a phenomenon that is governed only by the relative position of r and g and which has nothing to do with the ownership of capital or any such class-related concept. Our simplified model, in spite of the above-mentioned logical complication, clearly demonstrates the fundamental contention of the Weizsäcker theory of exploitation.

It has been a running theme of all bourgeois economic theories that capitalism in its pure form is an exploitationless system. The argument of Adam Smith, Ricardo and Mill in this respect will be given below. The neoclassical economists have tried to prove it in terms of the marginal productivity theory of distribution. And as for the neo-neoclassical economists, of course, Weizsäcker is their chief spokesman on this matter, with Samuelson standing by. See Sau (1974); also Dobb (1973).

14. Weizsäcker (1973). He ventures even further to state that no matter whether the production relations are capitalist or socialist there would be no exploitation so long as $r = g$; by contrast there would be exploitation if r and g diverge.

15. Marx (1867), vol. 1, pp. 589–90; Marx (1885), vol. 2, pp. 364, 366–95; and Marx (1894), vol. 3, pp. 832–51. There the relevant theory of Smith, Ricardo and Mill is critically reviewed.

16. Marx (1867), vol. 1, pp. 589–91.

17. Marx (1885), vol. 2, p. 393.

18. Marx (1867), vol. 1, p. 590.

19. See also Sraffa (1960), p. 94 for the implication of this error in another branch of theory.

20. Under capitalism, labour itself is a commodity. However, to maintain consistency with the earlier discussion of bourgeois theories, where labour is taken as a primary factor rather than strictly a 'commodity', we shall continue with that usage, unless there is a possibility of creating confusion.

21. Marx (1867), vol. 1, pp. 218, 531–4.

22. Sau (1974); Wolfstetter (1973).

23. Sau (1974).

24. Robinson, J. (1969), p. 99.

25. A word about the impossibility of the Golden Age under the Pasinetti condition. If the capitalists' propensity to save is positive and, of course, numerically less than one, then the steady state investment is equal to the volume of total profits multiplied by their saving propensity, regardless of whether or not the workers consume all their incomes (Pasinetti (1962), pp. 99, equation 14). In that case, obviously, equation (9) in our text above does not hold, and the Golden Age recedes out of sight.

Should the capitalists' consumption out of profits be matched in amount by workers' savings (in which case the workers also get a part of profits as their income), even then investment rises only up to the share of profits received by the capitalists; and still it falls short of total profits by an amount equal to the share accruing to the workers on account of their past accumulation of savings.

And, of course, all this is turned upside down in the anti-Pasinetti MSM land, named after Meade, Samuelson and Modigliani, where workers' saving dominates the accumulation process and the capitalists' property relative to the workers' approaches zero (Harcourt (1972), p. 221).

26. When the growth rate and interest rate diverge, the choice of technique by the capitalist is inoptimal. So the 'capitalist exploitation takes two forms: one is the capitalists' acquisition of consumption of goods through straightforward command over other people's labour; the other more subtle form of exploitation is the lower average level of consumption per head associated with a suboptimal technical choice, whenever consumption out of profit prevents the fulfilment of the Golden Rule. ... If the rate of interest differs from the growth rate, in such conditions consumption per head is not necessarily located on the outer boundary of frontiers.' See Nuti (1970a), pp. 328 and 337.

27. Weizsäcker (1971 and 1973), Weizsäcker–Samuelson (1971), and Sau (1974).

28. Sweezy (1942), pp. 121–2.

29. Sraffa (1960); Eatwell (1974; 1975); Medio (1972). See also Rowthorn (1974); Brunhoff (1974); Laibman (1974); Sau (1974).

30. Sraffa (1960), p. 20.

31. Medio (1972), p. 338.

32. Sweezy (1942), pp. 145–6.

33. *Ibid.* pp. 68 and 96.

34. Medio (1972), p. 340.

35. Lenin (1916); Magdoff (1966), pp. 27–31; Magdoff (1974), pp. 15–16.

36. These findings of the German scholar Herman Levy are reported in Sylos-Labini (1969), pp. 1–3. See also Lenin (1916).

37. Hymer (1972), p. 45.

38. For the situation in India then, once the largest colony in the world, see Habib (1975).

39. Hymer (1972), p. 45. Cf. Sweezy's opinion that one of the most important general effects of monopoly on the functioning of the capitalist system is that 'the labour-saving bias of capitalist technology is enhanced' (Sweezy (1942), p. 285). Also: 'The forces which tend to reabsorb the workers gradually liberated or made redundant by technical progress are weaker when the oligopolistic or monopolistic mechanism operates than when the mechanism of competition operates.... [Besides,] in a highly concentrated economy there is a bias in favour of labour-saving investment' (Sylos-Labini (1969), pp. 159 and 186).

40. Magdoff (1974), pp. 17–18; Tugendhat (1971).

41. Radice (1975), p. 9.

42. United Nations (1973), pp. 15–16, cited in Chattopadhyay (1975), pp. 21–2; see also Griffin (1974).

43. Baran–Sweezy (1966), p. 65; Sylos-Labini (1969), p. 183.

44. This is an oft-repeated, well-documented observation. See Keynes (1936); Sylos-Labini (1969); Baran–Sweezy (1966); Amin (1974).

45. Cf. 'It may then happen that the most progressive entrepreneurs become the allies of the trade unions for, even with rising wages, their costs are lower than those of their competitors, and the rise in wages speeds up the rate at which high-cost producers are squeezed out of existence' (Robinson, J. (1969), p. 94). Also: 'In oligopoly cost reduc-

tions are not necessarily translated into higher profits. They may be and often are translated into higher wages for the workers. This may be due to strong trade-union action, to government intervention, or to any combination of the two causes. It may also happen as a result of "political" decisions on the part of the management of large oligopolistic firms' (Sylos-Labini (1969), p. 108).

46. For the impact of monopoly on the nature of technical progress, see note 39 above.

CHAPTER 3

1. Marx (1867), vol. 1, pp. 8–9.
2. Marx, *Capital*, vol. 1, part 4, Chapter 13, section 7 of the original German edition, cited in Baran–Sweezy (1966), p. 20n.
3. Amin (1974), pp. 40–1.
4. Bukharin (1973), p. 21.
5. Marx (1867), p. 352.
6. This section draws heavily upon a brilliant paper, Habib (1975).
7. *Ibid.* p. 25.
8. *Ibid.* p. 28.
9. *Ibid.* p. 40.
10. Bagchi (1972).
11. Cf. 'Under mercantilism the characteristic type of colonial exploitation was through the regulation of trade in such a way that prices of goods exported to the colonies were kept up by artificial means, mainly through the intervention of the State, and those imported from colonies were kept down' (Kemp (1967), p. 121). See also Owen and Sutcliffe (1972), p. 181.
12. Jalée (1968), p. 19.
13. Bukharin (1973), p. 20.
14. Baran–Sweezy (1966), p. 113.
15. Tugendhat (1971), pp. 31–3.
16. Jalée (1968), p. 29; see also Amin (1974), vol. 1, p. 67.
17. Jalée (1968), p. 58.
18. The amount of value transferred from the Third World to the developed countries through unequal exchange in the year 1966 is estimated by Amin to be of the order of $22 billion, which is nearly four times the total long-term capital, including official donations, private investments and the credits extended by such bodies as the IBRD, that came into the Third World in that year. Amin's computation is as follows.

  Total exports from the underdeveloped countries in 1966 were valued by the world market at about $35,000 million. Of these, the 'ultramodern' petroleum, mining, plantation and other export sectors accounted for above 75 per cent or $26 billion. Had the same products been produced by the developed countries with the same techniques and thus the same productivity (at 15 per cent profit on invested capital, seven year depreciation, capital coefficient of 3.5, and a 100 per cent rate of surplus value) the value price of these products would have been $8 billion more.

The underdeveloped countries' remaining exports, which are valued at $9 billion (the difference between the total of $35 billion and $26 billion from the 'modern' sector), would be valued at $23 billion, that is $14 billion more than the world market assigns to them, assuming a wage gap of 20 to 1 and a productivity gap of at most 2 to 1 if metropolitan techniques were, or could be, used.

The two underpayments the underdeveloped countries receive for the value they produce added together amount to: $8 + 14 = 22$ billion dollars. This is the quantum of value which is drained away from the underdeveloped countries through the mechanism of unequal exchange. It may be noted that this amount of $22 billion is equivalent to only 1.5 per cent of the net domestic product of the developed countries, but it is as much as 15 per cent of that of the underdeveloped countries, or nearly equal to their total gross investment (and hence much more than their net investment).

These calculations of Amin are cited in Frank (1976). Here 'developed countries' presumably include all countries outside the Third World.

19. Vaitsos (1971), pp. 211–13. The overpricing is defined with reference to the prevailing price in different world markets.

20. *Ibid.* p. 211.

21. Jalée (1968), p. 34; Amin (1974), p. 69, gives about the same figure as the 1960–5 average.

22. Jalée (1968), p. 38. These figures are as of 1962.

23. Jalée (1968), p. 38.

24. *Ibid.* p. 27.

25. It should be noted that the measurement of capitals remains the same for value as well as price calculation. Strictly speaking this is not permissible as first pointed out by Bortkiewicz. See Sweezy (1942), pp. 115–25. For the sake of simplification we are abstracting from the Bortkiewicz problem. See also Emmanuel (1972), p. 61.

26. See Sweezy (1942), pp. 290–1.

27. *Ibid.* p. 291.

28. *Ibid.*; emphasis added.

29. Emmanuel (1972), pp. 160–3. 'Inequality of wages...is alone the cause of the inequality of exchange' (*ibid.* p. 61).

30. *Ibid.* p. 160.

31. *Ibid.* p. 60.

32. *Ibid.* pp. 61 and 64.

33. The same comment applies to the two-sector–two-country model of Saigal (1973). See Sau (1975 and 1976a).

34. Braun (1972). It is understood that Amin (1972) has grafted the Sraffa model on to the Marxian schema of expanded reproduction; unfortunately, this paper is not yet available to us. However, Amin (1974) hails the Emmanuel theory as a fundamental contribution, and then

proceeds to use unequal exchange as a corner-stone of the centre–periphery relationship. He argues that unequal exchange is the modern instrument for primitive accumulation by the metropolitan centre of world capitalism, and that such primitive accumulation is not a thing of the past but quite contemporary.

Two other models have been attempted recently. To begin with, Evans (1976) considers two steady state economies engaged in trade. Apart from the anomalies which appear in case the growth rates of the two steady state economies do not tally, it is also not at all clear as to why the exchange is called unequal. This endeavour of Evans (1976) to recast the Emmanuel model in such a form therefore remains far from convincing.

Diwan–Marwah (1976) also have tried to quantify inter-country transfers on account of unequal exchange. However, their theoretical structure and methodology leave much to be desired. As they put it: 'In our conceptual framework, implicit subsidies [transfers] depend upon only non-market factors such as inequality between trading partners, international demonstration effects, transfer of inappropriate technology, domination etc. Market price, again conceptually, should involve equivalent exchange....We define "implicit transfers or subsidies or grants" as that part of the trade flow which is accounted for only by changes in exports....The argument is that the non-market factors that generate transfers take effect through the growth rate of exports. These are transfers in the sense that one of the trading partners obtains a portion of the export of others without exchanging equivalent values. These are implicit because these are obtained through non-market factors' (*Ibid.* p. 195). Again, one fails to see how these transfers are effected in their model through non-market factors.

35. Braun's model is as follows. Retaining his notations, suppose the imperialist country produces commodities $A, B, \ldots E$; and the dependent country of the Third World, commodities $F, G, \ldots K$. Let $A_A, B_A, \ldots K_A$ be the amounts of commodities $A, B, \ldots K$ respectively which are required as inputs to produce output A. (Note that a letter, say, A or B, denotes the name of the commodity and also the volume of its output.) The production matrix of the imperialist country is given by:

$$A_A, \quad B_A, \quad C_A, \quad \ldots K_A, \quad L_A \longrightarrow A$$
$$A_B, \quad B_B, \quad C_B, \quad \ldots K_B, \quad L_B \longrightarrow B$$
$$\cdots \qquad \cdots \qquad \cdots$$
$$A_E, \quad B_E, \quad C_E, \quad \ldots K_E, \quad L_E \longrightarrow E$$

where $L_A, L_B, \ldots L_E$ are labour inputs, Similarly, the production matrix of the dependent country is given by:

$$A_F, \quad B_F, \quad C_F, \quad \ldots K_F, \quad L_F \longrightarrow F$$
$$A_G, \quad B_G, \quad C_G, \quad \ldots K_G, \quad L_G \longrightarrow G$$
$$\cdots \qquad \cdots \qquad \cdots$$
$$A_K, \quad B_K, \quad C_K, \quad \ldots K_K, \quad L_K \longrightarrow K$$

Wage rates in the two countries are different, but the profit rate is the same. Let W_I and W_D be the wage rates in the imperialist and the dependent countries respectively, and R the uniform profit rate. Then the Sraffa-type price equations are given by (see Sraffa (1960), p. 11, section 11):

$$(A_A P_A + B_A P_B + \ldots K_A P_K)(1+R) + L_A W_I = AP_A$$
$$\ldots \qquad \qquad \ldots$$
$$(A_E P_A + B_E P_B + \ldots K_E P_K)(1+R) + L_E W_I = EP_E$$
$$(A_F P_A + B_F P_B + \ldots K_F P_K)(1+R) + L_F W_D = FP_F$$
$$\ldots \qquad \qquad \ldots$$
$$(A_K P_A + B_K P_B + \ldots K_K P_K)(1+R) + L_K W_D = KP_K$$

where P_A, P_B, $\ldots P_K$ are the prices of the commodities. This is a system of K equations with $(K+2)$ unknowns, with one of the commodity prices being taken as the numeraire. From this system one can derive the following equation:

$$R = R(W_I, W_D)$$

which shows the relationship between R, W_I and W_D. Braun goes on to specify the properties of this equation as follows:

$$\frac{\delta R}{\delta W_I} < 0, \quad \frac{\delta R}{\delta W_D} < 0;$$

and for a given value of R,

$$\frac{dW_D}{dW_I} = - \left(\frac{\delta R}{\delta W_I} \right) \Big/ \left(\frac{\delta R}{\delta W_D} \right) < 0.$$

Finally, in the above systems of price equations, given any arbitrary value of R, if W_I rises and hence W_D falls, then the prices of commodities A, B, $\ldots E$ will *rise* on an average, and those of commodities F, G, $\ldots K$ will *fall*. In note 36 below we cite these results as the four propositions of Braun.

36. Now Braun takes a numerical example of two goods, namely, iron and corn produced respectively in the imperialist country and the dependent country. The technology is as follows:

13 tons of iron, 2 tons of corn, 10 man years → 27 tons of iron.
10 tons of iron, 4 tons of corn, 10 man years → 12 tons of corn.

Let P_H be the price of iron, P_T the price of corn, W_I and W_D the two wage rates, and R the rate of profit. The price equations are:

$$(13 P_H + 2 P_T)(1+R) + 10 W_I = 27 P_H$$
$$(10 P_H + 4 P_T)(1+R) + 10 W_D = 12 P_T$$

Iron is taken as the numeraire; hence $P_H = 1$. The profit rate is arbitrarily fixed at 20 per cent; that is, $R = 0.20$. In the two equations above there are now only three unknowns, namely, W_I, W_D and P_T. For any preassigned value of any one of these three variables, the solution for the other two can be computed from the two equations. Setting six alternative values for W_I, Braun has computed the corresponding values of W_D and P_T.

In the above example, the capital invested in the imperialist country is measured by $(13\ P_H + 2\ P_T)$, and that in the dependent country by $(10\ P_H + 4\ P_T)$. The rate of profit R being known, the volume of profit also can be calculated. Let G_I and G_D denote the volumes of profit in the two countries respectively.

Braun's simulation with six alternative values of W_I and the variables W_D, P_T, G_I and G_D is presented below.

W_I	W_D	P_T	G_I	G_D
0.00	2.22	4.750	4.50	5.80
0.15	1.77	4.125	4.25	5.30
0.30	1.32	3.500	4.00	4.80
0.45	0.87	2.875	3.75	4.30
0.60	0.42	2.250	3.50	3.80
0.70	0.12	1.833	3.33	3.46

Note that as W_I rises, W_D and P_T fall, and so does G_D. See Braun (1972), Table 5.

What one may ask here is: Why would the bourgeoisie of the dependent country continue to engage in trade if the volumes of their capital and profit go on declining with every rise in wages in the imperialist country?

37. Sau (1975 and 1976a).
38. Amin (1974), vol. 1, p. 57. Emphasis added.
39. Sraffa (1960); pp. 34–5; Sau (1973–4).
40. Weizsäcker (1971), pp. 18–19.
41. Emmanuel (1972), pp. 57, 59, 62, 63, 76–81, takes total capital invested in some of his exercises.
42. Baran and Sweezy (1966), p. 193; see also Sweezy (1942), pp. 291–2.
43. Kidron (1965), p. 247.
44. Gulbrandsen (1973); Griffin (1974).
45. Adam (1975), p. 89.
46. Lall (1973), Penrose (1968), Sutcliffe (1972), Turner (1973).
47. Vaitsos (1970), pp. 318–19.
48. *Ibid.* p. 319.
49. See Hymer (1972) for uneven development under the dominance of multinational corporations.
50. Sweezy (1942), p. 202.
51. Luxemburg (1951), p. 350.
52. *Ibid.* p. 452. Emphasis added.
53. *Ibid.*
54. Sweezy (1942), p. 205.
55. *Ibid.* p. 204.
56. Amin (1974) goes to the extent of claiming that primitive accumulation

is an on-going feature of world capitalism even today; and that unequal exchange is the main instrument thereof.

57. Preobrazhensky (1965); see also Mitra (1975).
58. *Ibid*. p. 124.

CHAPTER 4

1. Bernal (1965), pp. 712, and 854 f.
2. Bernal (1965), pp. 718–19; Mansfield (1968a), pp. 43–5.
3. Mansfield (1968), pp. 8–9; Mansfield (1968a), p. 55.
4. Mansfield (1968a), p. 15. See also Mandel (1970), p. 34.
5. Mandel (1970), pp. 35–6; Steindl (1969), p. 200.
6. Servan-Schreiber (1969), p. 59; see also Bernal (1965), p. 715, and Mansfield (1968), p. 111.
7. Bernal (1965), p. 715.
8. Baran–Sweezy (1966), p. 40; Magdoff (1966), Ch. 2.
9. Steindl (1969), p. 200.
10. Sau (1973), pp. 45–6.
11. Mansfield (1968), pp. 8–9.
12. Steindl (1969), pp. 201–2.
13. Mansfield (1968), pp. 55–6.
14. Mansfield (1968).
15. *Ibid*. p. 13.
16. Sylos-Labini (1969).
17. *Ibid*. p. 123.
18. *Ibid*. pp. 123–87.
19. Sweezy (1942), p. 276. Emphasis added.
20. Bernal (1965), p. 715.
21. Baran–Sweezy (1966), p. 102.
22. Salter (1960), pp. 72–3. For a theoretical discussion of the replacement problem, also see Bhattacharyya (1965).
23. Using the notations of Nuti (1970a), let a_i be the input supplied to labour at period i ($i = 0, 1, 2, \ldots k-1$) to produce machines, and then a_i be the output at period i ($i = k, k+1, \ldots n$). A 'technique of production' is represented by a time flow of a_i ($i = 0, 1, \ldots k, \ldots n$) where the input appears with the negative sign and the output with the positive sign. The sequence of the time pattern of labour required first to make machines, then to operate them to produce the flow of output, is given by $\{l_i\}$, where $l_0 > 0$ and $l_i \geqslant 0$ for $i = 1, 2, \ldots n$. Assume that $\sum_0^n a_i > 0$. The scale of a technique of production is taken so that $l_0 = 1$.

The present value (v) of starting a unit scale process, $\{a_i\}$, $\{l_i\}$, is given by:

12

$$v = \sum_{i=0}^{n} (a_i - wl_i) \ (1+r)^{-i} \qquad\qquad (i)$$

where w is the wage rate and r the profit rate. The wage–profit frontier can be derived by setting v of equation (i) equal to zero.

Now suppose that there is a positive salvage value (θ) for the machines at the end of period n. Then the equation for the new wage–profit frontier is given by:

$$0 = \sum_{i=1}^{n} (a_i - wl_i) \ (1+r)^{-i} + \theta \qquad\qquad (ii)$$

For any given r, the w of equation (ii) is higher than that of equation (i) with $v = 0$. Thus a positive resale value of the machines at the end of their economic life causes the wage–profit frontier to shift up.

24. We are considering what is called embodied technological progress, where the machines of younger vintage are more productive.
25. Sen (1962), p. 346; Sen (1975), p. 66.
26. Adam (1975), pp. 92–3.
27. Sen (1962), p. 346.
28. Sen (1962), p. 347; Sen (1975), p. 65. This inter-country 'disequilibrium' continues because of the limits that apply to the availability of capital in underdeveloped countries.
29. Smith (1972); Sen (1975), p. 66.
30. See above, Ch. 3, notes 42 and 43.
31. Sen (1962), p. 346, interprets the data of Table 6 as follows: 'A similar transfer quite often takes place *within* an economy, from its advanced to its backward sector.' We are extrapolating a sector into a country.
32. Sau (1975d; 1976a).
33. NCAER (1971), p. 2.
34. *Ibid*. Figure 1, p. 3; and Mansfield (1968a), p. 201.
25. Mansfield (1968a), p. 201.
36. NCAER (1971), p. 2.
37. Dunning (1970), p. 391.
38. *Ibid*.; see also Gruber, Mehta and Vernon (1967) and Kessing (1967).
39. Adam (1975), p. 89; and Mansfield (1968a), p. 201, for the 1961 figure of royalty; see also Vernon (1970).
40. Vaitsos (1971), p. 184.
41. *Ibid*. pp. 183–214.
42. NCAER (1971), p. 17.
43. Sau (1973c). The petty bourgeoisie in India operates outside the organized financial market; so it does not occur in the RBI sample.
44. Here 'wages' include wages, salaries, bonus, provident fund, gratuity and other employees' welfare expenses. Total output includes wages, gross profit after depreciation, managerial remuneration and interest payment as given in the income, expenditure and appropriation account published by the RBI.
45. NCAER (1971), pp. 14–17.

46. Individuals and partnerships were excluded from the survey. The coverage was confined to Indian joint stock companies, and so it excluded branches of foreign firms since a branch organization forms part of an enterprise operating abroad and does not entail collaboration with local enterprise. See RBI (1968), p. 6.

47. Dunning (1964), p. 85; Layton (1969), p. 16.

48. Vaitsos (1971), p. 185.

49. Dunning (1964), p. 65, Table 2.

50. *Ibid.* p. 71.

51. *Ibid.* p. 76.

52. *Ibid.*; Brown (1972; 1974 and 1974a); Blaug (1968), pp. 264–71.

53. Dunning (1964), p. 77. It is debatable whether the credits extended by socialist countries can be called 'capital' imports.

54. Cairncross (1953); Sweezy (1972), pp. 22–3; Frank (1967), p. 294.

55. Magdoff (1972), p. 153, and also pp. 150–2.

56. Dunning (1964), p. 76.

57. Hayter (1971), p. 9.

58. *Ibid.* p. 10.

59. *Ibid.*

60. *Ibid.* pp. 9–10.

CHAPTER 5

1. Owen–Sutcliffe (1972); Baran–Sweezy (1966); Magdoff (1966); Sweezy–Magdoff (1965). However, Robinson (1972) makes an attempt to analyse the non-European foundations of European imperialism in terms of a theory of collaboration, where a group of colonial elites works as a mediator of imperialism. It is our view that this so-called 'ex-centric' approach to European imperialism has much to recommend it; however, it cannot be any more than what it is—an opposite reaction to the traditional 'in-centric' approach. To understand the essence of imperialism one has to have an integrated, unified theoretical frame where both the 'ex-centric' and the 'in-centric' factors are coordinated. And this is what we are trying to develop in this essay.

2. Brown (1974a), pp. 69–71.

3. Schultz (1964).

4. Lewis (1954), and Fei–Ranis (1964).

5. This view is reflected most in Gunnar Myrdal's survey of the South Asian scene. See Myrdal (1968), especially p. 1380.

6. For instance, see Krishna (1963); and Schultz (1964), pp. 41–52.

7. Krishna (1963), Table 2.

8. Schultz (1964), p. 106.

9. *Ibid.*

10. 'Schultz's account of optimizing peasant communities implies that traditional agriculture is close to neo-classical perfect competition: *neo-classical* because fixed factor proportions are implausible (Schultz

rightly rejects them when he dismisses the possibility of zero marginal product of labour); *perfect competition* because otherwise individual profit-maximizing actions do not add up to a social optimum, so that Schultz's conclusion—that interference with the allocation of traditional resources is almost useless—would not follow' (Lipton (1968), p. 113; emphasis added).

11. Schultz (1964), p. 39.
12. Harberger (1959); see also Schultz (1964), p. 34*n*. Emphasis added.
13. A member of the Chicago group, Cheung (1968) has tried to prove that tenancy has no bearing upon resource allocation in agriculture. This has given rise to a controversy in the pages of *EPW* between P. K. Bardhan and T. N. Srinivasan on the one hand and Amiya Bagchi on the other; see *EPW*, (*a*) special number, August 1973, (*b*) March 9, 1974, (*c*) October 4, 1975, and (*d*) January 17, 1976.

   On the question of farm productivity under semi-feudalism, see Chandra (1974) and Sau (1975a).
14. Sau (1973), Ch. 3.
15. See Sen (1975).
16. Sau (1973), pp. 56–8.
17. The arithmetic is as crude as follows: 66 per cent of 86 per cent is 56.76 per cent, or nearly 60 per cent.
18. In this category also belongs the argument that a big farm is likely to have a high proportion of inferior land whose productivity is extremely meagre after the main season.
19. See Sau (1976c).
20. *Ibid.*; and also Sau (1973, p. 19; and 1975h).
21. Notwithstanding the substantial scale of irrigation work, irrigated areas account for only 21 per cent of all cultivated land in Sri Lanka, and also in Indonesia, 18 per cent in Thailand, 16 per cent in Mexico, 12 per cent in the Philippines, and 3 per cent in Morocco, for instance. See Tyagunenko (1973), p. 59.
22. Fei–Ranis (1964).
23. Myrdal (1968).
24. *Ibid.* p. 1062.
25. *Ibid.* pp. 1063–4.
26. *Ibid.* p. 1380.
27. Engels (1894), p. 207; Marx (1847); see also Sau (1973e).
28. Mao (1937).
29. Brown (1974a), p. 71.
30. *Ibid.*; see also Baran (1962); Frank (1967; 1969; 1972; 1975); and also Amin (1974). Cf. 'Underdevelopment as we know it today, and economic development as well, are the simultaneous and related products of the development on a world-wide scale and over a history of more than four centuries at least of a single integrated economic system: capitalism. I suggest that the experience with mercantilism and capitalism should be understood to be part not only of a single historical process, the development of capitalism, but of the development of a

single integrated system, the capitalist system, which came to attain world-wide scope' (Frank (1975), p. 43).

31. Frank (1967), pp. xiii, 219–77.
32. Cf. 'The present analysis of the Brazilian situation may also find application elsewhere in Latin America and perhaps even in Asia and parts of Africa' (Frank (1967), p. 269).
33. Frank (1975), p. 88.
34. See Sau (1975d).
35. Alavi (1975), p. 1253.
36. Amin (1974) seems to have been the first to coin the terms 'articulation' and 'disarticulation' of an economy.
37. Alavi (1975), p. 1253.
38. *Ibid.* p. 1243.
39. *Ibid.*
40. *Ibid.* p. 1259.
41. *Ibid.* p. 1243.
42. *Ibid.* p. 1260. The *post-colonial* mode is essentially the same as the colonial mode except for the fact that there is now a new basis of subordination of the indigenous capital by metropolitan capital. Within the hierarchical relationship under the post-colonial mode, there is a convergence of interests between the big bourgeoisie of the former colony and the imperialist bourgeoisie, a basis which is radically different from that which determined the subordination of the 'comprador' bourgeoisie in the *colonial* situation.
43. See Ho (1973); Le Duan (1970); and Truong-Chinh (1969). Lenin also emphasizes the simultaneous existence of more than one mode of production in pre-revolution Russia. According to him the landlord economy in Russia combined the features of both capitalism and serfdom. He specifically refers to the semi-feudal elements in the then Russia. As for China and Vietnam, Mao and Ho Chi Minh not only recognized the prevalence of feudalism along with capitalism but they called feudalism the mainstay of imperialism.
44. For an analysis of the behaviour of semi-feudal landowners, see Bhaduri (1973) and Sau (1973), pp. 19–21.
45. See Sau (1974c and 1975f).
46. Lenin (1899b), p. 189. Emphasis added.
47. Baran (1962), pp. 202–3.
48. Lenin (1899a, p. 111; 1903, pp. 342–3 and 347). See also Chandra (1974) and Sau (1975a).
49. Lenin (1899a), pp. 134, 136 and 146. See also Sau (1973d).
50. Lenin (1899), pp. 183–5.
51. Habib (1975), pp. 43–5; see also Ch. 3 above.
52. Dobb (1967), pp. 194–5.
53. See Chandra (1975) and Sau (1973d). See also earlier in this chapter our hypothesis to explain the inverse relationship between intensity of cropping and farm size. When a rich farmer has multiple modes of profit-making he does not resort to full utilization of land, and the

inspiration for him to become a capitalist farmer is considerably reduced.

54. Myint (1972), pp. 45–7. A report entitled 'Arrested Green Revolution' by a special correspondent in the *Economic and Political Weekly* (*EPW*), vol. 10. nos. 25 and 26, dated June 21 and 28, 1975, also narrates how the once prosperous capitalist farmers in the green revolution region of Punjab are transforming themselves into a group of moneylenders.

55. Frank (1967), p. 222; and Kenner–Petras (1969), pp. 137–67. Cf. 'In our countries are two conditions: an underdeveloped industry and an agrarian regime of *feudal* character.... [However,] in the actual historic conditions of Latin America, the national bourgeoisie cannot lead the anti-feudal and anti-imperialist struggle. Experience shows that in our nations that class, even when its interests are in contradiction to those of ... imperialism, has been incapable of confronting it, for it is paralysed by fear of social revolution and frightened by the cry of the exploited masses' (*Second Havana Declaration*, in Kenner-Petras (1969), pp. 161–3; emphasis added).

Debray echoes this part of the second Havana Declaration when he describes Latin America as 'the superimposition of different levels of development, an enclave of capitalist and mercantile penetration combined with an interior of *feudal* mono-production' (Debray (1967), p. 14; emphasis added). Again, 'agrarian feudalism is an integral moment of the development of the commercial and agrarian export bourgeoisie, and even of industrial bourgeoisie, as in Colombia and Brazil' (*ibid.* p. 145). However, he at the same time warns that the recognition of the presence of feudalism in Latin American agrarian economy should not be construed as a plea for, first bourgeois democratic revolution and then socialist revolution. In his own words: 'As it has been said of Russia before 1917, Latin America today is pregnant with two revolutions, the bourgeois-democratic and the socialist revolution, and cannot release one without releasing the other: "at the birth of the first, it cannot withhold the second". Thus it is perilous to count on the "national bourgeoisie"— even in those countries where one is developing—to make a bourgeois-democratic revolution, since it is well aware of the process which it would be unleashing' (*ibid.* p. 178).

56. Lenin (1899), p. 237. Emphasis added.

57. Malinin (1974), p. 191; and Sau (1973a).

58. Lenin (1916), p. 274. For Indian data, see Habib (1975), p. 42.

59. Cf. 'While we correctly defined the *trend* of development, we did not correctly define the *moment* of that development. We assumed that the elements of capitalist agriculture have already taken full shape in Russia, both in landlord farming ... and in peasant farming which seemed to have given rise to a strong peasant bourgeoisie and therefore to be incapable of bringing about a "peasant agrarian revolution". The erroneous programme was not the result of "fear" of the peasant agrarian revolution, but of an *over-estimation of the degree* of capitalist

development in Russian agriculture. The survivals of serfdom appeared to us then to be a minor detail, whereas capitalist agriculture on the peasant allotments and on the landlords' estate seemed to be quite mature and well-established. The revolution [of 1905] has exposed that mistake; it has confirmed the trend of development as we have defined it [but not the *moment* of that development]' (Lenin (1907), pp. 291–2).

60. See Sau (1973; 1973a; and 1973d).

61. Lenin (1908), p. 129. This quotation is followed by: 'And the crux of the matter concerning the Russian agrarian crisis and the forthcoming upheaval is *not* what degree of development has been reached by capitalism or what the rate of that development is, but whether it is, or is not, a capitalist crisis and upheaval, whether it is, or is not, taking place in conditions in which the peasantry is being transformed into a rural bourgeoisie and a proletariat, and whether the relations between the various households within the commune are, or are not, bourgeois relations. In other words: the primary object of any study of the agrarian question in Russia is to establish the basic data for characterizing the class substance of agrarian relations' (*Ibid.*). Clearly, Lenin here is talking about the uneven nature of capitalist development in the agrarian economy of Russia. On the basis of the first law of uneven development, that is, the law of uneven development of capitalism, Lenin, in 1908, deduced also the character of the then forthcoming upheaval in Russia.

62. See Lenin (1916), p. 241. Invoking the second law, the law of uneven development *under* capitalism, Lenin, in September 1916, formulated the doctrine of 'socialism in one country'. In his own words: 'The development of capitalism proceeds extremely unevenly in different countries. It cannot be otherwise under commodity production. From this it follows irrefutably that socialism cannot achieve victory simultaneously *in all* countries. It will achieve victory first in one or several countries, while the others for some time remain bourgeois or pre-bourgeois' (Lenin (1916a), p. 79).

63. Frank (1967), p. 7.

64. *Ibid.* pp. 7–8; also p. 19.

65. Marx also analyses how 'one capitalist kills many', how the surplus of one capitalist is expropriated by another as market price fluctuates, and how differentiation among the bourgeoisie goes on. But Frank's model of hierarchical exploitation where one stratum of capitalists exploits another is a different pattern of century-old relationship which continually produces development in one part of the world at the expense of another.

66. See Sau (1976; 1976a).

67. Ulyanovsky (1971), pp. 102–3. Emphasis added. See also Ulyanovsky (1974).

68. Ulyanovsky–Pavlov (1973), p. 158. Emphasis added.

69. See Sau (1974a).

70. Ho (1973); Le Duan (1970); Truong-Chinh (1969).

71. Sau (1974a); and also Sau (1976b).
72. Ulyanovsky–Pavlov (1973), p. 154. See also Ulyanovsky (1974).
73. Solodovnikov–Bogoslovsky (1975), p. 97.
74. Kalecki (1967).
75. *Ibid.*
76. Shirokov (1973), p. 313.
77. Sau (1976b).

CHAPTER 6

1. Sau (1974c). See also Moore (1966) for the contradictions among the ruling classes at different phases of development in Britain, France, the United States, Japan, China and India.
2. Sau (1975c), Table 1. Our data of the market for industrial consumer goods are drawn primarily from those of the National Sample Survey (NSS) which gives itemwise consumer expenditures by various groups for the following: (*a*) foodgrains, (*b*) milk and milk products, (*c*) meat, egg and fish, (*d*) edible oil, (*e*) sugar, (*f*) salt, (*g*) other food, (*h*) clothing, (*i*) fuel and light, (*j*) miscellaneous, (*k*) rent, and (*i*) taxes. By *industrial* goods we mean items (*d*) to (*j*), subject to the condition that only a certain part of item (*g*), namely, other food, is included hereunder, the remaining of it being considered as non-industrial, that is, agricultural product. By *agricultural* goods we mean the first three items and the remainder of item (*g*).

In a preliminary report (Sau (1974b)), we took three-fourths of item (*g*), namely, other food, to be industrial goods. Subsequently, we found more detailed information about the components of 'other food' in the 20th, 22nd and 23rd rounds of the NSS. According to the NSS definition, 'other food' consists of pulses and products, vegetables, fruits and nuts, spices, and beverages and refreshments. This holds up to the 17th round. But in the 18th and 19th rounds some other items also have been included under this head. On the basis of the more detailed information of the 19th, 22nd and 23rd rounds, we have now taken one-fifth of the expenditures on 'other food' to be on industrial goods for all rural expenditure groups. For the urban expenditure groups the percentage rises from 20 per cent to 60 per cent, with 40 per cent as the average for all expenditure groups.

For the methodology behind Tables 17–19, see Sau (1973), pp. 30–1, and Sau (1974b). It may be mentioned here that Mundle (1975) has done some calculations of consumption of agricultural and industrial goods using a slightly different method; but he confirms our conclusions.
3. Sau (1973), pp. 52–3.
4. Sau (1973c and 1975b).
5. UN (1966), p. 5.
6. *Ibid.*
7. *Ibid.*

8. *Ibid.*
9. *Ibid.* p. 14.
10. See Kidron (1965), pp. 240–2.
11. In this context see Bagchi (1972a); Patnaik (1973); Radice (1975); Dos Santos (1969); Frank (1972; 1975); Baran (1962); Sweezy (1967); Rhodes (1970); Amin (1974); Sutcliffe (1971; 1972); Hymer (1972); Klochkovsky (1975); and Vakhruschev (1973).
12. Marx–Engels (1848), p. 117.
13. Frank (1972), p. 5.
14. The irrelevance of traditional economics—classical, neo-classical, and Keynesian—in such a context is all too glaring.

CHAPTER 7

1. Magdoff (1974), p. 8.
2. Luxemburg (1951).
3. For a summary of the debate in India, see Cleaver (1976). The author of this paper appears to be under the wrong impression that the concept of mode of production is devoid of the dialectics of class relations (*ibid.* p. A-8). Alavi (1975) also gives a summary.

BIBLIOGRAPHY

Acharya, S. S. (1975). 'Green Revolution: Farm Income Distribution', *Economic Times*, New Delhi, 12 December.

Alavi, H. (1975). 'Indian and the Colonial Mode of Production', *Economic and Political Weekly* (hereafter, *EPW*), Bombay, vol. 10, special number, August.

Amin, S. (1972). *A Propos de l'accumulation* (mimeo), cited in Saigal (1973). Dakar: United Nations African Institute for Economic Development and Planning.

——(1974). *Accumulation on a World Scale*, vols. 1 and 2. New York: Monthly Review Press.

Bagchi, Amiya (1972). *Private Investment in India, 1900–1939*. London: Cambridge University Press.

——(1972a). 'Some International Foundations of Capitalist Growth and Underdevelopment', *EPW*, Bombay, vol. 7, special number, August.

Baran, P. A. (1962). *Political Economy of Growth*, 2nd ed. New Delhi: People's Publishing House.

——and Sweezy, P. M. (1966). *Monopoly Capital*. Harmondsworth: Penguin.

Bernal, J. D. (1965). *Science in History*, 3rd ed., vols. 1-4. Harmondsworth: Penguin.

Bernstein, H. (ed.) (1973). *Underdevelopment and Development*. Harmondsworth: Penguin.

Bhaduri, A. (1973). 'Agricultural Backwardness under Semi-Feudalism', *Economic Journal*, London, vol. 83.

Bhattacharyya, S. K. (1965). *Capital Longevity and Economic Growth*. Calcutta: Bookland.

Blaug, M. (1968). *Economic Theory in Retrospect*, 2nd ed. London: Heinemann.

Braun, O. (1972). *Unequal Exchange* (mimeo). Dakar: United Nations African Institute for Economic Development and Planning.

Brown, M. Barratt (1972). 'A Critique of Marxist Theories of Imperialism', in Owen and Sutcliffe (1972).

——(1974). 'New Trends in Trade and Investment', in Chattopadhyay (1974).

——(1974a). *The Economics of Imperialism*. Harmondsworth: Penguin.

Brunhoff, S. de (1975). 'Controversies in the Theory of Surplus Value: A Reply to John Eatwell', *Science and Society*, N.Y., vol. 38.

Bukharin, N. (1973). *Imperialism and World Economy*. New York: Monthly Review Press.

Cairncross, A. K. (1953). *Home and Foreign Investment*, 1880–1913. London: Cambridge University Press.

Chandra, N. K. (1973). 'Western Imperialism and India To-day', *EPW*, Bombay, vol. 8.

——(1974). 'Farm Efficiency under Semi-Feudalism: A Critique of Marginalist Theories and Some Marxist Formulations', *EPW*, Bombay, special number, vol. 8, August.

——(1975). 'Agrarian Transition in India', *Frontier*, Calcutta, vol. 8, November 22 and 29.

Chattopadhyay, B. (ed.) (1974). *Imperialism in the Modern Phase*, vol. 1. New Delhi: People's Publishing House.

——(1975). 'Multinational Corporation and Sovereignty', *Mainstream*, Delhi, December 20.

Cheung, S. N. S. (1968). 'Private Property Rights and Sharecropping', *Journal of Political Economy*, Chicago, vol. 76, November/December.

Cleaver, H. (1976). 'Internationalisation of Capital and Mode of Production in Agriculture', *EPW*, Bombay, vol. 11, March 27, under 'Review of Agriculture'.

Debray, R. (1965). 'Problems of Revolutionary Strategy of Latin America', in Debray, R. (1973), *Strategy for Revolution*. Harmondsworth: Pelican.

Diwan, R. K. (1973). 'Trade between Unequal Partners', *EPW*, Bombay, vol. 8, annual number, February.

——and Marwah, K. (1976). 'Transfers from Poor to Rich Countries: An Analysis of World Exports', *EPW*, Bombay, vol. 11, annual number, February.

Dobb, M. (1967). *Studies in the Development of Capitalism*. London: Routledge and Kegan Paul.

——(1973). *Theories of Value and Distribution Since Adam Smith: Ideology and Economic Theory*. London: Cambridge University Press.

Domar, E. D. (1946). 'Capital Expansion, Rate of Growth and Employment', *Econometrica*, Bristol, vol. 14, reprinted in Sen (1970).

Dos Santos, T. (1969). 'The Crisis of Development Theory and the Problem of Dependence in Latin America', in Bernstein (1973).

Dunning, J. H. (1974). 'Capital Movements in the Twentieth Century', in Dunning (1972).

——(1970). 'Technology, United States Investment and European Economic Growth', in Dunning (1972).

Dunning, J. H. (ed.) (1972). *International Investment*. Harmondsworth: Penguin.

Eatwell, J. (1974). 'Controversies in the Theory of Surplus Value: Old and New', *Science and Society*, N.Y., vol. 38.

——(1975). 'Mr Sraffa's Standard Commodity and the Rate of Exploitation', *Quarterly Journal of Economics*, Cambridge, Mass., November.

Emmanuel, A. (1972). *Unequal Exchange: A Study of the Imperialism of Trade*. New York: Monthly Review Press.

Engels, F. (1894). *Anti-Dühring*, 3rd ed. Moscow: Foreign Languages Publishing House, 1962.

Evans, D. (1976). 'Unequal Exchange and Economic Policies', *EPW*, Bombay, vol. 11, annual number, February.

Fei, J. C. H. and Ranis, G. (1964). *Development of the Labour Surplus Economy: Theory and Policy*. Homewood: Richard D. Irwin.

Feinstein, C. H. (ed.) (1967). *Socialism, Capitalism and Economic Growth*. London: Cambridge University Press.

Findlay, R. (1963). 'The Robinsonian Model of Accumulation', *Economica*, London, N.S., vol. 30, February.

Frank, A. G. (1967). *Capitalism and Underdevelopment in Latin America*. New York: Monthly Review Press.

——(1969). *Latin America: Underdevelopment or Revolution*. New York: Monthly Review Press.

——(1972). *Lumpen-Bourgeoisie and Lumpen-Development*. New York: Monthly Review Press.

——(1975). *On Capitalist Underdevelopment*. Bombay: Oxford University Press.

——(1976). 'That the Extent of Internal Market is Limited by International Division of Labour and Relations of Production', *EPW*, Bombay, annual number, February.

GOI: Government of India, Ministry of Food and Agriculture. *Studies in the Economics of Farm Management, U.P. (1966–67), Orissa (1967–68), Maharashtra (1967–68), Punjab (1967–68), Assam (1968–69), Tamilnadu (1968–69)*, New Delhi.

Griffin, K. (1974). 'The International Transmission of Inequality', *World Development*, Oxford: Pergamon Press, vol. 2, No. 3.

Gruber, W., Mehta, D. and Vernon, R. (1967). 'The R&D Factor in International Trade and International Investment of United States Industries', *Journal of Political Economy*, Chicago, February.

Gulbrandsen, O. (1975). 'The Main Streams of the World Economy' (mimeo), *XV International Congress of Agricultural Economists*, Sao Paulo.

Habib, I. (1972). 'Potentialities of Capitalistic Development in the Economy of Mughal India', *Enquiry*, New Delhi, N.S., vol. 3, no. 3.

——(1975). 'Colonisation of the Indian Economy, 1757–1900', *Social Scientist*, Trivandrum, no. 32.

Harberger, A. C. (1959). 'Using the Resources at Hand More Effectively', *American Economic Review*, vol. 49, reprinted in Wall, D. (ed.) (1972), *Chicago Essays in Economic Development*. Chicago: University of Chicago Press.

Harcourt, G. C. (1972). *Some Cambridge Controversies in the Theory of Capital*. London: Cambridge University Press.

——and Laing, N. F. (ed.) (1971). *Capital and Growth*. Harmondsworth: Penguin.

Harrod, R. (1939). 'An Essay in Dynamic Theory', *Economic Journal*, London, vol. 49. Reprinted in Sen (1970).

Hayter, T. (1971). *Aid as Imperialism*. Harmondsworth: Penguin.

Hazari, R. K. (ed.) (1968). *Foreign Collaboration*. University of Bombay.

Ho Chi Minh (1973). *Selected Writings*. Hanoi: Foreign Languages Publishing House.

Hopper, D. W. (1965). 'Allocative Efficiency in Traditional Indian Agriculture', *Journal of Farm Economics*, Wisconsin, vol. 47.

Hunt, E. K. and Schwartz, J. G. (eds.) (1972). *A Critique of Economic Theory*. Harmondsworth: Penguin.

Hymer, S. (1972). 'The Multinational Corporation and the Law of Uneven Development', in Bhagwati, J. (ed.) (1972), *Economics and World Order from the 1970s to the 1990s*. Calcutta: Orient Longman. Reprinted in Radice (1975).

Jalée, P. (1968). *The Pillage of the Third World*. New York: Monthly Review Press.

Kalecki, M. (1962). 'Observations on the Theory of Growth', *Economic Journal*, London, March.

——(1967). 'Social and Economic Aspects of Intermediate Regimes', in his *Selected Essays on the Economic Growth of the Socialist and the Mixed Economy*. London: Cambridge University Press, 1972.

Keesing, D. B. (1967). 'The Impact of Research and Development on United States Trade', *Journal of Political Economy*, Chicago, February.

Kemp, T. (1967). *Theories of Imperialism*. London: Dennis Dobson.

——(1972). 'The Marxist Theory of Imperialism', in Owen and Sutcliffe (1972).

Kenner, M. and Petras, J. (eds.) (1969). *Fidel Castro Speaks*. Harmondsworth: Penguin.

Keynes, J. M. (1936). *The General Theory of Employment, Interest and Money*. London: Macmillan.

Kidron, M. (1965). *Foreign Investments in India*. London: Oxford University Press.

Klochkovsky, L. L. (1975). *Economic Neocolonialism*. Moscow: Progress Publishers.

Krishna, R. (1963). 'Farm Supply Response in India–Pakistan: A Case Study of the Punjab Region', *Economic Journal*, London, vol. 83, September.

Lall, S. (1973). 'Transfer Pricing by Multinational Manufacturing Firms', *Oxford Bulletin of Economics and Statistics*, August.

Laibman, D. (1975). 'Controversies in the Theory of Surplus Value: A Comment', *Science and Society*, N.Y., vol. 38.

Layton, C. (1969). *European Advanced Technology: A Programme for Integration*. London: Allen and Unwin.

Le Duan (1969). *Forward Under the Glorious Banner of the October Revolution*, 3rd ed. Hanoi: Foreign Languages Publishing House.

——(1970). *The Vietnamese Revolution: Fundamental Problems, Essential Talks*. Hanoi: Foreign Languages Publishing House.

Lenin, V. I. (1893). *On the So-called Market Question*, reprinted in Lenin, *Collected Works*, vol. 1. Moscow: Progress Publishers, 1963.

——(1899). *The Development of Capitalism in Russia*, reprinted in Lenin, *Collected Works*, vol. 3. Moscow: Progress Publishers, 1964.

——(1899a). *Capitalism in Agriculture*, in Lenin, *Collected Works*, vol. 4. Moscow: Progress Publishers, 1964.

——(1899b). 'Review of S. N. Prokopovich's Books', in Lenin, *Collected Works*, vol. 4. Moscow: Progress Publishers, 1964.

——(1903). *Marxist Views on the Agrarian Question in Europe and in Russia*, in Lenin, *Collected Works*, vol. 6. Moscow: Progress Publishers, 1964.

——(1907). *The Agrarian Programme of Social Democracy in the First Russian Revolution, 1905–1907*, in Lenin, *Collected Works*, vol. 13. Moscow: Progress Publishers, 1962.

——(1908). *The Agrarian Question in Russia towards the Close of the 19th Century*, in Lenin, *Collected Works*, vol. 15. Moscow: Progress Publishers, 1963.

——(1915). *New Data on the Laws Governing the Development of Capitalism in Agriculture*, in Lenin, *Collected Works*, vol. 22. Moscow: Progress Publishers, 1964.

——(1916). *Imperialism, the Highest Stage of Capitalism*, in Lenin, *Collected Works*, vol. 22. Moscow: Progress Publishers, 1964.

——(1916a). *The Military Programme of the Proletarian Revolution*, in Lenin, *Collected Works*, vol. 23, Moscow: Progress Publishers, 1964.

Lewis, W. A. (1954). 'Economic Development with Unlimited Supplies of Labour', *The Manchester School*, May. Reprinted in Agarwala, A.N. and Singh, S. P. (eds.) (1958), *The Economics of Underdevelopment*. Delhi: Oxford University Press.

Lipton, M. (1968). 'Strategy for Agriculture: Urban Bias and Rural Planning', in Streeten, P. and Lipton, M. (eds.), *The Crisis of Indian Planning*. London: Oxford University Press, 1968.

Luxemburg, R. (1951). *The Accumulation of Capital*. New York: Monthly Review Press.

Magdoff, H. (1966). *The Age of Imperialism*. New York: Monthly Review Press.

——(1972). 'Imperialism without Colonies', in Owen and Sutcliffe (1972).

——(1974). 'Imperialism: An Historical Survey', in Chattopadhyay (1974).

Malinin, V. A. (1974). *The Fundamentals of Marxist–Leninist Philosophy*. Moscow: Progress Publishers.

Mandel, E. (1970). *Europe vs. America*. London: New Left Books.

Manfred, A. Z. (ed.) (1974). *A Short History of the World*, vol. 1. Moscow: Progress Publishers.

Mansfield, E. (1968). *Industrial Research and Technological Innovation*. New York: W. W. Norton.

——(1968a). *The Economics of Technological Change*. New York: W. W. Norton.

Mao Tse-tung (1937). 'On Contradiction', in *Selected Works of Mao Tse-tung*, vol. 1. Calcutta: Nabajatak Prakashan, 1973.

Marx, K. (1847). *The Poverty of Philosophy*. Moscow: Foreign Languages Publishing House.

——(1867, 1885, 1894). *Capital*, vols. 1-3. Moscow: Progress Publishers, 1965, 1967 and 1966 respectively.

——and Engels, F. (1848). *Manifesto of the Communist Party*, in Marx, K. and Engels, F. (1969), *Selected Works*, vol. 1. Moscow: Progress Publishers.

Medio, A. (1972). 'Profits and Surplus-Value: Appearance and Reality in Capitalist Production', in Hunt and Schwartz (1972).

Mitra, Ashok (1975). 'Terms of Exchange, Accumulation, and Growth: Some Comments on the Soviet Debate in the 1920's' (mimeo). Calcutta.

Moore, (Jr.) B. (1966). *Social Origins of Dictatorship and Democracy*. Harmondsworth: Penguin.

Mundle, Sudipto (1975). 'Intersectoral Flow of Consumer Goods: Some Preliminary Results', *EPW*, Bombay, vol. 10, annual number, February.

Myint, H. (1972). *Southeast Asia's Economy*. Harmondsworth: Penguin.

Myrdal, G. (1968). *Asian Drama*, vol. 2. New York: Pantheon.

NCAER: National Council of Applied Economic Research (1971). *Foreign Technology and Investment*. Delhi.

Nuti, D. M. (1970). 'Vulgar Economy in the Theory of Income Distribution', *De Economist*, vol. 118. Reprinted in Hunt and Schwartz (1972).

——(1970a)). 'Capitalism, Socialism and Steady Growth', *Economic Journal*, London, vol. 80. Reprinted in Harcourt and Laing (1971).

Owen, R. and Sutcliffe, B. (eds.) (1972). *Studies in the Theory of Imperialism*. London: Longman.

Pasinetti, L. L. (1962). 'Rate of Profit and Income Distribution in Relation to the Rate of Economic Growth', *Review of Economic Studies*, Edinburgh, vol. 29. Reprinted in Sen (1970).

Patnaik, P. (1973). 'On the Political Economy of Underdevelopment', *EPW*, Bombay, vol. 8, annual number, February.

Pavlov, V., Rastyannikov, V., and Shirokov, G. (1975). *India: Social and Economic Development (18th–20th centuries)*. Moscow: Progress Publishers.

Phelps, E. S. (1961). 'The Golden Rule of Accumulation: A Fable for Growthmen', *American Economic Review*, vol. 51. Reprinted in Sen (1970).

Prasad, P. H. (1974). 'Limits to Investment Planning', in Mitra, Ashok (ed.) (1974), *Economic Theory and Planning*. Calcutta: Oxford University Press.

Preobrazhensky, E. (1965). *The New Economics*. Oxford: Clarendon Press. Partly reprinted in Nove, A. and Nuti, D. M. (eds.) (1972), *Socialist Economics*. Harmondsworth: Penguin.

Radice, H. (ed.) (1975). *International Firms and Modern Imperialism*. Harmondsworth: Penguin.

RBI: Reserve Bank of India (1968). *Foreign Collaboration in Indian Industry*. Bombay.

——*Bulletin* (monthly). Bombay.

Rhodes, R. I. (ed.) (1970). *Imperialism and Underdevelopment: A Reader*. New York: Monthly Review Press.

Robinson, J. (1969). *The Accumulation of Capital*, 3rd ed. London: Macmillan.

——(1963). 'Findlay's Robinsonian Model of Accumulation: A Comment', *Economica*, London, N. S., vol. 30, November.

Robinson, R. (1972). 'Non-European Foundations of European Imperialism: Sketch for a Theory of Collaboration', in Owen and Sutcliffe (1972).

Rowthorn, B. (1974). 'Neo-Classicism, Neo-Ricardianism and Marxism', *New Left Review*, no. 86.

Saigal, J. C. (1973). *On the Theory of 'Unequal Exchange'* (mimeo). Dakar: United Nations African Institute for Economic Development and Planning.

Salter, W. E. G. (1960). *Productivity and Technical Change*. London: Cambridge University Press.

Sau, Ranjit (1973). *Indian Economic Growth: Constraints and Prospects*. Calcutta: Orient Longman.

——(1973a). 'On the Essence and Manifestation of Capitalism in Indian Agriculture', *EPW*, vol. 8, March 31.

——(1973b). 'And Quiet Flows Orthodox Economics', *EPW*, Bombay, vol. 8, June 30.

——(1973c). 'Growth and Fluctuation in the Indian Economy', *EPW*, Bombay, vol. 8, special number, August.

——(1973d). 'Can Capitalism Develop in Indian Agriculture?', paper presented at the *Seminar on the Political Economy of Indian Agriculture*, Calcutta.

——(1973e). 'Political Economy of Indian Agriculture: What Is It All About?', *EPW*, Bombay, vol. 8, May 19.

——(1973–4). 'A Note on the Unequal Exchange in International Trade', *Arthaniti* (a bi-annual journal of economics), Calcutta University.

——(1974). 'On Value, Capital and Capitalism', *EPW*, Bombay, vol. 9, annual number, February.

——(1974a). 'Non-Capitalist Path and All That', *EPW*, Bombay, vol. 9, April 13.

——(1974b). 'Some Aspects of Inter-Sectoral Resource Flow', *EPW*, Bombay, vol. 9, special number, August.

——(1974c). 'Arthanaitik Sankat O Shoshak Shreneer Antardwanda' (Economic Crisis and the Internal Contradictions of the Exploiting Classes), *Ekshan*, Calcutta, Autumn.

——(1975). 'Unequal Exchange and the Class Alignment in the Capitalist World', *Frontier*, Calcutta, vol. 8, May 3.

——(1975a). 'Farm Efficiency under Semi-Feudalism', *EPW*, Bombay, vol. 10, Review of Agriculture, March.

——(1975b). 'The Dialectics of Class Relations and Economic Development in India', paper presented at the *Annual Conference of the Canadian Society for Asian Studies*, Montreal.

——(1975c). 'On the Inter-Sectoral Resource Flow: Some Aspects of the Linkage between Agriculture and Industry', paper presented at the UN-IDEP Conference on *An Appraisal of the Relationship between Agricultural Development and Industrialization in Africa and Asia*, Tananarive.

——(1975d). 'The Dialectics of Underdevelopment', *EPW*, Bombay, vol. 10, July 5.

——(1975e). 'Capitalism, Imperialism and Underdevelopment', *EPW*, Bombay, vol. 10, special number, August.

——(1975f). 'Tritiya Bishwey Shrenee Binyas' (Class Alignment in the Third World), *Samatat*, Calcutta, no. 26.

——(1975g). 'Notes on Some Aspects of the Strategy of Economic Development in India', in Association of Indian Universities (1975), *Higher Education and Development*. New Delhi.

——(1975h). 'The Small Farmer and the Market', *Economic Bulletin for Asia and the Pacific* (United Nations), vol. 26, September/December.

——(1976). 'Contradictions and Development in the Third World: The Scope and Method of Its Political Economy', paper presented at the *First Congress of Third World Economists*, Algiers.

——(1976a). 'The Theory of Unequal Exchange, Trade and Imperialism', *EPW*, Bombay, vol. 10, March 6.

——(1976b). 'Intermediate Regime: Act II, Scene 1', *EPW*, Bombay, vol. 11, July 10.

——(1976c). 'Land Utilization: A Note', *EPW*, Bombay, vol. 11, September 4.

Schultz, T. (1964). *Transforming Traditional Agriculture*. New Haven: Yale University Press.

Sen, Amartya (1962). 'On the Usefulness of Used Machines', *Review of Economics and Statistics*, Cambridge, Mass., vol. 44.

——(ed.) (1970). *Growth Economics*. Harmondsworth: Penguin.

——(1975). *Employment, Technology and Development*. Delhi: Oxford University Press.

Servan-Schreiber, J. J. (1969). *The American Challenge*. Harmondsworth: Penguin.

Shirokov, G. K. (1973). *Industrialisation of India*. Moscow: Progress Publishers.

Smith, M. A. M. (1972). 'Wage Differentials and Trade in Second Hand Machines' (mimeo). London School of Economics.

Solodovnikov, V. and Bogoslovsky, V. (1975). *Non-Capitalist Development*. Moscow: Progress Publishers.

Sraffa, P. (1960). *Production of Commodities by Means of Commodities*. London: Cambridge University Press.

Steindl, J. (1967). 'Capitalism, Science and Technology', in Feinstein (1967).

Sutcliffe, B. (1971). *Industry and Underdevelopment*. London: Addison-Wesley.

——(1972). 'Imperialism and Industrialisation in the Third World', in Owen and Sutcliffe (1972).

Sweezy, P. M. (1942). *The Theory of Capitalist Development*. New York: Monthly Review Press.

——(1967). 'Obstacles to Economic Development', in Feinstein (1967).

——(1972). *Modern Capitalism and Other Essays*. New York: Monthly Review Press.

——and Magdoff, H. (1965). *The Dynamics of U.S. Capitalism*. New York: Monthly Review Press.

Sylos-Labini, Paolo (1969). *Oligopoly and Technical Progress*, revised ed. Cambridge, Mass.: Harvard University Press.

Thomas, B. (1967). 'The Historical Record of International Capital Movements to 1913', in Dunning (1972).

Thomson, D. (1966). *Europe since Napoleon*. Harmondsworth: Penguin.

Toynbee, A. J. (1965). *A Study of History*, abridged by Somervell, D. C., vols. 1 and 2. New York: Dell.

Truong-Chinh (1969). *Forward Along the Path Charted by K. Marx*. Hanoi: Foreign Languages Publishing House.

Tugendhat, C. (1973). *The Multinationals*. Harmondsworth: Penguin.

Turner, L. (1973). *Multinational Companies and the Third World*. London: Allen Lane.

Tyagunenko, V. L. and others (1973). *Industrialisation of Developing Countries*. Moscow: Progress Publishers.

Ulyanovsky, R. (1971). 'The Leninist Concept of Non-Capitalist Development and Our Time', *Social Sciences* (a journal of the USSR Academy of Sciences), Moscow, no. 2(4), April–June.

——(1974). *Socialism and the Newly Independent Nations*. Moscow: Progress Publishers.

——and Pavlov, V. (1973). *Asian Dilemma*. Moscow: Progress Publishers.

UN: United Nations (1966). *Report of Expert Group on Second-Hand Equipment for Developing Countries*. New York.

——(1973). *Multinational Corporations in World Development*. New York.

Vaitsos, C. (1970). 'Bargaining and the Distribution of Returns in the Purchase of Technology by Developing Countries', in Bernstein (1973).

——(1971). 'The Process of Commercialisation of Technology in the Andean Pact', in Radice (1975).

Vakhruschev, V. (1973). *Neocolonialism: Methods and Manoeuvres*. Moscow: Progress Publishers.

Vernon, R. (ed.) (1970). *The Technology Factor in International Trade*. New York: Columbia University Press.

Weizsäcker, C. C. von (1971). *Steady State Capital Theory*. New York: Springer-Verlag.

——(1973). 'Modern Capital Theory and the Concept of Exploitation' *Kyklos*, Basel, vol. 26.

——and Samuelson, P. A. (1971). 'A New Labour Theory of Value for Rational Planning through Use of the Bourgeois Profit Rate', *Proceedings of the National Academy of Sciences, USA*, vol. 68. Reprinted in Samuelson, P. A. (1972), *The Collected Scientific Papers*, vol. 3, MIT Press.

Wolfstetter, E. (1973). 'Surplus Labour, Synchronised Labour Costs and Marx's Labour Theory of Value', *Economic Journal*, London, vol. 83.

INDEX

Accumulation of capital, 22, 31, 63
Africa, 1–3, 12, 13, 36, 40, 41, 43, 99,
    100, 118, 123, 130, 134, 136, 158
Aid, 95, 96
Algeria, 2, 136
America-centricity, 8
Amin, S., 35
Antithesis between town and country, 36
Asia, 1, 3, 12, 13, 32, 36, 40, 41, 43,
    80, 99, 100, 118, 123, 130, 136,
    158
  South, 110, 111
Atomic bomb, 70
Australia, 3
Average commodity, 28

Baran, 114, 115, 117
Bauer, Otto, 50
Belgium, 69, 84
Bengal, 38
Bombay, 150
Bonn, 70, 130
Bourgeoisie, 53, 89, 113, 115, 118,
    155,
  (in) advanced capitalist countries,
    81, 82
  agricultural, 117, 142
  big, 82, 84, 85, 137, 138
  differentiation of, 89
  domestic, 11, 141, 151, 153
  European, 4
  fragile, 152
  imperialist, 116, 117, 118, 141, 155
  Indian, 85
  indigenous, 118
  industrial, 142
  metropolitan, 82
  middle, 82, 84, 85, 89, 90, 135,
    136, 139, 155

  nascent (in India), 40
  petty, 137, 138, 156
  small, 82, 84
  Third World, 82, 84, 89, 97, 142,
    146, 150, 152, 154, 155
Bourgeois economists, 9 100, 160
Braun, 53, 54, 55, 59, 153
Brazil, 80, 114, 117, 161
Britain, 2, 7, 32, 37, 43, 64, 69, 76,
    83, 93, 121, 149, 161
Burma, 136

Cairo, 150
Calcutta, 101
Cambodia, 3
Canada, 3, 97
Capital, 8, 9
Capital, 2, 27
  accumulation of, 31
  constant, 24, 27, 30, 63
  flow of, 33, 42, 43, 67, 93–5, 97
  foreign private, 93–6, 100, 153
  merchant, 153
  organic composition of, 28, 30,
    35, 48, 50, 63, 116
  variable, 24, 27, 63
Capital–labour ratio, 31, 74
Capitalism, 2, 8, 10, 13, 17, 26, 27, 29,
    34, 36, 63, 71, 100, 122, 129, 131,
    152, 160, 163
  agrarian, 122, 123, 125, 153
  British, 39, 64
  competitive, 102, 111
  crisis in, 29
  dynamics of, 115
  efficient, 100, 110
  essence of, 126
  growth of, 131
  industrial, 5, 31, 118, 144, 146
  manifestation of, 126